PICASSO

Picasso

by ANTONINA VALLENTIN

Editorial Consultant: Katherine Woods

CASSELL · LONDON

CASSELL & COMPANY LIMITED

35 Red Lion Square · London WC1

and at

MELBOURNE · SYDNEY · TORONTO
JOHANNESBURG · CAPE TOWN · AUCKLAND

First published 1963

Printed in Great Britain by
Ebenezer Baylis and Son, Limited
The Trinity Press, Worcester, and London
F. 1062

Contents

Illustrations

Our thanks are due to Pierre Cailler, and the publishers of *La Point*
for granting permission to reproduce these photographs.

CHAPTER I 1881–1895

Precocious Childhood

THE child born at Malaga, Spain, on the evening of 25th October, 1881, was apparently still-born. Every attention was lavished on it, but the body remained inert, the lips frigid, the breathing non-existent. The baby's uncle, Dr. Salvador Ruiz Blasco, bustled about while the parents gazed in anguish at the silent, motionless child. 'In those days,' relates Picasso, 'doctors used to smoke fat cigars. My uncle was smoking one. He blew the smoke at me. I made a face and began to cry.'

According to Spanish custom the child was baptized with a whole rosary of names: Pablo, Diego, José, Francisco de Paula, Juan Nepomuceno, Maria de los Remedios, Cipriano de la Santissima Trinidad. Picasso finds it perfectly natural for saints to be mobilized in this way. He believes that children everywhere possess as many names as he does.

The father, José Ruiz Blasco, was the son of a very ancient family that came from the mountains of León, that traced its history from the end of the fifteenth century and counted among its ancestors an illustrious Archbishop, Viceroy and Captain-General of Peru who had died in the odour of sanctity at Lima. The family also proudly cherished the memory of another saintly man, departed in the middle of the nineteenth century, whom Pablo heard referred to with respect as 'Uncle Perico who led an exemplary life as a hermit in the Sierra de Cordoba'.

Picasso's paternal grandfather, however, was in business in Malaga as a glove manufacturer. Passionately fond of the violin, he seems to have been the first member of the family to show any artistic talent. He was also a tireless worker and toiled ceaselessly to support a large family. Picasso's father, on the other hand, with Nordic physique and reddish hair—'an English type', as Picasso once told Gertrude Stein—seems to have been a contemplative man, averse to struggle and easily discouraged. In him the artist prevailed over the family saints and business men. He chose painting as a profession, but to make both ends meet accepted a post as teacher in the provincial school of Arts and Crafts. According to the family, he was as famed for his wit as he was respected for his art—like his son, a dealer in *bons mots* which dazzled or disconcerted his friends.

From his mother, Maria Picasso Lopez, Picasso has inherited physical vigour and southern vivacity. Following Spanish custom, he signed his first pictures with his mother's name after his father's. Then one day he dropped the 'Ruiz'—on the day, perhaps, when he found himself as an artist.

The double *s* in his mother's name is unusual in Spain, and attempts have been made to trace Italian ancestry. There was, in fact, a Genoese painter named Matteo Picasso who was fairly well known as a portraitist in the nineteenth century, but so far as is known Maria Picasso's family had always lived in Malaga. At one time Picasso himself took a passing interest in the possibility of an Italian connection and he asked a friend to get him some reproductions of Matteo Picasso's paintings, as though to make sure of his quality as an artist before adopting him as an ancestor. But the longer his voluntary exile from Spain, the more conscious he becomes of his Spanish nature.

His restlessness probably comes from his maternal grandfather whom a contemporary photograph shows as a prosperous-looking citizen with full cheeks, a bushy black moustache and, beneath the domed forehead, a burning, imperious gaze. One day, finding life in Malaga too cramped for him, Francisco set off for Cuba. Nothing is known of what he did there, how he lived or even of how he died. At any rate, he was the first of the solid bourgeois family to make his escape, and when Picasso had achieved such fame that everyone was eager to do him service he had inquiries made in Cuba for the vanished Francisco. But in vain—the disturbing gaze which he seems to have bequeathed to his grandson continues to defy curiosity. There is a photograph in existence of Maria Picasso, standing as a timid young girl beside her formidable and massive mama, which shows her resemblance to her father.

One day, Gertrude Stein met Picasso and his mother in Antibes. The old lady spoke only Spanish, but managed to make herself understood when talking of her son. Gertrude Stein was struck by their resemblance and mentioned how good-looking Picasso had been as a youth. 'Ah,' said his mother, 'if you thought him handsome then, I can assure you that was nothing compared with him as a child. He was an angel, or a devil for beauty. You couldn't take your eyes off him.' 'And now?' asked Picasso. 'Oh, now,' said the ladies in unison, 'the beauty has all gone!' 'All the same,' added his mother impulsively, 'you are a nice boy, and you are a perfect son.' This blind admiration of his mother's has no doubt been a permanent feature of Picasso's life. A letter she wrote him in 1936, three years before she died, reveals the intimacy between them even when they seldom met or corresponded: 'I hear you are doing some writing. I can believe anything of you. If they told me you had sung Mass I should still believe it.' It seems that, amongst other qualities, Picasso's sense of humour has been inherited from his mother.

At Malaga, following Spanish custom, different generations of the family lived under the same roof. Picasso's maternal grandmother, Doña Inès Picasso, and her two daughters, Elodia and Heliodora, lived with his mother. They had possessed some fairly lucrative vineyards, but these had been ravaged by phylloxera, so to help their brother-in-law they took to embroidering braid for the caps and uniforms of railway officials. Long after, Picasso still remembered this embroidery and the fascination it had held for him as a child and drew on scraps of paper the wheels and other designs which his aunts had worked interminably to earn their living.

But among the child's most vivid impressions were the pictures painted by his father. Don José, according to his son, painted 'pictures for dining-rooms': partridges, rabbits, hares, flowers (preferably lilac), but above all pigeons. Those pigeons made a huge impression on the child. There was one enormous canvas representing a pigeon-loft with the birds resting on their perches. He can still see it, he says: 'A cage with hundreds, thousands, millions of pigeons.' Actually, there were nine, as he realized many years later when he saw a reproduction of the painting which had meanwhile been relegated to the attic of the Malaga City Hall. The craftsmanship was timid and finicky. It might have been a photograph: the yard, the pigeon-loft, the plump and pompous birds.

The child was obsessed by painting. School was a nightmare, whether the dank, dark communal school or the bright, modern private school which he attended later. Picasso swears that he learnt nothing at either. He hated to concentrate, as he was perpetually told, as it blocked his soaring imagination, and he kept his eyes glued to the clock and the crawling minute hand. 'I got muddled about the time school was to finish,' he says, 'and I was obsessed with the fear that no one would come to fetch me.' But he was an intelligent child. Surely, friends ask, some ideas must have penetrated? 'No,' says Picasso vehemently. 'Nothing. I swear to you. Nothing whatever.' But the friends remain sceptical. After all, the child did learn to read and write. He can count. . . .

But Picasso's memory is probably accurate in recalling his school days as a void. Throughout his life he has been dependent on visual impulses which have been transformed in his mind into images. His most daring ideas, those which have jolted a whole era out of its rut, have not come to him through books, abstract thought or intellectual argument, but often through those exceptionally gifted people whom he has chosen as his friends and his intuitive skill in discerning their quality. The lightning grasp of his mind is as remarkable as his ability to resist assimilating what he cannot use or make his own. This ability to select from experience what is of creative value to him explains his refusal as a child to absorb random knowledge. In the strange surroundings of school the small boy yearned for familiar sights. Loneliness obsessed him, and it was increased by the surrounding crowd and by premature attempts to discipline his mind. In this anguish lies the key to his whole life.

But despite his chronic inattention, the pupil received a leaving certificate. 'That was a real comedy,' is Picasso's comment. But the headmaster of the private school was a friend of the family and, thanks to an arrangement perhaps common in Malaga, the child was formally credited with the necessary knowledge to embark on life. But his course was, in fact, set in advance and his first picture, which Picasso still possesses, was painted when he was eight years old.

It was a Spanish scene that was already familiar to him. Don José never missed a bull-fight and the passion for bulls—*la afición* as the Spanish call it—laid hold of his son in childhood. The *Picador* (property of Picasso) by the eight-year-old shows a torero clad in sumptuous yellow. The horse he rides is fairly accurate in its proportions. The onlookers in the tiers of seats are represented by a man and woman, seen half-length, and a third person in a big hat who appear behind the barrier. What is striking in the little picture is the choice of colours, a scale of warm tones: soil tinted with mauve, the barrier of pink with purplish blue which sets off the yellow of the torero's costume. Despite childish awkwardness, a gift of observation is clearly foreshadowed. The horse's hoof-prints are plain on the ground. But in the place where the people's eyes ought to be there are clumsy little holes in the wood on which the picture is painted. 'My sister did those with a nail,' Picasso explains. 'She must have been five or six at the time.'

In the first childish efforts there was no hint of the future revolutionary. One day, around 1946, Picasso visited an exhibition of children's drawings organized by the British Council. He looked at the pictures with his ambiguous smile. 'I could not have taken part in an exhibition of this kind when I was a child,' he said. 'At twelve I was drawing like Raphael.'

His first attempts, indeed, were reassuringly academic. And it was the ability to take pains, acquired at such an early age, together with the fact that he served his man's apprenticeship as a child, which helped Picasso to achieve mastery of his craft.

Picasso was ten when the family moved to Corunna. The provincial museum of Malaga had closed its doors and the post of curator, which had been his father's main source of income, had been abolished. The family had also increased during the Malaga years: his sister Lola had been born in 1884 and Conchita in 1887. In Corunna, therefore, Don José hastened to accept a job as teacher of drawing at the Instituto da Guarda. But children and parents had been spoiled by the mild climate of Malaga and the weather in Galicia proved a sore trial. It rained unceasingly, Picasso recalls. His father never went out except to go to the School. 'The rest of the time he watched the rain through the window.' Young Pablo, too, was disgusted with the weather. One day he drew a group of people cowering with hunched shoulders under an umbrella. Underneath he wrote: 'It has already begun to rain. Now it will go on until summer.'

All his life long, Picasso has kept his southerner's loathing for a low sky and a hostile climate, a loathing mixed with contempt for the people who endure them without complaining. He has always longed for light and felt an exile where the sun was not shining, a recluse drowning his nostalgia in work. As a child he took the foul weather of Corunna as a personal offence. He vented his rage in caricatures. 'Now the wind has got up,' he wrote, 'and will go on blowing till there is no

5

Corunna left.' But already he was finding refuge in work. The courses he took under his father's supervision at the secondary school of Arts and Crafts were those inflicted on all children in all provincial studios at that time. They had not changed very much since Goya worked in Lujan's studio in Saragossa. Most of the time was taken up with studies from plaster casts: statues with blind eyes, torsos of recumbent warriors, a clenched hand, a leg. Picasso's pencil drawings at the age of twelve or thirteen hardly differed from those any child of that age might have achieved from the same models. For anyone else, these exercises would have been so much lost time. But it is one of the basic laws of Picasso's nature that with him nothing is lost that has once been accepted, nothing is useless to him that has once been his own. He is dominated also by a sense of permanence and—a surprising trait in a man given to breaking abruptly with the past—by a feeling for continuity, and it is this which has made him preserve the picture he painted at the age of eight and the drawings done at Corunna of plaster casts.

Even at that early age, work meant everything to him. His father's patience, on the other hand, seems to have been strictly limited. Boredom, lack of friends in Corunna, the severity of the climate combined to plunge him into idleness. He still painted from time to time, but could no longer be bothered to finish the details of his pictures. Pigeons were his everlasting theme because he could find a sale for them. Even then he would cut off a dead pigeon's feet and nail them to a board, demanding that his son should reproduce them accurately in the unfinished picture, watching over the work until it was done to his satisfaction.

When he was about fourteen, Pablo began to paint from living models. These were no doubt school models; old people with sharpened features were preferred in the studios because it is easier to catch the likeness of a distinctive face than of smooth cheeks. A painting of one of these old men, with a puffed and furrowed face, is in the Sala Collection in Barcelona. Modelled with little touches conveying the roughness of the skin and the bumps in the sunken flesh, the head contrasts with a white low-necked shirt treated in large masses.

The same type of old man appears in another picture now in the Malaga provincial museum: *The Two Old People*, probably painted around 1894. The small picture is a family present dedicated to a female cousin. The composition of the bare interior is awkward, the workmanship timid. At that age, the boy was not even bold enough to simplify. But in this conventional, studied work in which an old man leaning on a stick is speaking into the ear of a blind old woman there is an indefinable feeling: pity, perhaps, for old people and their acceptance of infirmity, or fear of the ravages of age—a strange fear to find in so young a boy, but one which Pablo Picasso has never overcome.

Soon the boy was trying his hand at what was to be the great subject of his mature work: still life. But a copper bowl of fruit, a china jug in relief, apples scattered over a tablecloth no more than reflected the bad taste of the period, that passion for a cunningly contrived muddle which derived from the work of Hans Makart. The boy painted landscapes on diminutive wooden panels, a bird, a man with a dog. He was sufficiently sure of himself and already well enough thought of to assay portraits of family friends. Soon the moment came when Don José recognized his son's superiority. He not only realized that he could teach him nothing further, he also saw that what he had so laboriously acquired his son had instinctively at his finger-tips. 'Then,' in Picasso's own phrase, 'he gave me his paints and his brushes and never painted again.'

Picasso did several paintings of his father at this period and the result helps to explain Don José's decision. He is revealed as a handsome and distinguished-looking man, but with a perplexed expression deriving from a mass of lines above the thin bridge of the nose. In one painting he is shown as a man who has lost his way in life, sitting wearily with his elbows on a table, his head resting on one long hand, the other idly before him, with abstracted gaze. From now on he pottered about doing things with his hands, both to while away the time and because he enjoyed it. He would make his son boxes—useless objects which got in the way—out of cardboard, paper and glue. Or he would amuse himself by prettying up whatever came to hand. One day, according to Picasso, he seized on the plaster cast of an Italian woman, removed the corners of the square head-dress, repainted the head, draped it with material and glued crystal tears to the cheeks.

The taste for transforming things and the ingenuity in which Picasso was one day to excel, were probably awakened in the child by watching his father toying with objects in this way. Half a century later, when confronted with the portrait of an Italian woman of the nineteenth-century Lyonese school, he remembered perhaps his father's antics with the plaster cast and, the conventionality of the picture awaking echoes in his mind, he drew on the edge of the portrait a faun playing his pipe and a Hercules leaning against the woman's high breasts.

After a life of obscurity, Don José was to die on the eve of the First World War. He had been a modest craftsman who had yet succeeded in laying a good foundation for his son's future fame.

The same precocious virtuosity, akin to the Lenbach manner, which is visible in Picasso's portraits of his father is seen also in his portrait of Don José's best friend, Ramón Perez Costales, the doctor who tended Pablo's sister Conchita during her fatal attack of diphtheria. It was at Costales's house that the author of *Songe et Mensonge de Franco* first set eyes on a Spanish Republican flag. An ardent republican himself and Minister of Labour in the First Spanish Republic, the doctor was the first man of importance to be painted by Picasso. The portrait shows a man with a Francis Joseph beard gazing benevolently beneath knitted eyebrows, the very incarnation of the enlightened bureaucrat.

Apart from his serious work, the boy took pleasure in drawing. He delighted to translate his experiences into visual images, but seldom into words. Like most children he loathed writing letters, particularly to order, and his family kept nagging him to write to his relatives and his grandmother who had stayed behind in Malaga. But what could he say to them? Writing to them felt like walking on stilts. He ran a 'newspaper', admittedly, a piece of paper folded in two on which, at the age of thirteen, he recorded his impressions, but they were altogether too private, and too mocking. The eternal rain at Corunna, for instance; he described the women wrapped in their shawls, cautiously skirting the puddles. He called the piece: 'Bathing at Betanzos'. And then, a martyr to his father's feathered friends, he wrote in the 'Small Ads' under the family address: 'Thoroughbred pigeons for sale.'

One of the last pictures painted at Corunna epitomizes the maturity of his gifts: *The Barefoot Girl*. The model had been supplied to him as to an adult painter, but also as a reward for his good behaviour during the Christmas holidays. The little girl can hardly be called pretty. She seems more used to earning a living by hard work than by posing for a painter. She is wearing a cloth over her head. The hands resting on her lap are those of a child, but the skin is already roughened by work. The large bare feet are planted heavily on the ground. 'The poor girls at home always went barefoot,' Picasso recalls, 'and this little thing had her feet covered with chilblains.' The face with its childish contours is sullen, the mouth droops as with children who have been scolded too often. Only the wide-open eyes have beauty, but their gaze is fixed, as though prematurely resigned.

Thus one day a boy of fourteen and a tired, harassed little girl came face to face. How did he manage to convey the suffering in this silent child? Clearly his eyes understood more than his brain could assimilate.

CHAPTER II 1896–1900

The Creative Urge

PICASSO'S real career began with a performance that most other artists would consider a *tour de force*. The Barcelona School of Fine Arts, an institution with a high reputation, founded in 1775, divided its art courses into successive grades. From general drawing the student graduated into more advanced classes where he painted from living models. But before he could progress he was required to pass an examination of such an exacting standard that students were given an entire month to prepare one drawing. 'I finished mine the first day,' says Picasso. 'I looked at it for a long time and thought whether there was anything I could add to it. But I could see nothing, absolutely nothing.' As he speaks he shakes his head slightly and looks puzzled, as he always is by slow methods of work alien to his own rapidity.

Extreme concentration of effort is his creative law and he cannot imagine long-drawn-out toil. His is a tide which expends itself in a single surge. He covers a large canvas in one day, just as the schoolboy took only one day to complete what was intended to be a month's work. When a friend asked him recently if he had finished a version of the *Femmes d'Alger* which he had sketched out the day before, he replied with a smile: 'Finished? Yes, if you like. It would not be a finished canvas for Michelangelo, for instance, but it is for me.'

If the vision he sets down so swiftly does not satisfy him, if it seems to him incomplete, capable of extension or modification, he will embark on a different approach to the same subject the next day. But the first treatment will be complete in itself, balanced in its different parts and possessing a calculated unity. He has said everything in a single breath. He cannot modify the expression without destroying the balance of that unity. If he feels the need to say it all again, quite differently, he makes a new beginning. And paints a new picture.

In that examination for entrance to the upper class of La Lonja, the law of Picasso's creativity was established once for all. His rapidity of execution is not due simply to a precocious mastery of his craft, to acuity of observation or sureness of touch, it is due above all to the clarity and completeness of his vision. His continuity of stroke has, admittedly, a sensual side, his treatment of a canvas or a sheet of paper seems almost like a sexual assault, but it is not the fury of his masculine temperament which forces a work into being, but his lucidity. This lucidity, this sudden release of a mysterious creative process, is one of the keys to Picasso.

He knows this himself. 'People believe,' he said laughingly one day, 'that a painter is in a perpetual state of excitement!' But he has surprised all those who thought to find in him a hurricane turned into a man. Doctors who have examined him, even those who have taken his electro-encephalograph, have found him unusually well balanced, while palmists who have bent over his magician's hands have pronounced him imperturbably calm. To illustrate the process that takes place from the initial vision to definitive form, Picasso touches his forehead. 'Everything that happens is here,' he says. 'Before it reaches the end of the pen or the brush, the most important thing is to have it at one's finger-tips, all of it, without losing anything.' And he will rub his finger-tips with his thumb, as though to conserve the force in them.

Picasso was to know blind alleys and, for a short time, to retrace his steps, he was to advance and withdraw. But, as in the examination at Barcelona, he was never to hesitate about the immediate task, about the necessity of the moment.

When a professor at the School of Fine Arts in Barcelona offered to change places with him, Don José moved his family from Corunna. But though the post in Barcelona was better paid, he was hardly happier in that lively city than he had been under Corunna's dismal sky. He still felt an exile from Malaga. He felt he had wasted his youth. And now the painters who had been his friends were forging ahead while he remained in a backwater. Successful, prosperous, spoken of in the newspapers, some of them even members of the Royal Academy, they made him aware of his failure, that he had abandoned painting for good. His son can remember how he felt

11

discouraged and cheated by life. He had lost everything: 'Malaga, the bulls, and his friends.'

Pablo himself seems to have been disappointed by his first experience of a large city. He was suspicious of the numerous and contradictory impressions which Barcelona offered and, though only fifteen years old and still untouched by life, he resisted them.

A mere stroll through the streets of the city, however, confronted him with a phenomenon unique in the world, that paroxysm of architectural exuberance which Gaudí had expressed in stone. As Cassou says of Gaudí: 'He is one of those eccentric individuals whom Spain delights in producing.' His work seems to defy the most ancient architectural traditions, the very laws of matter, the most firmly established relations between man and space. Amongst other exterior influences, Barcelona had already been stamped by the neo-Gothic with its superimposed gables, high roofs and pointed turrets and it was the Gothic which inspired Gaudí, but an opera-stage Gothic more plausible in canvas and papiermâché than in bricks and stone, a Gothic which eliminated buttresses and flying buttresses and so defied its own principles. Gaudí's free and easy treatment of his materials, producing convulsions in stone, slanting columns, meandering chimney-stacks and heavy roofs undulating like desert sand-dunes, making rocks look like animals and wrought-iron like thick-leaved bulbous plants, might have made an enormous impression on a young painter. But Picasso seems to have been repelled by Gaudí's very extravagance.

Nevertheless, in this mad art of Gaudí's there is a foretaste of many future artistic adventures. Expressionism might have quoted it as its authority, and surrealism and naturalism have drawn their inspiration from that plethora of sculptured figures jostling beneath the porticos of the Cathedral of the Holy Family. With Gaudí there is also the same return to the sources of primitive art which was later to precede the decisive change in Picasso's art. Gaudí himself said: 'Originality is the return to origins,' and the dizzy cones with which he crowned the Cathedral were inspired by primitive African architecture. Apart from Gaudí's search for original forms there is another aspect of his flamboyance which might have impressed Picasso: the achievement of the impossible, the frenzied dream given material shape. But Picasso has denied being influenced at all by Gaudí's art or example. 'No,' he says, 'I was not in the least impressed by him. He did not influence my youth in any way. Perhaps it was just the opposite.' In a posthumous Gaudí exhibition held in Barcelona some of his projects clearly show the influence of a younger artist on the acclaimed master. 'It is curious, isn't it?' adds Picasso thoughtfully.

Like all ports, Barcelona seems to have welcomed every extravagance, and the bad more readily than the good. As Cassou has said: 'The peculiarity of this city is that it has never heard of good taste. Bad taste, on the other hand, is expressed there in a highly aggressive fashion.' At that time, Pablo was probably incapable of passing judgment on his surroundings, but he knew, or at least he sensed that those first years in Barcelona were not favourable for his work. Much later, when he came upon a landscape dated 1896, he seemed both shocked and pained. 'I hate that period of my studies,' he said to Kahnweiler. 'The work I was doing before was much better.'

In that same year, Picasso, at fifteen, felt no longer able or willing to work at home. So his father rented a studio for him in the Calle de la Plata. But in moving he did not escape Don José's tutelage. The subjects which he chose could not have been more hackneyed or their execution more conventional. Conventional, too, were his drawings in Chinese ink and in charcoal and his watercolours. One of the first large canvases that he painted then, with life-sized figures, was called *The Bayonet Attack*. It is said to have been so huge that it could not be taken down the stairway, but, to the great delight of the passers-by, had to be lowered from a window with ropes.

But young and inexperienced though he was, Picasso did not find this scene of bellicose fervour worthy of preservation and in the following year he painted it over—or is said to have done so—with a more peaceable subject which was at first entitled, *The Visit to the Sick*. It was Don José who conceived this composition and he also who served as model for the bearded and distinguished-looking physician who is taking a sick woman's pulse while a nun leans over her, holding a baby in her arms. Pompously renamed *Science and Charity* for the occasion, the picture was sent to the Exhibition of Fine Arts in Madrid where it received honourable mention.

Picasso feels no indulgence for the trial and error of his early years and, as his sense of irony turns as readily on himself as upon others, he recalls with amusement that when the picture was exhibited one critic scoffed at 'the doctor who is taking the pulse of a glove'.

In that same year of 1897, no doubt encouraged by his modest success, young Pablo left home for Madrid. There he succeeded in gaining admittance to the advanced classes in the Academy of San Fernando just as easily as he had done in Barcelona: by doing the work of several days in a few hours. Well-to-do relatives paid the expenses of his journey and clubbed together to cover the cost of his stay. But he only had a few pesetas, he recalls, 'barely enough to keep me from starving to death, no more'. From now on, he knew the meaning of privation and at times perhaps real starvation. For, once removed from his family who had mapped out the road to success for him with travelling scholarships and the Prix de Rome, the young man revolted, stayed away from the Academy and so sacrificed even the meagre allowance which his relatives paid him. Only his father, 'the poor man', continued to send what he could.

In the spring of 1898, he caught scarlet fever, a grievous ordeal for an adolescent, and the subsequent exhaustion made him depressed. Ever since then he has suffered from the fears which beset a fundamentally healthy person in the face of illness or rather, feeling the need to have all his powers continually at his disposal, he has worried at the least sign of indisposition in himself or in those who are close to him.

To recuperate after his illness he accepted the invitation of a friend, the painter Manuel Pallarès, to spend some time at La Horta de San Juan. He stayed there for several months, taking a full part in the life of the village, learning how to milk a cow, groom a horse and look after the chickens. 'Everything I know,' he says, 'I learnt in Pallarès's village.'

This contact with simple things was to leave a permanent stamp on him. There is always something about Picasso which suggests the wide open spaces. He seems to have stored the sun and the breezes in himself. Even his gestures are spacious and on first meeting him one would imagine him to be a Highlander or a sailor. After days or even weeks spent in his Paris studio with a view of lowering skies, grey roofs and leafless trees through his windows, he still enters a room with big strides as though he had just come back from a long walk, bringing with him a sniff of the breezes or the warmth of the sun in his clothes.

A sketch of himself, perhaps one of his first self-portraits, shows him as he was in this year of 1898. In this figure of a seventeen-year-old boy seated in the act of drawing, there is still something of the awkwardness of adolescence in the thrust of the head and the bony wrists. He does not seem to be at home in his city clothes, his detachable collar and his broad artist's tie. His hair has been parted in the middle and plastered down. But the rapid sketch shows all his own peculiar obstinacy and the fixity of the eyes when he is working.

On his return from Horta he worked in the studio of an older friend, Joseph Cardona Iturro, a sculptor under the influence of the German Pre-Raphaelites. But young Pablo was more interested in the technique of his craft than in aesthetic theories and a friend describes him at that time as 'painting and drawing indefatigably'. When Jaime Sabartés came to see him he found him 'lost under a pile of drawings'.

The studio in which he was then working was only a room in the apartment of a corset-maker, Cardona's mother. Always fascinated by manual skill, Picasso watched the employees punching eyelets in the long whalebone corsets thought necessary in those days as a framework for feminine curves, and with his perennial interest in trying his hand at other people's work, he even operated the machine himself. The simplest materials also intrigue Picasso. All his friends know his habit of tinkering with a bit of wire or paper to make it emerge as a human face or some other object, particularly as a pastime when he loses interest in the talk around him.

Some of his permanent characteristics were beginning to appear in Picasso at that age. At eighteen or nineteen he already belonged to the literary and artistic *élite* of Barcelona, though as an Andalusian it was not easy for him to get adopted by exclusive circles in Catalonia and he was looked on somewhat askance. But slowly he gained an ascendancy—just how or why no one later would have been able to say. He was reticent rather than communicative, not forthcoming either in his speech or his affections and more addicted to the barbed shaft than to compliments. But he was a personality and as time went on, an increasingly dominant one.

By fits and starts after his own fashion, alternately eager and reluctant, he absorbed the influence of his surroundings. At that time, at the turn of the century, material civilization with its immutable values, its bourgeois complacency and its pride in industrial progress was everywhere being questioned. Doubt, defiance and a certain emotional and spiritual anguish were in the air and nowhere more than in Barcelona which lay at the cross-roads of conflicting currents.

'May the Sacred Disquiet be with you,' Eugenio d'Ors was preaching, in capital letters, of course. In Barcelona, Nietzsche's influence was paramount. The painter Santiago Rusinol, with whom Picasso was later to be associated, was preaching the triumph of 'man carried away by a rightful iconoclastic pride', and his duty to 'snatch brilliant, frenzied, paroxysmal visions from life . . . to translate eternal truths into crazy paradoxes and to make the abnormal and the unheard-of the foundations of existence'. From Germany the whole mythology of Wagner was being imported and his works were becoming widely known at concerts and in the opera house. German-inspired nostalgia for a mythical past and for the misty Middle Ages made all the greater impression on the Catalans because their own autonomist movement looked on the Middle Ages as the golden era of their national independence.

Two contradictory movements, both Nordic in origin, were alive in Barcelona: on the one hand, an escape into the past from the *malaise* of the present and on the other, a revolt against the established order which made up in daring for what it lacked in a sense of reality.

In the plastic arts the northern influence was particularly strong. Artificiality was encouraged by admiration for the English Pre-Raphaelites with their alleged discovery of a lost pictorial innocence, and for the German Pre-Raphaelites. A form of symbolism shrouded in the trappings of an over-facile mystification became fashionable. The prevailing taste submitted to this strait-jacket. Decorative arabesques took precedence over the search for reality. In Vienna this was called the *Jugendstil*, in Latin countries, the 'noodle style'. Far-sighted Catalans emphasized the havoc wrought in contemporary popular taste by this artificiality in artistic and literary aspirations, this borrowed *optique*.

In the long, warm evenings, young people in search of mutual encouragement used to foregather in cafés and taverns and while away the time in impassioned aesthetic discussions. These scenes play a large part in Picasso's early works. There is a little picture painted in 1897 with swift and vigorous strokes reproducing a bluish, smoke-filled *Intérieur de café* (Junyer Vidal Collection, Barcelona). The *Café chantant du Parallèle*, with patches of colour in relief, conveys the atmosphere of a typical pleasure-haunt in any country. Picasso was touching here on what was to be his own special world in years to come.

The favourite resort of artists, on which they were to confer passing fame, was a restaurant-cum-cabaret to which its founders—mostly painters, artists and men of letters—had given the name of 'Els Quatre Gats', The Four Cats. The name derived partly from the Chat Noir in

Paris, whence the principal founder of the place, Papa Romeu, had just returned after working with Aristide Bruant. With his ruddy face and picturesque appearance, Romeu attracted the professional interest of several painters among his friends. Picasso painted him in water-colour and made a number of drawings. In an advertisement he did for Els Quatre Gats, Papa Romeu is to be seen enthroned in an armchair, smoking a large pipe and surrounded by his friends, among whom are Picasso himself and Sabartés, his future biographer who became his faithful friend at this time.

Els Quatre Gats became a second home for Picasso and a very lively one, for the cabaret proved a dazzling success. To attract the public, Romeu got Miguel Utrillo to do shadow plays and a puppet theatre was installed on which the best known pieces by Barcelona writers and also by Richepin were played to a packed room, Albeniz himself sometimes accompanying the marionettes on the piano.

Picasso's inseparable friend at this time was another *habitué* of Els Quatre Gats, a young man less than a year older than himself by the name of Carlos Casagemas. Interested in all the literary aspirations of the day and receptive to the seething mass of ideas with which Picasso perpetually bubbled, Casagemas was sufficiently well-off to have time to listen to the younger artist and to accompany him on his long walks in Barcelona. In 1900, Casagemas was able to rent a studio and Picasso left the corset-maker's apartment and moved in with his friend, sharing the expenses. This studio was on the top floor of an old house in the upper part of the city. The room was large and the young men's resources could not meet the cost of furnishing it. Instead, Picasso covered the walls with paintings depicting the furniture which was not there, the heavy wardrobes, the sofas. The pictures overflowed on to the stairway where they were intended to serve as signposts to possible patrons.

The walls of Els Quatre Gats were also covered with portraits of clients done by Picasso. These now began to attract attention. A critic mentioned them in the newspaper *La Vanguardia* and Picasso saw his name in print for the first time. In the preceding year or two his work had undergone a change. The conventionality of his student years had dropped away from him and he had also changed his subjects. He now did a series of coloured drawings in bold strokes which bore the title: *Scènes de la vie de bohème*. In 1899 he also painted the interior of Els Quatre Gats, the *Rencontre* of two ladies (Sala Collection,

17

Barcelona) and, though he returned to portraiture in *Portrait de Lola* (his sister) now in the Modern Museum, Barcelona, he painted her in the same elegant manner, in broad planes, as the other two pictures. Several combined influences are reflected in this new technique: the large flat places of the *Rencontre* are inspired by the Japanese print which the interior of Picasso's family home in the *Portrait de Lola* shows to have been as much in vogue in Barcelona at that time as in Paris.

The elongated figures then evident in his work were also due to contemporary influences. To the return to the past which was such a powerful current of the times, the Catalans had added as their personal contribution the rehabilitation of El Greco, who had been relegated to scorn and oblivion. Santiago Rusinol, already famous as a painter —Picasso later made a drawing of him wearing a turban and smoking a pipe—had managed to buy two of El Greco's paintings in Paris, *Saint Peter* and *Saint Mary Magdalene*. In 1893 these two pictures were carried on litters in solemn procession to Cap Ferrat, Picasso at the time being only twelve years old. But the artists who took part in the pilgrimage later became *habitués* of Els Quatre Gats: Papa Romeu, Ramon Casas, whose vigorous portraits and posters inspired by his stay in Paris had a great success in Barcelona, and, amongst many others, Casas's pupil and Picasso's great friend in years to come, Ramon Pichot.

The first trace of El Greco's formal influence on Picasso is seen in the elongation of the figures, the way the child appears welded to its mother and the upward sweep of the mantle's fluted folds in the small pastel, *Mère et fils*, of 1898 (Stransky Collection, New York). The same elongation is visible in a drawing of the same year, *Vieillard avec un enfant malade*. But here the distribution of the planes in blacks and whites reveals a definite Nordic influence, that is, of the English Pre-Raphaelites and of German graphic art. This was a temporary phase, due no doubt to a combination of circumstances. Among the artistic periodicals published in Barcelona at that time there was one called *Joventud*, of clearly German inspiration. Even the title was printed in Gothic letters.

In *Joventud* the first reproduction of a Picasso drawing appeared on 19th July, 1900. It had been commissioned to illustrate an English Pre-Raphaelite poem entitled 'The Clamour of the Virgins', by one Joan Oliva Bridgeman. Both the poem and its author have been rescued from oblivion by the choice of artist, which was due either to chance or the recommendation of a friend. A typical product of the times, the poem demanded the right to free love:

> We are virgins, forced
> To be so by abhorréd laws
> Which turn us into slaves. . . .
> . . . Let us free ourselves! Let us enjoy love,
> And rend the white robe that wraps our bodies:
> It is the shroud that conceals a treasure.

Picasso's illustration was less daring than the text. It shows a nude woman of delicate profile asleep with 'shroud' already torn, flabby breasts and the rest of the body blurred. In her dream she evokes a phantom man of whom only the head and the upper part of the body are visible.

Soon after, Picasso was commissioned by another Barcelona review, the *Catalunya Artistica*. To illustrate a rustic tale by a Catalan author, he drew *La Folle*. The distribution of blacks and whites is still obedient to the prevailing taste. The figure is wooden according to the demands of the neo-Gothic style. But the picture represents Picasso's first encounter with the theme of his future work: human decadence. The eyes are sunk deep in their sockets, the nose is delicate but irregular and the wide mouth is like a dark wound slashed in a white expanse. This drawing anticipates Picasso's later work. But the theme was not his own invention, but, once again, was suggested by his surroundings. One of the biographers of his Barcelona years speaks of the 'wind of folly' which was blowing in those days. Several of his friends were to commit suicide or suffer mental collapse. And to those who, like Rusinol, made a cult of the abnormal and preferred madmen to solid citizens, lack of mental balance was positively attractive. Melancholy was in the air, and under the blue Mediterranean skies a Catalan poet was singing this dirge *à la Verlaine*:

> The sky is grey, my heart is grey, all is grey without end,
> Grey is around me, grey in myself,
> Even my thoughts are grey.

At the age of nineteen young Pablo seemed in perfect accord with the decadent poses and languorous airs of such surroundings. A self-portrait (Barbey Collection, Barcelona), done in 1900 in charcoal and watercolour, shows him as he was at that time: the typical Byronic hero wrapped in gloom, though a little young for the part. He wears a very high-cut waistcoat beneath a wide, short overcoat with an upturned collar and his long hair is topped by a broad-brimmed hat. His hands are thrust into his pockets, his young head is slightly bowed and a pair of large eyes gaze at the world more in disenchantment than with curiosity.

In fact, however, Picasso was alive to the artificiality of these morbidly elegant poses. The future creator of nightmares was basically healthy, proof against neuroses and already armed with an unshakeable sense of humour which made him flee pathos in all its forms and avoid the traps of sentimentality. If he felt himself succumbing to hocus-pocus, if the surrounding atmosphere weighed too heavily on him he could get rid of it with a vigorous shrug of his broad shoulders.

Sabartés knew the mechanics of this process. The two friends were seeing a lot of each other at that time and Picasso made his first portrait of Sabartés in the studio he was sharing with Casagemas. In spirit, the large charcoal drawing was akin to his self-portrait. The very manner in which the young man was leaning against the back of a chair with one hand on the top seemed to indicate a flight from the realities of life. The hair parted in the middle fell over his high forehead, the eyes were mournful, and even the mouth of the model with its pouting lips was caught in an expression of disillusioned melancholy. At that time, Picasso was doing a lot of portraits of his friends and colleagues, mostly in charcoal or watercolour. Then one day he suddenly got bored with this gallery of romantics. When Sabartés arrived at the studio, he was told abruptly: 'Take a brush. Hold it in your fingers as if it was a flower. A little higher. Yes, like that. Good. Now don't move.' The quick charcoal drawing shows a youth wearing a full cape, his long hair encircled by a garland of flowers. One slender hand is raised in a precious gesture, holding a flower between the finger-tips. A pair of pince-nez athwart the pointed nose lend a ludicrous touch. There are also some lighted candles in the picture and some white crosses scattered around. The whole bears the inscription in capital letters: POETA DECADENTE. . . .

In the previous year, at the age of eighteen, Picasso had got hold of a copper plate no larger than the palm of his hand. For his first engraving, as for his first painting, he chose a typically Spanish theme: a picador, his legs wide astride and planted firmly on the ground, with the lance in his hand. An engraver pulled some prints of it and Picasso, who had not remembered that the picture would be seen in reverse, saw that his picador was now holding the lance in his left hand. . . . Unabashed, he added a new title to the plate: *Left-handed Picador* (El Zurdo).

From his friends' recollections of these early years, the young man emerges with clearly marked characteristics. 'He can make himself understood without the use of words,' said one of them. He listened much and spoke little. Ideas and information gravitated towards him without him displaying or even admitting what he had acquired. He seemed to be familiar with the latest intellectual trends and all the recent publications, yet no one remembered seeing him with a book in his hand. He was alternately all attention or absent-minded. 'In the café or the street,' we are told, 'he would suddenly lose contact in the middle of a conversation and go off without a word.'

He always had a horror of wasting his time, hating to linger over impressions he had already made use of and absorbing new ones like a sponge. He stayed up late at night as though afraid to miss the chance of a nocturnal encounter or of some new experience. He was the last to leave a café table and in the early hours of the morning often sought out a friend to roam La Rambla, the main street of Barcelona, with him. Late every evening he would visit the Eden Concert, the *bistrots* of the Paralelo or the popular shows. 'The girls', too, claimed his attention.

Picasso's sex life began at a very early age. 'Yes,' he says, smiling broadly with a sparkle in his eyes, 'I was still quite small'—and he indicates a diminutive height with his hand. 'Obviously, I didn't wait for the age of reason. If I had, I might not have begun at all!' He seems to be very amused by the memories he revives, to have no regrets either at missed opportunities or over his precocious pleasures. His amorous experiences have left no bitterness.

From the start, sensual pleasure was inseparable from his creative work, and instead of becoming a slave to it he used it as he uses all those people and things that can serve his art. Thus his friends and those who are dear to him have their definite place in his life. He does not seem to encroach on their independence, he uses no compulsion, he does not interfere with anyone's natural bent. But he assesses what other people have to give him in accordance with his own needs. 'He uses his friends,' it has been said, 'as he uses colours in painting a picture: some are used for one thing and others for another.' No doubt he would be very surprised if any of them tried to object. He is probably barely conscious of having introduced this system into his life, or too absorbed in his work to think of it.

It is this total self-surrender to the task of the moment, a characteristic already strongly marked in the young Picasso, which best explains the man he has become. 'Whether he is drawing,' it has been said, 'or painting, reading a newspaper or sewing on a button, he is always absorbed in what he is doing and indifferent to everything else.' The power of concentration, which Bergson defined as genius, is particularly striking in Picasso because his creative urge is a constant, a continuous tension. With him, the surge of inspiration is not a gift of heaven patiently and humbly awaited, but a pressing need and a vital necessity. From an early age he was possessed by a frenzy for work. There is an urgency in him which allows no relaxation. What relaxation he does allow himself, the pleasure he enjoys, in short the life he lives, is his means of recharging a battery which he insists must always be ready for use. Any interruption in the flow of current seems like a catastrophe. If he is not straining every nerve in creative effort, he collapses. 'If he is not working,' a friend notes, 'if he is not in the mood for work, he has no taste for anything. Fortunately it is not like that every day; otherwise it would be a calamity.'

All his life, Picasso has striven to compel the total engagement of his powers, this continuity of expression. All his friends have experienced his sudden bouts of evil humour when inspiration was at a low ebb. At such moments he feels poised above a void, a total prey to misery as though his creative impotence was to last for ever. All the experience of a lifetime does not suffice to relieve the torture of these sterile hours. It is useless for Picasso to tell himself that they will pass: at the height of his fame he is as close to despair as the youth who lost his taste for living with the taste for work.

One day a few years ago, Tristan Tzara called to see him. He found Picasso in a state of abject distress. He had spent hours in his studio waiting in vain for that mysterious release of the creative trigger that would make him seize brush or charcoal. He was waiting passionately for a miracle that was slow to come. The hours ticked by. 'Nothing,' he said. 'I have done nothing but read the newspaper. I have even read the personal column.' He confessed himself defeated. All his past triumphs meant nothing to him, and in the days that followed he was to renew this vigil, alone with a distress that no promise of a better tomorrow could relieve.

From adolescence onwards, Picasso's great spiritual adventure consisted in this need to create, a hunger and thirst that were never satisfied.

CHAPTER III 1901–1902

Forging a Style

A SKETCH of himself done at the age of nineteen —since stolen from one of his friends—showed Picasso with his head ringed with the words: 'Yo el Rey' (I the King) several times repeated. No doubt referring to his creative independence, a man very much attached to him said to me earnestly one day: 'And he *is* a king!'

This sketch is said by one of Picasso's Catalan biographers to have been made on the eve of his departure for Paris. None of his friends seems to have understood at the time why he chose to go. He gave up his studio and forsook them all—for what? To them it remained an inexplicable venture. But despite Nordic tendencies and German philosophy and aesthetics, which exercised so powerful an influence in Barcelona, Paris had, of course, retained an unparalleled prestige among painters, and in the discussions around café tables and at Els Quatre Gats, it was the authority of the men who had come back from Paris that prevailed. Though their equal or superior in talent, no doubt the young man was made to feel ashamed that he had not yet crossed the Pyrenees. At any rate, though equally uncomprehending, his father gave him the money for the journey at his mother's insistence, and she told him later than Don José had handed over all the cash he had in the house except for a few pesetas to keep the family going until the end of the month.

Picasso left Barcelona for Paris in October, 1900, with Casagemas and his friend of La Horta, Pallarès. Though it was a leap in the dark, the hazard of the trip was somewhat lessened by the fact that the three young men were sure of a roof over their heads: a painter friend, Isidro Nonell, had just returned to Barcelona from Paris and turned over his studio at 49, Rue Gabrielle to them.

In Paris, ignorant of the language and limited to the fellowship of his compatriots, Picasso had the good luck to meet Pedro Manyac, the son of a Barcelona manufacturer, who had come to France after a family quarrel and was making use of his association with artists from his home town to do business as a picture dealer, and also Berthe Weill who had been employed in an antique shop which also bought and sold pictures. Later, Berthe Weill had started a small shop of her own. But finding that furniture and other antiques did not sell well and being ignorant of art herself, she had asked Pedro Manyac to put her in touch with some 'unpretentious' painters. Picasso seemed to fit this description, but as it happened the only pictures he had brought with him were of Spanish scenes which he thought would sell well: bull-fights, bull-fighters and bull rings. An afternoon appointment was arranged. Berthe Weill climbed six flights of stairs, knocked on the door and went on knocking. . . . No answer. Furious, she went down again—to meet Manyac at the bottom who told her that his friends Picasso and the sculptor Manolo were probably asleep and advised her to try again.

Berthe Weill was the first person to buy pictures from Picasso: three for 100 francs. And their association continued until ultimately she found him and his friends too expensive. Moreover, she said that Picasso frightened her. 'He puts a pistol under your nose and asks for money. Admittedly, it was a toy pistol. But it was not really that which frightened me. It was his terrible eyes.'

This purchase of three bull-fight scenes was an unexpected success and, realizing that Picasso would one day be a commercial asset, Manyac promised him an income of 150 francs a month in exchange for his output, just enough to make him independent of his family.

Picasso left Paris at the end of December in time to spend Christmas at home, telling his friends that it was Manyac's offer which had decided him to leave: he could work just as well for him in Barcelona as in Paris. This was his official explanation, but no doubt he was moved by some obscure instinct which made him choose the most propitious environment for his work. The many sketches which Picasso made in Paris have women and wine as their principal theme. If these represented temptations to him in the ordinary course of life, it seems that they were sublimated in the process of recording them on paper. But with Casagemas it was otherwise. At an age when triumph and disaster seem to be absolutes, he became involved in an unhappy love affair, took to drink and ceased to paint. Picasso was greatly affected by his friend's predicament.

The two young men spent the Christmas holidays with their parents in Barcelona, but the return to familiar surroundings brought no relief to Casagemas and after a few days, hoping perhaps that the sun and the countryside would have a better effect, Picasso took his friend to Malaga. But the trip was lost on Casagemas, while to Picasso the reunion with his relatives was painfully disappointing. In their staid respectability, they seemed shocked by the appearance of the two artists, and Picasso was forced to realize that he and his relatives no longer spoke the same language. Still drinking heavily, Casagemas, meanwhile, seemed to abandon the last shreds of self-control and Picasso realized that he could do no more for him. The fortnight they spent together at Malaga must have been a severe trial on his youthful patience and a highly distressing experience for him with his lust for life. It was an object-lesson also in the destructive power of uncontrolled passion and all his life thereafter he was to have a horror of sentimental complications, a horror which, according to one of his women friends, often made him cut short his amorous adventures.

Sensing perhaps that he would not see him again, Picasso bade farewell to his friend and Casagemas returned to Paris. Some days later he shot himself, some said on discovering the girl he loved in the arms of another man. His sudden, tragic end, his wasted life made a profound impression on Picasso and his sorrow is shown by the many drawings of Casagemas still to be found among his sketches. As late as 1903, the memory of Casagemas inspired a large picture symbolizing the rejection of life by a young man in despair. Casagemas appears naked with compressed lips and a bitter expression on his face. One hand is open in a gesture conveying uncertainty, perhaps about the reality of a happiness in which he could not believe. A young woman with a beautiful body is clinging to him, but he disregards her as he does another young woman who is gazing at him, her eyes full of reproach, with a child in her arms. Between these two groups—the man and the woman, and the woman alone with her child—two plaques or pictures are seen against the wall, one showing a passionate embrace and the other, a man crouching, apparently overwhelmed with loneliness. The whole scene (Cleveland Museum of Art, gift of Hanna Fund) bears the title *La Vie*. 'I did not give it that title,' says Picasso. 'I did not set out to paint symbols. I simply painted the images which rose before my eyes. It is up to others to find a hidden meaning in them. To me, a picture speaks for itself. What is the point of trying to explain it after it has been painted?'

Picasso may well have expected some material assistance from his relatives in Malaga, but their hostile reception and the death of his friend now convinced him that he could rely henceforth on nobody but himself, and that he would have to be completely independent. He therefore decided to settle in Madrid, taking a year's lease on an attic room there which he furnished as best he could with a palliasse, a table and a kitchen chair. There was neither light nor heat. 'I have never been so cold in my life,' he said later. And he went hungry. At the age of twenty he was certainly prepared to pay the price of his decisions.

Like Barcelona, Madrid was dominated at that time in the artistic and literary sphere by German influences. The Munich reviews *Jugend* and *Simplicissimus* set the tone. Picasso conceived the ambition to found a review of similar but independent character and in Madrid met a Catalan writer who was prepared to back the publication. This was Francisco de Asis Soler and his independent means appear to have derived from his father, who—exotic touch!—manufactured an electrical apparatus designed to preserve masculine virility. In a contemporary drawing by Picasso, Soler looks very much the man of letters, a dandy rather than a Bohemian, complete with top hat and walking stick, a long distinguished visage and an upturned moustache like Kaiser William's. In a self-portrait, on the other hand, Picasso accentuated—one would say deliberately—his own uncouth appearance: hands in pockets, straggling forelock and a square jaw. Together, he and Soler founded their review, assuming the artistic and literary direction respectively. The title, *Arte Joven* (Young Art) indicated their programme, while their approach was shown in an introductory article which stated: '*Arte Joven* will be an honest periodical.' But the first number, dated 31st March, 1901, differed little, except for the impressions which Picasso had gained in Paris, from all the other contemporary reviews which imitated the *Jugendstil*, and in any case *Arte Joven* expired after two or three issues. The last number came out in June, but by then, despite the fact that he had rented his room in Madrid for a year, Picasso had already been back in Barcelona a fortnight.

During his absence his friends seemed to have realized that he had not received the recognition he deserved in his adopted city and they had organized an exhibition of his pastels—his favourite mode of expression at that time—at the Salon Parès, the best gallery in Barcelona, where on Sundays solid citizens were in the habit of casting an eye at the pictures on their way home from Mass before buying their Sunday cake, the famous *tortell*, at a nearby *patisserie*.

'Some promising talent among the young strangers to our city has already emerged from the modern artistic centre concentrated at Barcelona,' wrote Miguel Utrillo when introducing this exhibition in the June number of *Pel y Ploma*, an art review of French inspiration. From his Parisian friends Utrillo must have learnt that Frenchmen—those few that Picasso met during his brief stay in Paris—had called him 'the little Goya', for he noted: 'We hope that the external resemblance will not be deceptive, and our heart tells us that we will be right.' He underlined Picasso's great qualities as a painter and his extremely youthful art, 'the product of his spirit of observation which detects beauty even in the horrible', and he added: 'The pastels represent merely one aspect of Picasso's talent which will be much discussed but no less appreciated by those who, abandoning ready-made moulds, seek art in all its aspects.' But Picasso was no longer in Barcelona when this eulogistic article appeared. He seems merely to have stopped there before setting out again for Paris, perhaps to look for a better livelihood than the monthly payments sent him by Manyac who, incidentally, was complaining that he was not receiving the promised pictures.

Picasso persuaded Jaume Andreu to accompany him to Paris and a drawing shows their arrival there, standing on the banks of the Seine in front of a bridge with the Eiffel Tower in the distance. With a long neck emerging from a full overcoat, Jaume Andreu looks more like an English traveller with his check cap, pipe and a beard fringing his face. Although it was spring it must have been cold, for Picasso has turned up the collar of his overcoat and his face is invisible except for the piercing eyes and strands of black hair escaping beneath the broad-brimmed hat. A woman in a large hat is turning round as the two strangers pass. Andreu carries a valise, but Picasso's only luggage seems to be a walking stick and a huge portfolio of drawings under his arm.

Picasso did indeed bring with him a large selection of pictures. Manyac was waiting for him—and his works—in a studio he had rented for them both at 130, Boulevard de Clichy. He at once put

Picasso in touch with an art dealer who was later to become famous, Ambroise Vollard, who forthwith arranged an exhibition for him in his gallery in the Rue Laffitte.

The Parisians' first encounter with Picasso took place on 24th June, 1901. Iturrino, a Basque painter considerably older than himself, was exhibiting at the same time, but with seventy-five canvases—an extraordinarily varied and rich collection for a young man still several months short of twenty—the day was, in fact, Picasso's. He showed the brightly-coloured pastels of Spanish scenes which he had brought with him: *The Picador, The Bull Ring*—a brilliant mixture of blues and reds that seemed to emprison the sunlight—and *The Toreadors*.

There were also works inspired by the theme which haunted Picasso's youth and on which he was continually trying new variations, as though seeking its perfect expression: the embrace of lovers. One of his first versions (Moscow Museum) showed a young man in a blue jacket standing beside an unmade bed in a shoddy attic with blue-washed walls, holding in his arms a woman with reddish-brown hair in a long red skirt. The man's bronzed skin and his powerful brown hands contrast with the pale, slender arms of the woman. But Picasso soon got bored with feeble anecdote. In the *Embrace* (Swarzenski Collection, Boston), he painted two lovers in the street, welded by the impulse that draws them together. In the pastel in the Modern Museum at Barcelona, the embracing couple form a monolithic block cut into large planes by colour alone: the blue jacket of the workman, the woman's red jacket and green skirt. In his search for greater intensity Picasso achieved a charcoal (Junyer Vidal Collection, Barcelona) in which the young woman is clinging to the man in a passionate frenzy.

The first Paris critic to notice Picasso's work was Félicien Fagus in the *Gazette d'Art*. He listed all the painters who he thought had influenced him: Delacroix, Manet, Monet, Van Gogh, Pissarro, Toulouse-Lautrec, Degas, Forain and Rops. 'But each one,' added Fagus, 'a passing phase, taking flight again as soon as caught. It is evident that his enthusiasm has not left him time to forge a personal style; his personality resides in this frenzy, this juvenile and impetuous spontaneity (they say that he is not yet twenty and that he covers as many as three canvases a day).' In the flower pieces also exhibited, Fagus mentions particularly 'the furious surge towards the light of the flowers out of their vase and of the vase itself and of the table which supports the vase, and the luminous air which surrounds them all'. But, as if to curb his own enthusiasm and not to anticipate too much the future of so brilliant a talent, Fagus goes on to ask whether such prodigious skill may not lead the young Spaniard into facile virtuosity.

Picasso himself seems to have mistrusted his own gifts. Though he had brought a rich production with him from Barcelona, he considered that his real apprenticehsip was now beginning: he had told Utrillo on the eve of his departure that he was going to Paris to work. He knew, at all events, that he could no longer be satisfied with reproducing street scenes and chance encounters, and that he would have to plunge deep to find himself through the experiences that Paris offered.

One of the Paris influences which affected him while still in Barcelona, was that of Steinlen. 'I knew the illustrated *Gil Blas* very well,' he recalls, 'and Steinlen's drawings made a great impression on me at that time.' Like Picasso himself in later years, Alexandre-Théophile Steinlen was one of those foreigners who take possession of Paris more fully than those who are born there. Of Swiss origin, through his drawings in *Gil Blas* he acquainted Picasso with the violent contrasts in joy and misery to be found in Paris, with the flotsam of the city, with women prematurely old and defeminized, with the brief and loveless embraces that take place in deserted streets.

Steinlen also interpreted the nocturnal and Bohemian aspects of the capital, but it was Toulouse-Lautrec, whose influence Fagus duly noted, who revealed Paris at night to Picasso in all its disturbing glamour.

Toulouse-Lautrec, who died in the autumn of the same year that Picasso reached Paris, was one of his first great discoveries. In his own words, Picasso realized 'what a great painter he had been'. He was fascinated by his precise and formal mastery, and in his sparsely furnished room in the Boulevard de Clichy he pinned a painting of Toulouse-Lautrec's to the wall—a poster representing the dancer May Milton in her swirling robe which Picasso, it seems, had torn from a public hoarding. But apart from this, in the streets of Paris Picasso was discovering for himself the living models of the creatures rejected by bourgeois morality whom Toulouse-Lautrec had made famous; people whose trade had existed from ancient times, but who seemed not to have been alive at all before a painter gave them the freedom of the city. From their artificial world of nocturnal pleasures Picasso took the subjects for his pastels and oil paintings, such as *Les Soupeurs*

(A. Lefèvre Collection, Paris), *Les Plastrons* (Stransky Collection, New York), *Les Rastaquouères*, a coloured pen-and-ink drawing (Barcelona Museum), or the many cabaret scenes, such as *Le Cancan* (Masoliver Collection, Barcelona) or *La Diseuse* (Modern Museum, Barcelona).

But even as a young man, Picasso was only influenced by other painters in the partial and limited sense that he took from them what he could make entirely his own. The influence of Toulouse-Lautrec was confined to the choice of subjects. The women in the portraits that Picasso painted at that time wore hats loaded with feathers or flowers above a towering coiffure: they looked like harmless *midinettes* disguised as women of evil life. When vice appears in Picasso it is marked by the sadness of human decadence, as in the extraordinary *Femme maquillée* (Museum of Modern Art, Barcelona), with her wide mouth closed in a crooked smile and her arms hugging her body as though to preserve its failing warmth.

Picasso's autonomy in relation to the world of pleasures seen by Toulouse-Lautrec is apparent in one of the masterpieces of this very rich year of 1901, *The Dwarf Dancer* (Museum of Modern Art, Barcelona). In this picture a child's body is seen surmounted by a large woman's head. The face is made-up and looks like that of a cripple, as though elongated in a distorting mirror towards the high cheekbones. The face clashes appallingly with the red dancer's dress bordered with little flowers. The Spanish heritage appears here beneath the Parisian theme and *The Dwarf Dancer* recalls the jesters of Velasquez rather than the atmosphere of the Moulin Rouge. But the first real monster appears in Picasso's work with the *Femme aux bas bleus*, a crippled creature with bandy legs and a greenish face under a shock of carroty hair.

The most marked difference between Toulouse-Lautrec and Picasso at this time was one of technique. Picasso's oil paintings were done with little abrupt touches of pure colour dabbed on the canvas, the backgrounds seem to be composed of square pieces of confetti stuck on haphazardly, and the technique is nearer to pointillism than to Toulouse-Lautrec's large planes. The tones are violent and often brutally juxtaposed. The yellow of the sofa in the *Femme aux bas bleus* clashes with the red hangings in the background, and her greenish shawl shouts at her orange hair.

This stridency of colour was something Picasso had only recently acquired and Sabartés was shaken by it when he came to Paris in the autumn to see his friend. He saw then a series of canvases which had been done in four or five months, of violent colouring similar to that on playing cards. 'What do you say to it?' asked Picasso and with his characteristically delicate and patient smile Sabartés replied: 'I shall get used to it.'

On several occasions the violence of the colours in Picasso's work has been the prelude to a change in subject-matter which has then established itself in monochrome. He was on the eve of such a change now and his technique of clashing colours, furious brush-strokes and twisting lines painted in relief in contrast to the shape of the figures reflected the powerful stimuli which he was then receiving. Asked later what had been the predominant influence on him during the early days in Paris, he unhesitatingly replied: 'Van Gogh!'

The Vollard exhibition had virtually no success, material or moral, in spite of Fagus's eulogy. Picasso continued to live among his compatriots like many foreigners who for years, perhaps indefinitely, live in the watertight compartment of their own nationality. But in spite of his bad French, he made some valuable contacts. The influential art critic, Gustave Coquiot, took an interest in his exhibition and Picasso painted his portrait twice. The exhibition also attracted a young man named Max Jacob, who had visited it out of professional interest. Jacob was an occasional art critic and also acted vaguely as secretary to a philanthropic lawyer, who was organizing an exhibition called 'The Child through the Ages' at the Petit Palais. Jacob noticed and was impressed by the exceptional vigour of Picasso's paintings, and on a visiting card wrote a few words expressing his admiration. So far, Picasso had met few spontaneous enthusiasts and this tribute meant a lot to him.

Soon after, Max Jacob received a letter from Pedro Manyac—who was the only one among the Spaniards who could write French—inviting him to call at the studio in the Boulevard de Clichy. At first sight, it seemed unlikely that he and Picasso would have much in common. The young Pablo came from a country of almost instinctive anti-Semitism and Max Jacob was no doubt the first Jew to cross his path. Their origins, moreover, were very different: Jacob came from Lower Brittany, and their temperaments were also poles apart. Though he was six years older than Picasso, Max Jacob was an essentially vulnerable human being, unable to control his appetites, anxious for affection, but at the same time proud and suspicious, the very antithesis, it seemed, of Picasso who knew what he wanted and knew how to observe life without becoming too involved in it.

Yet, strangely, they took to one another at their first meeting. Neither could speak the other's language, so they merely shook hands and then, for lack of words, shook hands again. One by one, Max Jacob examined the pictures that littered the studio. He was told that Picasso painted as many as two in a day, or a night. He seemed to be exploring a new and limitless world. So the evening passed. Later on, Picasso's Spanish friends began to arrive. They urged Max Jacob to stay for supper, which consisted of beans. There were no chairs, so they sat on the floor. As conversation was difficult and there was at least a tacit understanding with the newcomer, everyone began to sing —airs from Beethoven, apparently. Everyone, that is, except Picasso who is no musician. But though he kept silent, he felt content.

Max Jacob was to preserve a glowing memory of the young Spaniard. 'He was extremely handsome,' he recalled later, 'with a face like ivory, without a wrinkle, and his shining eyes, which were larger then than they are today, and the raven's wing of hair hanging over his low forehead.'

Next day, Picasso returned the visit, accompanied as usual by his Spanish friends including Manyac, the indispensable interpreter. Max Jacob was living in a small, shabby room on the Quai aux Fleurs, the walls covered with lithographs by Daumier and Gavarni—they were cheap in those days. The Spaniards left late in the evening. Manyac went to sleep in a chair. Picasso and Max Jacob conversed in signs made eloquent by looks and smiles. Of his new-found friend, Picasso knew only that he was a poet, but he had a profound respect for magicians with words and he has always felt closer to them than to his painter friends. So, although he understood hardly a word of French, he asked Max Jacob to read some of his poems. An odd request, certainly, in view of the language difficulty, but nothing loath, Max Jacob complied and when they separated at dawn, he felt so flattered by Picasso's close attention that he was encouraged, as he said later, 'for the rest of my life. I believed in him more than I did in myself.' Overflowing with gratitude, he was determined to show it. In his room Picasso had admired a woodcut of Dürer's, perhaps his most precious possession; Max Jacob gave it to him and, seeing his interest in the Daumiers and the Gavarnis, he pressed those on him too.

But it was not only mutual admiration which linked Picasso and

33

Max Jacob, nor their poverty. They shared also a sense of moral isolation. 'We were both equally lost children,' Max Jacob has said. But if he drew strength from the younger man, he also gave him a great deal. Max Jacob was the first spiritual intermediary between Picasso and Paris, and also between Picasso and France. For although Picasso remained authentically Spanish in his reactions and emotions, his great spiritual adventure in the sphere of creation could have taken place nowhere but in France, where the aesthetic climate was favourable to his development, so enabling him to absorb the influence of other artists more easily and in due course to find the necessary recognition to exert his own. But fame and pride in the triumph of his efforts never made him forget that in the initially hostile atmosphere of Paris, it was a Frenchman and a poet who had welcomed him as a brother.

Soon after their first meeting, Picasso painted a portrait of Max Jacob sitting on the floor amongst his books in front of a large fire, but later the picture was painted over. Canvases were, indeed, expensive and there were never enough to satisfy Picasso's creative fury. Over the portrait of his friend he painted one of his finest Maternities of that period, a picture whose composition expresses perfectly the communion between a mother and her child. The woman is crouching, her long feet planted firmly on the ground, and the child is nestling among the heavy folds of her cloak, supported by one very long and delicate hand. The mother's head leans forward heavily against the child's forehead so that the two form a single block (Maurice Wertheim Collection, New York).

At the time when Picasso painted Max Jacob, they were seeing each other frequently and, as Picasso progressed in his knowledge of French, the characteristics which they had in common beneath their superficial dissimilarity became more apparent. They shared the same sense of humour, the habit of changing rapidly from melancholy to laughter and they shared a deep distrust of sentimentality. Each, finally, liked to baffle his friends with unpredictable sallies, with alternate malice and affection, and perhaps Picasso's abrupt transitions of mood in later years have their origin in those far-off days when Max Jacob set him an example. Nothing, at any rate, could be more delightful for two young men whose present was impecunious and whose future was uncertain than to enjoy laughter in common.

Meanwhile, Picasso was introducing Max Jacob to his Spanish friends who were flocking to Paris in increasing numbers. In the autumn, Sabartés arrived and Picasso met him at the station at about ten in the morning. Characteristically, Sabartés's first thought was that he had upset his friend's routine. 'Why did you get up so early?' he asked. From now on, life was lived with a new intensity.

Picasso with his young Spanish friends wandered through the streets of Paris, feeling their isolation in the great metropolis, seeking a spot which they could make their own, a rendezvous in the long empty evenings. In Montmartre, in the Place Jean-Baptiste-Clément—which was a square only in name—they found a tavern poor enough to accept their poverty-stricken selves. The site was a black hole without light or pavement. A board proclaimed simply, *Zut!* To the Spaniards, ignorant of French, it sounded pleasantly like a challenge. At the back of the premises, which were furnished with a counter and a few upturned beer-barrels in the guise of tables, opened a room of gloomy and squalid aspect. The floor was of beaten earth, a row of creaking, worm-eaten benches stretched along the walls which were spattered with filth and damp, and cobwebs were so thick on the lamps that light could barely penetrate. But the young men proved so assiduous that the room was soon reserved for them exclusively. Frédé, the proprietor, wandered about with a jug of beer in his hand, a beret crammed on his head and, over his shoulder, a guitar with which he sometimes accompanied his clients when they sang in an adjoining room. Soon, he was calling the newcomers 'mes petits', and later they were to make him famous.

One day, in a fit of extravagance, Frédé whitewashed the walls and the ceiling and cleaned the lamps. The Spaniards now felt thoroughly at home. Picasso and Ramón Pichot set to work to decorate the walls. With the end of his brush, in single strokes, Picasso drew the bodies of naked women, painting beside them the figure of a hermit. This his friends interpreted as the Temptation of Saint Anthony. Pichot, meanwhile, drew the Eiffel Tower in a corner of the room with Saint-Dumont's dirigible balloon hovering above it as a contemporary touch. There was still one empty space. In it Picasso sketched a portrait of Sabartés, half-length and more than life-size in a declamatory pose with a book in his hand. Above his head, a bat, taken from the coat-of-arms of his native city, spread its wings.

The friends now looked on their room in the 'Zut' as a corner of Spain. But they were not allowed to forget that they were still in Paris. One evening, shouts and screams came from the other side of the

35

wall where accounts were being settled with knives. On another occasion, some shots rang out. Frédé appeared, unperturbed. 'It is nothing, friends. Don't worry. Drink up!' One evening, Sabartés met Max Jacob in the two-roomed apartment which Picasso shared with Manyac in the Boulevard de Clichy. Max Jacob often came to see his friend, usually with a book under his arm. On this particular evening he had brought a volume of Verlaine to read the poems to his foreign friends. They were as ignorant of French as Picasso had been on his arrival, but the rhythm of the verses made up for their lack of sense. Max Jacob read slowly and deliberately. Then, as his enthusiasm mounted, he became more animated, began to raise his voice and gesticulate. Night fell, but when it was too dark to read he recited the poems by heart. With darkness came the cold, overpowering the feeble warmth of the stove. But Max Jacob read on gravely to his young friends who had their whole lives before them:

> *Un grand sommeil noir*
> *Tombe sur ma vie.*
> *Dormez tout espoir,*
> *Dormez toute envie. . . .*

They were strange lines to read to them, and to Picasso with his ambition and his zest for life.

In studying Picasso's latest pictures, Sabartés felt giddy as though he were skirting an abyss. He felt that something had happened to his friend and not merely in the pictorial sphere. Picasso seemed to have suffered an internal jolt, to have awoken to reality and to have said good-bye to his youth, although he was only twenty.

A new content, a new vision of humanity seemed to emerge from the splashes of colour, the fireworks that scintillated right into the background of his pictures. The change had not taken place overnight. Picasso's breaks with his past, abrupt though they seem, occur in stages, and in this process each picture seems like a step forward in a direction which he alone can foresee or which he inevitably follows. *La Femme maquillée*, for instance, with her crooked smile and her crouching body, is very different from the glamorous creature in the previous work, *Courtisane aux pierreries* (former collection of Ricardo Vines).

The theme of loneliness which was henceforth to dominate it, now appeared in Picasso's work. The contrast between the striped costumes of public entertainers and the distress which he discovered in them was particularly poignant. In *Harlequin leaning on his Elbow* (Henry Clifford Collection, Philadelphia), for instance, the figure sits with his chin in his hand, his wide mouth caught in a bitter expression, turning his head away from the woman who presses against him. *Harlequin and his Companion* are closely interlocked, their silhouettes forming a single mass. But this mass, with its flat, vivid colours is ringed by a black line and placed on one side of the picture, confronting a void, seemingly to indicate the isolation of the two lovers.

There was a new sensibility evident in these pictures, but even Picasso was at a loss to explain its origin. 'Can one ever say where an influence comes from?' he remarked one day. 'Or what can become a stimulus for a new work? Women certainly, but animals too, sometimes an object, sometimes a mere trifle. Not even a whole picture, but sometimes a spot in the picture which happens to be there by mistake or by chance.' And he studies a picture as though looking for some imaginary spot which might have released a new sense of vision in him.

In the course of that year, 1901, in the course, in fact, of a single summer, the colour was suddenly drained from his pictures. The picture dedicated to the memory of Casagemas, which his Barcelona friends saw in his studio in the autumn of 1901, was bathed in moonlight. But the ghostly tints had nothing specifically to do with the dead. It was a new vision of the living, a new sense of volume which demanded this economy of colour. A change of form preceded the change of tone, or, as he himself has said, 'the arabesques peculiar to the Blue period preceded the employment of monochrome, as, for instance, in *Harlequin and his Companion*.'

One day, Picasso saw the oblique rays of the sun falling on the blue walls of his room, planting splashes of gold and blue-green shadows on his picture, *Femme prenant son tub*. In this light the scene seemed to take on a peculiar significance, accentuated by the curve of the woman's body, the head lowered between the shoulders and the breasts hanging loosely between the arms (Phillips Memorial Gallery, Washington). With the advent of the Blue period, women's flesh became paler and the smile faded on their compressed lips. The *Woman with a Chignon* (Henry Bakwin Collection, New York) has broad-set eyes, a slightly crooked nose, a twisted mouth and a long, asymmetrical face with a slanting fringe over the forehead and a high chignon placed on one side which seems on the point of falling over. The woman is leaning her elbows on the table. The arms are excessively long and the heavy face is resting on large hands. The whole picture seems a symbol of hopeless resignation. The same effect is achieved in the picture, *Au Café*, where the woman sits before an empty glass with her chin in one hand and the other clutching her shoulder in a bony grip as though to protect herself from blows. She is a sister of the *Woman with arms crossed* (collection of Mr. and Mrs. Chauncey McCormick), where the head is thrust forward with a fixed expression and the mouth is distorted with weeping. There is, finally, the *Women drinking Absinthe* (Hamburg Museum), where the figures are slumped in their chairs and seem to be shivering under their heavy shawls as though death were already in them.

Since Sabartés's arrival in Paris, Picasso had started the habit of meeting his Spanish friends at the Lorraine, a café in the Latin Quarter frequented by many French intellectuals who liked to rub shoulders with the celebrities of the day. Picasso was always reluctant to leave his studio and, one evening, Sabartés had to wait a long time for the arrival of his friends. In imitation of the Bohemian artists of Paris, he wore his chestnut hair very long, falling straight on either side of the high forehead. He had on a corduroy jacket and a waistcoat with a high collar. He looked like one of the local artists, but he was feeling very lonely and uprooted. His eyes were gazing in boredom through the smoke-filled room. His chin rested on one hand and the other caressed a tall beer-mug as though it were a life-buoy. This was how Picasso saw him from a distance, with his head turned to one side and his lips sagging at the corners, and this was how he painted him in the portrait known as *The Bock* (Moscow Museum of Modern Ars).

At the age of twenty, Picasso had already created a very personal vision. 'If we demand sincerity from the artist, we do not admit that it can be found outside suffering,' wrote his friend. But this new conception of life and the discovery of omnipresent suffering accompanied by a darkening of his palette was disconcerting for his Paris friends, and above all, for his manager, Manyac, who had been delighted by the profusion of colour and the pleasant virtuosity of his early manner. The change seemed to him arbitrary and harmful to Picasso's interests and his own. The new manner was certainly less

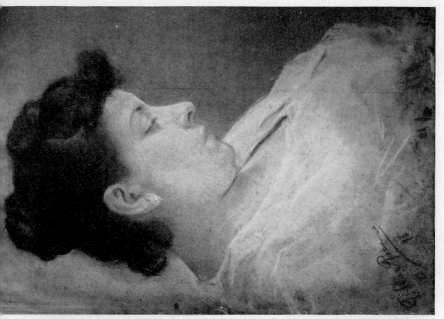

1 Picasso's mother, 1895

2 Picasso's father

3 Picasso's birthplace

4 Pablo and Lola

commercial. The indignation, however, which Picasso caused his financial adviser by choosing a path calculated to turn away clients was only the prelude to more spectacular challenges to come. But a little more adaptability might have been expected of an unknown young man of twenty, some preparedness to make concessions for the sake of emerging from poverty and obscurity.

Manyac was only the first who failed to understand Picasso's basic intransigence; many others concerned with his financial interests were to have the same experience. But Manyac felt the more justified in demanding consideration in that Picasso depended on him, lived in the studio which he had rented and existed on the monetary advances which he had made. That they lived together made relations more difficult and these were further aggravated by Picasso's habit of inviting his friends to the studio which Manyac paid for, and keeping them to lunch or supper, Soon, Manyac was ostentatiously absenting himself when he found guests had arrived.

The daily friction was finally too much for Picasso and he began to lose interest in work. Wandering through Paris, he got to know a Spanish sculptor, Paco Durio, who lived in a strange wooden building in the Rue Ravignan. Little suspecting that he would one day make the place famous, he used to call at nightfall and interest himself in the work of his friend as though he had only just discovered sculpture.

Gloomily, Picasso confided to his friends that he was only waiting for the money which his father had promised before leaving Paris. No doubt he had been reluctant to ask for money; it was confessing a failure, but the privations he was enduring were beyond his strength. The winter was a hard one and he could not even pay for coal to warm the studio. When his friends had stayed late at the 'Zut' or their journey home to the left bank seemed too long, Picasso put them up at the flat. Soto stayed the night there from time to time, also Sabartés. They used thick tomes for pillows and piled all the clothing they possessed on top of themselves. Pictures were wedged against the doors to keep out the draught. After sixty years, Picasso can still remember the horror of those glacial nights.

It was at the end of his stay in Paris, before he left for Barcelona in January, 1902, that Picasso painted a strange self-portrait (property of the artist). If his own testimony and that of his friends did not agree, one would never believe it to be the picture of a young man of twenty. He had grown a stiff moustache and a fringe of beard. In the square

D

face, the cheeks are hollow and the ringed eyes are sunk in their orbits. The gaze is forceful, but filled with sadness. The mouth, with full compressed lips, seems to be restraining painful confidences. The upturned overcoat is hardly necessary to suggest that it is the portrait of a man who has experienced extreme cold, who has probably gone hungry and who perhaps is recovering from an illness. It is also the face of a matured and disillusioned individual. It is no doubt significant, in the light of Picasso's future development, that he looked like this at the age of twenty.

CHAPTER IV 1902–1904

The Blue Period

'IAM working hard,' wrote Picasso from Barcelona to Max Jacob. 'I am showing what I do to my friends, the *local artists*'—he underlined the words—'but they find there is too much soul and not enough form: it is very odd. You know how to talk to people like that, but they write very bad books and paint ridiculous pictures.'

Thus if indifferent critics had any effect on him, it was to make him persevere in the path he had chosen and to increase his obstinacy. His contempt for them was his salvation because it prevented him making concessions. He got used to his isolation. That was life, he decided.

Christian Zervos was to say of him that he was 'the proudest man of our time'. But this pride does not seem to have come to him with fame or with his ability to shock with impunity or even with financial success. He possessed the same pride at a time when everything seemed to conspire to discourage him and to arouse in him legions of doubts. The future Picasso is perhaps only completely understandable in the light of this self-awareness. If he had made no impression in Paris, he now realized that he would never make any in Barcelona. None of his artist friends there ever enjoyed more than local success and they were quite unable to appreciate his talent. One day, those works in which they detected too much 'soul' would be fought for by collectors, but meanwhile they did not help him to gain material independence. He was still living with his parents and was using a studio rented by the brother of his friend Angel de Soto. Another painter friend of de Soto's paid half the rent. He worked in one corner and Picasso in another. Although the latter contributed little to the expenses, he monopolized the room with his drawings, his canvases, his paints and his feverish presence so that soon de Soto himself was calling the place 'Picasso's studio'.

But this hard work did not correspond to a search for oblivion. On the contrary, this was one of those rare periods when Picasso resumed contact with the outside world and took an interest in everything that came before his eyes. It seems to me that, after his beginnings when everything that confronted him became a subject for his art, the moment when he started to paint landscapes represented a turning-point in his life. And Picasso has confirmed this. Landscape was for him a kind of minor art. He seemed to reimmerse himself in visual impressions before attacking a new theme—rather like an orchestra tuning up before it plays a symphony.

One of the landscapes which he painted after his return to Barcelona was the view seen from the windows of his studio, *La Maison bleue*, with its blue roofs blending with the sky, its ochre façade and a street with bluish shadows.

This blue is much more intense than that of the canvases painted in Paris. Sabartés noted the change when he returned to Barcelona in the spring and saw Picasso's new pictures. He realized that it was a change of light which had led to this increased intensity. In full sunlight Picasso's shadows had become deeper. What had been grey-blue or greenish-blue under the mother-of-pearl sky of the Île de France, had become almost pure azure in Barcelona. There has been much discussion on the influences which provoked the Blue period; that of the Catalan painters has been stressed, for instance, Isidro Nonell or Sebastian Junyer or that of older men with whom Picasso was then associating. But the Blue period began in Paris and merely became more marked in Barcelona. The literary moonlights, so much in vogue at that time, and the Nordic reveries which saturated Catalan poetry at the beginning of the century may also have played a part. Whistler's monochrome technique might also have encouraged him to sustain that unity of colouring. Among many other reasons, the artist's poverty has been cited which did not allow him a wide choice of colours and forced him to be sparing with the light under which he worked at night-time.

But whatever the reasons for the change, the blue colouring was closely linked with a complete recasting of the relationship between human figures and the space surrounding them. From now on, Picasso's figures have their centre of gravity within themselves, they rotate on their own axes and they have no contact with anything outside themselves. The composition of the Maternities which he painted created the greatest possible unity between the folds of their garments, their heavy, sorrowful heads and the infants nestling in the folds.

These women of Picasso's are very similar to the Florentine virgins. The nape of the neck is bowed in the same way, the nose is in a straight line with the forehead, the eyebrows are heavily drawn, the wrists are too fragile, the hands are too long and too supple and the fingers are excessively elongated and of an equal thinness throughout their length. The hands, particularly, are typical of the Blue period. But Picasso's children, too, with their heavy foreheads and serious expressions are reminiscent of the fifteenth-century Italian painters: it is clear that he remembered his visits to the Louvre.

In Paris he had argued a great deal with his friends from Barcelona about the sources of artistic inspiration. 'At that time,' writes Sabartés, 'we were staunch supporters of Picasso's idea that the genuine artist should be ignorant of everything, that knowledge gets in his way, stops him from seeing and prevents self-expression by robbing him of spontaneity. In the museums the works of the Primitives seemed to prove the truth of our doctrine; they showed an innocence uncontaminated by artifice.'

But this way of thought was contemporary, not personal, and it was alive particularly in Barcelona literary circles. Admiration for the artists then labelled 'Primitives' had given rise to the powerful Pre-Raphaelite movement. But the English painters and their German imitators had taken from the *Quattrocento* only its most showy and superficial side. Picasso was closer to a Botticelli, a Botticelli confused by Savonarola, than to the English painters and men of letters. His Mothers, for example in the pastel *Maternité* (Bernheim Collection, Paris), or in *Maternité au bord de la Mer* (Fontbona Collection, Barcelona), have that protective fervour for their precious burdens and the sense of the precariousness of life which overwhelms the grieving virgins of the religious painters.

But Picasso's Mothers, draped like antique statues, are nevertheless sisters to those fallen women that he began to paint in Paris and continued to evoke in Barcelona. The same model seems to have sat for the pastel, *Maternité* and for the *uveuse Bassoupie*, even to the lock of hair which falls over their cheeks. The *Femme assise* (former Vollard Collection), looking as though petrified, with her heavy straight nose, is close to the horror-stricken *Confidente* of Moscow. *La Femme accroupie près de la mer* (Stein Collection) expresses to the maximum the distress of all those women cowering with crossed arms before a hostile world. The street-walkers, like the fallen women and the sorrowful mothers, are bathed in a blue half-light. According to Karl Jung this is the blue of night, of moonlight or the Toual-blue of the Egyptian infernal regions. Speaking later of a Picasso exhibition in Zürich, the Swiss psycho-analyst called his art 'a typical expression of schizophrenia with its contradictions of feeling and even a total absence of sensibility'. Jung saw evidence in Picasso's paintings of moral dissociation revealed 'in the so-called "broken" lines, that is, a kind of psychic fissure running across the image'. And this image 'leaves one cold or astonishes by its paradoxical, disturbing, frightening or grotesque audacities'. Professor Jung, who lived aloof from modern art, seldom visited exhibitions of contemporary artists and was not well acquainted with literary tendencies, compared Picasso's 'schizophrenic expression' to James Joyce's: 'The ugly, the morbid, the grotesque, the unintelligible, the commonplace are sought after not in order to express, but to conceal, and the veil is not meant to be pierced; it is like a cold fog spread over empty marshes, as pointless as a spectacle that can do without a spectator.' Jung saw in Picasso's art 'the demoniac force of attraction of the ugly and the evil'. According to him, the Blue period is bathed 'in a pessimistic, end-of-the-world atmosphere'. It is the symbol of *Nekya*, of the 'descent into hell', a disintegration of concrete forms with its 'mournful masterpiece of the adolescent prostitute, tubercular and syphilitic'.

This interpretation of Jung's has aroused a lively controversy between Picasso's admirers and his detractors. But if, like every true creator, Picasso is at home with monsters and brings them to life to impress them on our imaginations, it may well be that without his imperturbable mental balance he could not make them so persuasive. And the times he lived in were out of joint. Suicides were frequent amongst his acquaintances, others were dogged by mental illness and his friend Junyer actually went mad. But the young man living in the 'infernal regions' of his creative art emerged from this perilous blue night with all his youthful vigour, normal appetites and a contagious laugh. For him, the beautiful body of a woman remained the most effective artistic stimulus.

At that time, a spectacle was being performed in Barcelona called

'The Flea', in which a beautiful girl named Chelito was anticipating
the modern strip-tease. Each time she undressed, the public went mad.
Young Pablo did not miss a single show. One day about noon, Sabartés
called to see him. Picasso was still asleep and all around him, on the
table, the chair and even on the floor were piles of drawings inspired
by the provocative poses of the fair Chelito. But if he was already
obsessed with the contours of the female body, in Picasso mastery of
form seems to have been born at the same time as desire. That continuous stroke, done without raising the brush, which was later to
feature in his masterpieces, was already his. Was it inherited from the
seventeenth-century Spanish calligraphers who traced baroque orna-
ments and cherubims releasing captive birds, also without lifting the
pen, and who called this skill 'the new art of writing': *Nueva arte de
escrivir*? 'No,' says Picasso. 'It is much more simple than that. It is a
common habit with us. In Malaga I have seen children drawing in the
sand in the same fashion, with a single stroke.'

But the young admirer of female beauty was also a delightful companion. In his spare time he sought the company of young, carefree
people like the Junyer-Vidal brothers. He saw a lot of them at that
time. One of them, Sebastian, also a painter, was barely two years
Picasso's senior, but his big bushy moustache made him look older
and his round eyes under arched eyebrows gazed at the world with
solemn intensity. Picasso made several rapid pen sketches of Sebastian.
In one of them he is dressed as a torero. In another, he wears a toga and
stands on a rock with a lyre in one hand and a scroll in the other,
apostrophizing the sea. In another picture, which he called his *Vision
of Majorca*, he made fun of the heroic note which Sebastian liked to
strike in his paintings and depicted him contemplating rocks shaped
like the heads of antique sages while voluptuous women stretch their
legs below. Finally, Picasso painted a parody of Manet's *Olympia*: a
buxom negress is reclining on a huge bed; on one side appears the
naked figure of Sebastian Junyer holding a bowl of fruit, on the other
stands Picasso, also naked, stretching his hand towards the voluptuous
vision.

But meanwhile, Paris was beckoning again. Picasso's material
position had not improved in Barcelona and he was feeling shut in.
For a time he even did pot-boilers, and his Catalan friends remember
an advertisement he painted for a patent medicine against malfunction-
ing of the lymphatic glands in which a pierrot is sitting on a bench

45

beside a thin, painted girl. He also designed posters for a grocer's shop-front. Finally, in October, 1902, he persuaded Sebastian Junyer to accompany him to Paris.

Picasso stayed at first at the Hotel Champollion, then, for lack of money, shared a room with a Spanish sculptor named Sisket in the Hotel du Maroc in the Rue de Seine. The building was old and the room was an attic with a ceiling so low that it touched the floor on one side and on the other left just enough space for a small bull's-eye window. One huge iron bedstead filled the floor and Picasso or his companion had to lie in bed before the other could get into the room.

But meanwhile, thanks to Manyac, Picasso had resumed contact with the Paris public. An exhibition had been held from 1st to 15th April at Berthe Weill's gallery. Among the fifteen oil paintings and pastels by Picasso, which were shown with works by Louis-Bernard Lemaire, were several Parisian scenes—such as *Le Trottin*, *Le Quatorze Juillet*, *L'Hétaïre*—several portraits of babies, children and girls, a mother-and-child, a version of the *Vierge aux cheveux d'or*, some few Catalan subjects and a still-life. But in spite of all efforts, the closing day came and not a picture had been sold.

When Picasso met Max Jacob again, they resumed their friendly relations. Max was still earning a scanty living, now as tutor to a small boy. As soon as he had a few sous to spare, he would bring his friend some fried potatoes, for as he said later: 'Neither Picasso nor the sculptor used to eat.' In this difficult period, Max Jacob's wealthy family came to his aid. His uncle Gompel, who later was to be one of the first people to buy Picassos, gave him a job in a department store which he owned in the Boulevard Voltaire. Max rented a large room near his work and invited Picasso to share it with him. But this room, too, had only one bed, so at night Max slept while Picasso worked and Picasso went to bed at seven in the morning when his friend left for the shop. The wages paid must have been small, for Picasso still remembers the rare occasions when they were able to cook an omelette, fry some potatoes or eat some beans. He also remembers their disappointment when they bought some sausages in the street and took them home only to find they were bad.

But soon their situation was even more desperate. Like so many of his other jobs, Max Jacob had found business life uncongenial and had got the sack. Picasso's career seemed without a future. One day, they were both leaning over the balcony of their fifth floor overlooking the boulevard. The same thought struck them both. . . . But almost immediately, Picasso said: 'We must not have ideas like that,' although, indeed, Picasso had more reason to despair than his friend: he was earning nothing at all, nobody wanted his pictures and he was living on Max Jacob who was himself extremely poor. When they moved and went to the Boulevard Barbès they could not even afford to buy paraffin so that Picasso could work at night.

He now realized that he would have to return home again, but he could not pay for the journey. He tried to sell his pictures—all of them, those that had been exhibited, the product of the last few months, his drawings and his watercolours—for 200 francs, but nobody would buy them. It was very cold that winter and even by piling on all their clothes they could not keep warm in the draughty room. So, for the sake of a few moments' warmth, Picasso burnt all his drawings and watercolours. Finally, he succeeded in selling the pastel of the *Maternité au bord de la mer* for a price which just covered his railway fare to Spain. He rolled up his remaining canvases and entrusted them to his friend Ramòn Pichot who put them on top of a cupboard and forgot about them. 'If he had lost them,' says Picasso, 'there would have been no Blue period, for everything I had painted up to then was in the roll.'

After his return to Barcelona, Picasso kept in touch with Max Jacob by means of occasional letters. One of them was written on a printed form which his friend de Soto's father, who was Inspector-General of customs, used for official business. 'It is a long time since I wrote to you,' scrawled Picasso, 'but it is really not because I am not thinking of you. It is because I am working, and when I am not working, I amuse myself or get bored stiff.' The back of the form is covered with drawings showing the view from the studio which de Soto had rented in his absence, the same studio that Picasso had shared with Casagemas. Picasso closes the letter with an invitation: 'Do you get any holidays? If so, you must come and see me in Barcelona. You cannot think how much pleasure that would give me.' Picasso himself was not thinking of returning to Paris in the near future. 'I am going to stay next winter here,' he wrote, 'and do something.' In Barcelona, Picasso found his old friends and resumed his old habits. When de Soto returned from his office in the town hall he always met friends in the studio who had come to see him or Picasso and they used to take their meals together, a grocer sending up provisions in a bucket intended to draw water from a well. . . .

In Barcelona, too, Picasso was soon arm-in-arm again with his faithful friend Sabartés. Sabartés was living in a small apartment in an old house reached by a dark and winding stairway from a narrow street. The walls had been roughly whitewashed. One day, Picasso decided to cover them with pictures, as he had done in his first studio and at the 'Zut'. Dipping his brush in a rich flow of blue, he ran it over the wall without lifting it, as though following some clear path that only he could perceive. On one narrow strip of wall he painted a huge nude male, as rigid as an Assyrian bas-relief. On the opposite wall, he painted a half-naked Moor hanging from a tree with one slipper sliding off his foot. Along the wall, close to the floor, a nude couple are making love. A bull's-eye window was given lids and lashes so that it appeared like a gigantic eye watching the lovers. Above the window, Picasso traced the legend: 'The hairs of my beard, although separate from myself, are gods as much as I.'

These paintings on an attic stairway—long since removed—are a reflection of the sexual obsession which haunted Picasso at that time. The pair of lovers was repeated in another painting, *L'Etreinte* (Paul Guillaume Collection, Paris), in which two naked bodies are intertwined with the face of each hidden in the other's flesh. The woman's slender arms are flung round the man's neck and her small breasts rub against his arm. But the belly pressed against his is distended like that of a pregnant woman.

Picasso's frenzied lovers represent a flight from loneliness, which is the main theme of this period—the loneliness of the old, the poor, the sick and the disinherited. The large subjects he was painting then were treated as frescoes with simultaneous scenes, as in *La Vie* or *Les Parias* (Chester Dale Collection, New York).

Two years after Picasso's visit to Toledo, El Greco seems to have exerted a delayed influence in his blue-ink drawings of beggars, with their prophet-like faces, their uneven eyes and hollow cheeks, but above all with their excessively delicate and elongated fingers. But the relationship between the figures and the surrounding space shows Picasso's own very individual interpretation of the laws of bas-relief within a compact framework. His preference henceforth for characters placed side by side instead of in a single block is clear when the drawing in blue ink, from the Junyer-Vidal Collection, Barcelona, is compared with the picture of *Le Vieux Juif* (Museum of Modern Art, Moscow).

Privation and human suffering seemed strangely familiar to this young man of twenty-two. Picasso plumbed the abyss of human isolation in his *Repas de l'aveugle* (Metropolitan Mueseum of Art, New York). For a man like himself who lives through his eyes, blindness is the most tragic of all afflictions. The blind man's head droops with the same resignation as in all Picasso's pictures of suffering. His body is hunched between the parallel lines of his arms while one hand, like the branch of a withered tree, gropes towards a jug of water. In this picture, the lunar blue achieves its maximum effect, suggesting a mood of frozen solitude.

Meanwhile, Picasso's means of escape from suffering continued to be portraits, courtesy portraits done as presents for his friends. There is the portrait of Coriane Romeu, with her full lips and robust sensuality. The portraits of the elegant tailor Soler, Soler's wife and the large picture of their family almost represent a page from Picasso's autobiography, for the pictures were painted in exchange for clothes.

Picasso's Soler portraits are certainly evidence of his increasing credit and also of his considerable sartorial needs. Max Jacob has stressed that even in the days of their common poverty Picasso was extremely careful about his person. He had a great feeling for what was stylish and matched his socks and trousers as lovingly as he painted a picture.

Soler could not have suspected the value of this payment in kind. He sold the *Déjeuner sur l'herbe de la Famille Soler* to a Catalan dealer who took it to Paris where the Cologne Museum acquired it for, it was said, the sum of one million francs.

Meanwhile, Picasso was escaping more or less consciously from his blue twilight. He painted at this time one of those portraits of Sabartés which in the course of his life were often to play the role of experiment. His friend's features were so familiar to him, the understanding between them was so complete that he could use Sabartés as a means of taking stock of himself. The portrait was done in a peculiar blue, a periwinkle blue rather than a cold or greenish colour. Skin, clothing and hair all merge into this warm tone. The red lips stand out against a dull, pastel tint. Sabartés's tie-pin gleams with a metallic lustre. It seemed that, after long abstention, the taste for fine materials was reawakening in Picasso.

This portrait of Sabartés, which is dated 1904, was painted in a studio which Picasso had rented in January when he left the one he had been sharing with de Soto. At last he was able to satisfy his need for independence. It was the first studio that had been his own since his adolescence. Though he needed almost constant company as soon as he left his work, he had an even more urgent need to be alone when he was working. He now rejoiced in his own latch-key and kept it in his purse as a treasured possession.

'I am very fond of keys,' says Picasso. 'It seems to me very important to have one. It is true that keys have often haunted me. In the series of bathing men and women there is always a door which they try to open with a big key.'

But in spite, or because of this independence Picasso was soon becoming restless again. On 24th February, 1904, an exhibition of his works was held in Paris organized by the Galerie Serrurier in the Boulevard Haussmann. Encouraged by this, he decided in April to leave for Paris, taking Sebastian Junyer with him as companion. A sketch done at that time in ink and watercolour shows a naked man with a long skinny body jumping into the void with his arms glued to his sides. That, no doubt, is how Picasso felt, returning to the city where so far he had only known poverty and rejection.

CHAPTER V 1904–1905

Hardships and Harlequins

THE Place Ravignan, a small square on a hill-side planted with young trees, was well known to Picasso and also the curious wooden building, so out of place in the heart of Paris, which was then called the 'Maison du Trappeur' and was later known as the 'Bateau-Lavoir'. Here Picasso had often visited his sculptor friend, Paco Durio. His studio happened to be vacant when Picasso arrived in Paris and rather than waste time looking for somewhere else, he installed himself in the familiar surroundings. Not even a couple of suicides and a welter of squalid people who sought refuge under the same roof could drive him from it.

The only contents of his studio were a day-bed, a rickety table, a tub and a small, rusty iron stove which was supposed to serve for cooking, heating and as support for a wash-basin with a towel and a piece of soap lying beside it on a deal board. A wan light from a single window fell on festoons of cobwebs hanging from the ceiling. The furniture was completed by two dilapidated chairs. In the half-open drawer of the table Picasso, who always liked to have animals around him, kept a tame white mouse.

The pictures Picasso had brought from Barcelona with their sorrowful themes were in harmony with the place, and the proximity of down-at-heel working people suggested similar subjects of hardship and privation. Soon, Picasso was painting a cripple leaning on his crutch and carrying a basket of flowers on his back (since repainted), a blind man, a tragic figure no more than a skeleton, before an empty plate and a morsel of bread, and *Le Repas frugal*, where another blind man grips his woman companion with long, bony fingers.

Picasso himself was experiencing difficult times, but he had his friends, among them Paco Durio, who had taken over a large studio in the neighbourhood where he had installed a pottery kiln. Better off than Picasso and guessing his straits, Durio one day left a tin of sardines, a litre of wine and a loaf of bread before the artist's door. According to the girl he was then living with, 'Picasso used to accept as the homage due to him everything that his friends tried to do to make life more comfortable for him.'

Another of Durio's protégés was an individual so picturesque that he seems to have been invented to enhance literary memoirs. Picasso and Durio had recently got to know the illegitimate son of a Spanish general, by name Manuel Hugué, known to his friends as Manolo. His only schooling had been the streets of Barcelona and the company of vagabonds and thieves. But he was a sculptor of real talent and in his native city he had existed for a while, thanks to the affections of a dairyman's daughter who had got him the job of carving small objects in butter for display purposes in the family shop. Later, as an incorrigible rebel, Manolo had deserted from military service and was now living by his wits in Paris. Durio put him up in his studio for a while where there were a number of valuable Gauguins, leaving Manolo in charge while he himself went to Spain. On his return, the pictures had gone. Manolo had sold them, and he explained as the most natural thing in the world that he had been faced with the alternatives of either dying of hunger beside the beautiful pictures or else having something to put in his stomach, and that life had seemed to him the more attractive proposition. But Manolo always succeeded in giving the impression to those he abused that he was conferring a favour on them. He never managed to speak recognizable French; on the other hand he was eminently successful in existing in Paris without doing any work. He invented a lottery in which the prize was to be a bust which he was going to sculpt himself. The bust was never made, but the lottery continued on and off for years. He had a flair for battening on the gullible. He was always on the look-out for a chance to diddle his neighbours, a task he performed with invariable courtesy and flowery quotations from picaresque literature. One day, he was having a drink at the Mollard Café, opposite the Gare Saint-Lazare. At the next table two gentlemen were discussing their common passion for photography and one of them was deploring his inability to find a camera of a certain make. At this point Manolo joined in the conversation, confessing gravely that he had possessed a camera of that particular make, but had had to pawn it in temporarily straitened circumstances.

He showed them the ticket: it did not specify the object pawned, but the enthusiast seized on it delightedly, paid a fair price for it and at once sent a messenger to collect the camera. Manolo took courteous leave of the gentlemen and was already far away when the man returned, staggering under the weight of an enormous mattress. . . .

It was Manolo who one evening brought André Salmon to see Picasso. Towards 'little Pablo', as he called him, Salmon—who was ten years older—maintained an admiring but by no means a fawning attitude. Sure of his own judgment, he recognized in his young friend '*un immense artiste, considérable et indispensable*'. But he made no bones about criticizing him in his own outspoken fashion and later he never allowed Picasso's fame to disturb his attitude of detached but unenvious friendship.

Among his most faithful friends Picasso had found Max Jacob again. 'I was out of a job when he came back in 1904,' the latter recalls. 'I was writing verses—because Picasso had discovered a talent in me—and also children's stories.' But the stories seldom got finished. The only ones his friends can remember were a 'Diary of Jean-Pierre' and the 'Sun-Giant' who used to swallow the world at intervals and then spit it up again: he came to a stop in the second chapter.

Max Jacob was still living in the Boulevard Barbès and was always available when Picasso wanted him. Though a difficult man, alternating between suspicion, malice and hectic gaiety, he was discretion itself in his relations with Picasso and, though refusing to take a job himself and sinking ever deeper into misery, he busied himself about Picasso's affairs with devoted affection and undertook to contact dealers in his name.

The big art dealers had not yet discovered Picasso. When Vollard saw the latest works of the Blue period he shrugged his shoulders and said simply: 'Your friend has gone mad.' A landscape thought sufficiently inoffensive to please him—sent when Picasso was ill and completely broke—was barely glanced at. Vollard turned his back and said: 'The belfry is crooked.'

Max Jacob had more success in selling the drawings. In the Rue des Martyrs there was a junk-merchant who sold mattresses, wash-basins, stools, contraband tobacco and 'art'. Papa Soulier, a hirsute individual with the look of a jaded lion, did not guess the value of what was passing through his hands, but he knew how to bargain. He would pay 10 sous for a drawing, rising sometimes, according to the dimensions, to 2 or 3 francs: then Max Jacob would return to the studio loaded with foodstuffs. Later on, when a Picasso drawing would fetch as much as 50 francs, a rich art-lover was gazing one day at the drawings which littered the studio. 'But look!' he said. 'You have got the makings of a fortune.'

The fortune was still far off. But Picasso's needs were few. When he had worked hard during the day or before he started work at night— he was falling more and more into the habit of spending his nights painting—he would have liked some distraction, but he had no money to go out. Happily, however, Max Jacob was at hand. 'In the evenings,' he writes, 'since we could not afford to visit the theatre, we used to act plays under the paraffin lamp. We played all the parts in turn, including the stage manager, the director, the electricians and the stage-hands, all of whom we included in the play.' Pirandello, it seems, had invented nothing!

Max Jacob introduced Picasso to his young friends, the violinist Henri Bloch and his sister Suzanne. When he was short of money Picasso made use of the young musician to contact possible purchasers for him. He painted Suzanne and the portrait (São Paulo Museum) shows a woman with massive features, forceful gaze, full lips and a powerful neck below a storm-cloud of blue-tinted hair. One might think that she is dreaming of her future career as a Wagnerian singer, the picture is of such strange intensity and sombre violence.

But work and the company of his friends still left a void in Picasso which only a more permanent attachment could fill. The tenants of the Bateau-Lavoir had to fetch their water from a tap at the bottom of a long flight of steps. One day, water-jug in hand, Picasso met a young woman there who also lived in the house. She was, as she described herself later, 'health and youth personified'. Fernande Olivier's parents ran a millinery business, but what she describes as 'a most unfortunate matrimonial venture' had uprooted her from her *petit bourgeois* environment and brought her in contact with the artistic world whose tastes she believed she shared.

Picasso invited her to his studio and her eyes rested with amazement on the grim picture, *Repas frugal*. But she was not put off and she stayed, Picasso in due course being extremely proud of his conquest. But she was several years older than he and to him in his extreme youth she seemed a woman of ripe age. 'She is very beautiful, but she is old,' he used to warn his friends. Later, she recalled her lover as he

5 Picasso in sergeant's uniform

6 Picasso in 1910

was then with his clumsy gestures, his 'woman's hands' and the small feet of which he was rather proud. From the first she found him 'restless and disturbing', but her own placid temperament sufficed to maintain balance and stability.

Fernande Olivier possessed a statuesque and provocatively feminine beauty which fascinated and subdued Picasso. Many years later, after their stormy separation, he still spoke of the profound influence which her exceptional physical attractions exerted over him. A portrait of her (private collection) painted two years after their meeting shows the sensual force of their passion: the impeccable arch of her eyebrows is outlined on a low forehead; her wide almond eyes are narrowed a little as though in pleasure or tenderness; the nose with its heavy bridge has sensitive nostrils; between the wide and gentle curves of her cheeks blossoms a mouth whose full lips are closed on a faintly inviting smile. A small watercolour, *La Femme endormie* (Pellequer Collection, Paris), shows a man with a lock of hair sweeping his forehead seated, chin in hand, beside a bed, gazing fascinated at a woman in her night-gown sleeping the sleep of exhaustion with one arm under her head and the armpit broadly bared. There was an elemental fury in Picasso's love for Fernande Olivier. He was ferociously jealous. 'He used to keep me locked up like a recluse,' she remembers.

Perhaps Fernande did not understand her lover while she was living with him, but after their separation, with her sensibilities sharpened by her distress, she came to realize that there had always seemed to be a source of suffering in him. At the same time, she did not seem to appreciate how her mere presence had soothed the anxieties which strangled him and had hitherto found their sole outlet in work, and hence how grateful Picasso was to her for bringing him mental and physical release.

A small, dilapidated room with half-rotten floorboards opened off Picasso's studio and here Fernande used to take refuge when visitors arrived and she was still half undressed. This little room was both store cupboard and shrine. Beside a pen-and-ink drawing of Fernande (later stolen from an exhibition) was laid a crumpled white linen blouse which recalled a particularly happy moment. In front of the blouse, to which a dark red rose was pinned, stood two bright blue vases with artificial flowers. Later, Fernande wondered whether this altar of love was not Picasso's way of laughing at himself. It may have been, but it was also the basis for one of his future paintings and no doubt also

E

represented his love of symbols in which a certain amount of superstition was mixed. On this subject Picasso himself gives an indulgent, almost tender smile: 'When you are in love, at that age, you make gestures like that.'

Picasso bore all the practical burden of their life together which began at that time. Fernande confesses that she was very lazy and left her lover to arrange everything. Picasso has never liked to give orders and even later, when he had a large domestic staff, he preferred not to see the house cleaned at all rather than give instructions for it to be done. So now, rather than make any demands on Fernande, he did all the housework himself, sweeping the studio and fetching the provisions in sandals and a faded blue jacket, while she stayed in bed in a room that was like a Turkish bath in summer and was so cold in winter that in the mornings the previous night's tea would be found frozen in the cups.

According to her own account, Fernande followed his creative efforts with only moderate interest. In the same way as she watched him do the housework, she sat passively by while he painted, sitting, as he usually did, on the floor or a low stool, with his brushes, palette and paints scattered around him. Later on, her indolence was to weigh somewhat heavily on his intellectual friends. To them, when he was better off, her sole interest and sole subject of conversation seemed to be the hats and furs which he bought her. But after all, she had done without them for a long time. For two months she had stayed indoors without complaining because she had no shoes to put on, had stayed in bed when there was no fuel—until a coal-merchant had been touched by her splendid eyes and had sent some on credit. As soon as he was in the money, Picasso, moved by this devotion, would go out and buy her a large bottle of eau-de-Cologne—for perfume was another of Fernande's passions.

Art dealers were still difficult and in moments of embarrassment Picasso would contact one of those second-hand dealers who both exploit and assist artists whom the experts have been slow to recognize. Clovis Sagot, a former clown with the Medrano Circus who possessed a certain boldness of artistic taste, had set up as a picture dealer in a shop near his former place of work. The shop had once been a pharmacy and the only act of generosity in which he was ever detected was to give sick artists the patent medicines he had found on the premises. Picasso had several opportunities of learning how pitiless this man could be. One day when there was not a sou left in the house and his work was at a standstill because he could buy neither paints nor canvas, he took three pictures to Sagot who offered him 700 francs. Picasso refused to sell. A few days later, he was forced to accept this sum and returned: but now Sagot would only give 500. Again Picasso refused, again he returned, and finally accepted 300 francs for the three pictures: a lesson which no doubt Sagot considered well deserved.

Lack of money was general among the artists, but so were various dodges for obtaining credit. 'We never ate so well at Picasso's as when we hadn't got a bean,' Fernande recalls. 'A lunch would be ordered from the *patisserie* in the Place des Abbesses, with instructions to deliver it at noon sharp. When the delivery man arrived he would get no answer to his knock and would finally leave the basket at the door.' But some small tradesmen and even *restaurateurs* would grant credit generously. Picasso's friends used to foregather with their wives or girl-friends at Azon's in the Rue Ravignan where they could get a dinner for 90 centimes, and at Vernin's in the Rue Cavalotti, which was conveniently near the pawnbroker's, they would even be offered a drop of spirits at the end of the meal. This stimulated Max Jacob's muse and he would sing to a popular air:

> *Ça m'ennuie d'aller chez Vernin.*
> *Mais il faut y aller quand même*
> *Parce qu'on y prend des verr' nains*
> *Et des fromages à la crème.*

Perhaps Max Jacob was not exactly delighted to find Fernande installed in his friend's life. Women terrified him and according to Fernande, 'He always thought he was being persecuted, especially by his friends' wives.' He seemed to resent Picasso's indulgence in amorous adventures and with a malice prompted perhaps by envy of his friend's sexual normality, he claimed that, 'Picasso would have preferred fame as a Don Juan rather than as a celebrated artist.' But his tact or his fidelity never deserted him. He never arrived at meal-times unless he was specially invited. And better than anyone else he could entertain Picasso and make him laugh. He had a prodigious memory and could recite whole tragedies by heart. As a musician and a pianist who had also taught singing he could perform scenes from operas and operettas with the same facility. But the *pièce de résistance* in his repertoire was his imitation of a barefoot dancing girl in which, already going bald and with spectacles on his nose, he would roll up his trousers and perform intricate steps with comic accuracy. He also imitated the female singer in the village hall with a bit of gauze round his neck and a woman's hat on his head, intoning in a sugary falsetto and with many simpering smiles, ballads such as the following:

> *Ah! superbe Pandore,*
> *Brigadier que j'adore,*
> *Ah! si tu restes froid*
> *A mon amour pour toi,*
> *Je le dis avec franchise*
> *Je vais faire une bêtise. . . .*

Later, despite his privations at that time, Max Jacob was to look back with affection on his days in the Rue Ravignan. Meanwhile, the former proprietor of the 'Zut' had acquired a tavern in Montmartre called the 'Lapin Agile'. Here, beside the customers, was an assortment of wild life which delighted Picasso: a raven which was the inseparable companion of Frédé's daughter Margot and a moth-eaten donkey which followed Frédé everywhere, even on his visits to Picasso's studio. One day, the donkey—who was called Lolo—had his tail dipped in paint and was called on to drag it over a canvas. The 'picture', entitled *Sunset over the Adriatic*, was in due course exhibited at the Salon des Indépendants as the work of the mythical painter 'Boronali' and caused much amusement.

One evening, a young German who had been wandering about the Sacré-Coeur put his nose in at the Lapin Agile. He had just bought a painting from Papa Soulier's junk-shop where pictures by unknown artists were piled pell-mell in front of the door. This picture showed a nude, fair-haired young woman taking a tub in a blue room. The German, Wilhelm Uhde by name, had paid 10 francs for it. Despite the ridiculous price, he knew at once that he had acquired an important work, for this acute, distinguished, extremely reserved young man possessed a perception and an independence of judgment which was to make him one of those great collectors who live intimately with the pictures they buy. The name Picasso which he had seen at the bottom of the picture was unknown to him. This evening, when he entered the Lapin Agile, chance placed him at the big centre table where the artists foregathered. The low room was full of smoke. Above the conversation he could hear a voice reciting Verlaine. Realizing he was among artists and, like all strangers wandering through Paris, anxious to make contacts, he introduced himself and ordered some wine. During the course of the evening he learnt that the painter of the canvas he had just bought was sitting on his right. 'Since that time,' he relates, 'I have lived for many years in the blue kingdom of Picasso.'

But, being in the habit of abandoning everything that he has attained or mastered, Picasso was already leaving that kingdom. As he could not increase its formal or emotional intensity, he could only repeat himself. But Picasso only resumes the same subjects or varies the same plastic vision so long as he has not exhausted their possibilities. As soon as he touches a limit or reaches a degree of saturation which only he can perceive he makes a break, one of those 'tireless new beginnings', as Zervos has said. One of the keys to his art is in his remark: 'To copy others is necessary, to copy oneself—what a shame!' But when Picasso makes a change of idiom, in short preparatory stages or from one day to the next, he surprises those who see him every day as much as total strangers, for his art is his only real means of communication and even those who have been closest to him, the women with whom he has lived, have been excluded from the citadel of his creative secret.

The culminating picture of his blue world is *La Fillette à la corbeille fleurie* of 1905 (Gertrude Stein Collection). The girl's body rises like a pale and slender column of light, still a little tinged with blue, against a warm, grey, smoky background towards the red splash of the flowers in her basket which she holds before her as a timid offering. With her large feet and pointed knees, it seems to be a child of the people who has posed for Picasso. She looks rather frightened. Her mouth is a little tremulous, but there is a suggestion of insistent femininity in the sideways glance of her veiled eyes.

In Picasso's personal life, *La Fillette à la corbeille fleurie* represents an important turning-point, the beginning of his friendship with Gertrude Stein, of whom he said later that she had been his only woman friend. Gertrude Stein seems to have had the gift of exerting a considerable influence by her mere presence, acting as a stimulus and as an encouragement to talent that without her would have taken longer to unfold. In the artistic world of Paris she acted as a catalyst, not only by the material assistance she gave, but through her lucid realization of the need for new forms of expression. All those who met her received something from her and, from the moment she came to live in Paris with her brother in 1904, it seemed as though she had never been absent.

Yet, far from becoming assimilated by the French atmosphere, Gertrude Stein remained profoundly and incorrigibly American. A compatriot wrote of her: 'One of the first women of her generation to settle in Paris, she was among the most patriotic of the voluntary exiles.' More curious still, this woman who came from a well-to-do environment and possessed a solid university education felt closer to the hermetic American *petite bourgeoisie* than to the intellectual *élite*. In her book, *The Making of Americans*, she displayed a warmth of affection for the middle class which, as one of her American critics has said, 'met with almost no response'.

She came to Paris thanks to a typically American success story. Her father had been sufficiently well-off to be able to travel with his family on the Continent, allow his three children to complete their studies and endow them, especially the two youngest, with a total incapacity for making money. But when he died, all he left them was a tramway concession in San Francisco, an asset that could not be realized. At this juncture the older brother, whose only desire had been to continue his medical studies, took charge of the family. He turned out to be a financial genius, busying himself with the scant remains of the family fortune to such good effect that he was able to assure his younger brother and sister an income large enough for them to live comfortably in Europe where at that time the cost of living was much lower.

Gertrude Stein finished her university studies in 1903, after four years of medicine including practical surgery. To this, later biographers have attributed her highly developed powers of observation. William James, who had directed her studies, then offered her a post in a lunatic asylum, but it is said that contact with the patients frightened her and that was the reason for her trip to Europe.

While Gertrude was finishing her studies in Baltimore, her brother Leo was living in Florence where he did some painting and then specialized in art criticism. Both then decided to settle in Paris. There, rummaging among the art shops, he discovered that Clovis Sagot had two pictures by unknown Spanish artists. He bought a watercolour by one of them—name now forgotten—and haggled over a small picture signed Picasso which he thought too expensive. Sagot promised to have a larger picture painted for him by the artist which would be reasonably priced and some days later he produced the *Fillette à la corbeille fleurie*. The price was rather high—150 francs—but Leo was determined to have it. Not so Gertrude, who was with him. She said frankly she disliked the picture, the legs and the feet were ugly and she would not have it in the house at any price. Anxiously following this English discussion as best he could, Sagot then made a suggestion: as the lady disliked the lower part, let the canvas be cut, simply sliced in two, preserving the head which she thought attractive. This proposition did not meet with approval and the argument continued. Finally, as Leo was so keen on the picture, Gertrude gave way and the first Picasso appeared on the walls of the detached house in the Rue de Fleurus where one day, according to an American critic, Gertrude Stein was to 'personify the Mecca of most of the painters and writers of her time'.

It was at Sagot's that Picasso first met Leo and Gertrude Stein. 'He was at once attracted by the woman's physical personality,' Fernande recalls. They both came to see him at his studio, Leo tall and straight, bald, with gold-rimmed spectacles and a long reddish beard, looking like a professor; Gertrude, short and massive, with a handsome head and fine, strong features, masculine in voice and bearing. Fernande was much intimidated by these visitors from another world and felt that they were hostile. She was amazed, too, to see Americans—who must surely be rich because they were Americans—dressed in brown corduroy and wearing sandals. But she adds, in the after-light, that they were evidently too intelligent to care about ridicule and too sure of themselves to worry about what other people thought.

Even years later, Fernande was still staggered by the fact that on their very first visit the Steins paid 800 francs for some of Picasso's pictures. This encounter not only brought Picasso's years of privation to an end, but was the start of a friendship with the Steins which was to supply the stimulus for a new plastic vision at the very time when he was most ready for it. As he himself has said: 'I do not seek, I find.'

This transition was helped by a trip which he made to Holland in the summer of 1905. A wealthy Dutchman, Tom Schilperoot, who lived in the artists' quarter of Paris and was destined to squander his fortune there, wanted to show Picasso his country and took him to spend a few weeks at his home in Schoorl. It was Picasso's first glimpse of the flat countryside, criss-crossed by canals where the light filtered through the mist rising from the water, of Rembrandt's golden half-light and of Vermeer's silvered blues and golds. But he had eyes only for the women. 'It was a ridiculous sight,' he told Fernande on his return, perhaps to reassure her, 'to see those boarding-school girls filing down the street with figures like soldiers in armour.' But in fact he was much impressed by their pink, healthy skins and by the placid good temper of the Dutch girls.

In Schoorl Picasso painted several portraits in gouache of plump nudes, the *Hollandaise*, for instance (Stang Collection, Oslo), naked except for an embroidered head-dress, with large breasts and arms crossed over broad thighs. 'The most beautiful female breasts,' Picasso was to say later, 'are those that give the most milk.' The *Hollandaise*, with her sturdy neck, round shoulders and breasts eminently suited to motherhood, seems to mark the end of the emaciated women of the Blue period and, in the firmness of the drawing, particularly of the eyebrows, the nose and the eyes, to anticipate Cézanne's influence.

Picasso had seen some Cézannes soon after his arrival in Paris when he made his first contact with Vollard. But he was then just entering on the Blue period and the pictures had made little impression on him. Now, at the end of that cycle, when he made his first call on the Steins he found himself in a group of Cézanne's fervent admirers.

Leo Stein had first heard of a painter called Cézanne when he was living in Florence and had seen some of the artist's works at the home of the collector Charles Loeser. On their arrival in Paris the Steins had learnt that the only dealer who had Cézannes to sell was Ambroise Vollard. In due course they visited his gallery. They found a tall man with a pale and sombre face standing in a room almost empty of pictures. Vollard, it seemed, was not an eager salesman. Was that finesse or a genuine attachment to the pictures he owned? His visitors mentioned Cézanne. Then his face lit up: Cézanne was the great romantic adventure of his life. Could they see a Cézanne? With heavy tread, Vollard descended to the cellar—everything in his life took place in cellars: dinners, receptions, discussions with artists. When he returned he was holding a tiny picture representing an apple on a barely covered canvas. But Leo Stein wanted one of those sun-lit Provençal landscapes such as he had seen at Charles Loeser's. Again Vollard descended, to return with a magnificent nude seen from the back. It was a fine picture, but they wanted a landscape. A longer wait this time. Finally Vollard showed them an unfinished canvas with a bit of landscape in the corner. No, that would not do, either. Meanwhile, night was falling, it was near to closing time. An old charwoman came up the stairs, then another, crossed the shop with a 'Bonsoir, messieurs-dames', and vanished. Suddenly Gertrude Stein burst out laughing. The situation was too much for her. Did these old women, she wondered, paint Cézannes to order? At last, still laughing, the Steins bought a small landscape which Vollard reluctantly produced for them. Later he confessed that he could see no reason for their mirth, but he discovered that the Steins bought more readily when they were in a good humour, so on future occasions he waited for the first laugh before getting down to business.

When Picasso discovered Cézanne—or rather, when he became susceptible to his influence—he seems to have remembered how his sculpture attracted him in the days when he visited his friend Paco Durio in his studio. At any rate, in 1905 he did several sculptures himself, for instance, the classical head of a woman (Werner Bär Collection, Zürich) with flat hair in a single block, a delicate and slightly aquiline nose and a protruding upper lip. Vollard quickly grasped the interest of Picasso's first attempts at sculpture and had them reproduced in bronze. One of them, with rough modelling like Rodin's that catches the light and shade, represented a jester with an enigmatic smile wearing his pointed cap (Phillips Memorial Gallery, Washington). But realizing perhaps that he had not achieved a personal style in sculpture as he had in his paintings, Picasso soon abandoned it and, with one or two exceptions, did not resume it for twenty years.

In 1905, a year rich in experiments and as productive as the summer of 1901, Picasso tried his hand at etching—a mode of expression in which he was later to be extraordinarily successful. At first, as though uncertain of the result, he used old plates just as they came to hand, sometimes working on both sides. Of the fifteen or so etchings which he did at that time, almost all portrayed travelling circus folk, a new theme for him and one which he also used in his paintings. The circus had always attracted him, perhaps because of the skill of the acrobats and the contrast between its human and its artificial side, and being able to afford it now he often went three or four times a week.

He had his favourites in this circus world: boys with narrow hips, young girls, skeletal harlequins and their female companions who even when resting preserved a regal carriage, and a fat clown with treble chin and enormous paunch. The girls whose toes grazed the backs of their horses anticipated the nymphs of his future Classical period. Only a fraction of the plates he made were printed at that time. Of those acquired by Vollard, 250 prints were pulled in 1913 and immediately became famous.

In the long series of pictures, preparatory studies and drawings which he made of the *saltimbanques*, Picasso seldom depicted them in the ring, but more usually in their casual lodgings or trailing along the roads with their children and their animals. He chose these subjects at a time when most French painters had eyes only for landscapes and still-life. It was through this series on the circus folk that his pictorial manner was transformed.

But to start with, the new pictures were very close to the Blue period both in the colouring and the type of individuals portrayed: an emaciated *Actor* (Mrs. Byron Foy Collection) painted during the winter of 1904–5, a skinny harlequin and an equally slim young father sitting beside his wife with her child in her arms in the *Acrobat's Family with Ape* (gouache, Museum of Fine Arts, Göteborg). For a long time yet, the children, too, and the adolescents wear inconsolable expressions and with their dark eyes seem haunted by melancholy, as, for instance, in the *Jeune Arlequin assis* (private collection, Paris), with his pale skin and his heavy head balanced on a frail body.

But though these half-starved figures, with their bony elbows and shoulders and their skeletal fingers like bundles of sticks, continue for a time, the blue background becomes steadily lighter, is tinged with rose, mauve and pale yellow, human skin becomes whiter and suddenly, in the Göteborg picture, a red carpet bursts on the scene.

In the still-lifes which Picasso painted at this time the colouring is also extremely varied, like a musical scale or the introduction of individual motifs which will later be used in a symphony. Even his adolescents with their premature solemnity, their enigmatic smiles, sometimes hold a colourful vase or a bouquet.

Colour in the pure state was indeed returning to pictorial art. According to Zervos, Picasso was 'by far the most contemporary artist among his contemporaries and the most susceptible to current conditions'. These conditions were dominated by a reaction expressed in various ways against impressionism. It was also a period when the frontiers between the arts were more fluid than ever before. Poetry and painting supplied mutual inspiration and Max Jacob was at that time conducting a holy war against excessive symbolism in both forms of art, thereby perhaps helping to release Picasso from the symbolist hang-over from the Blue period and encouraging him to seek independent subjects that did not lend themselves to literary interpretation. In the pictorial field, the most violent assault against the impressionists was being conducted on the very ground where their own revolution had taken place: colour and its relation to light. The attack was launched by a dozen artists at the autumn Salon of 1905. Their canvases were explosions of colour straight from the tube, opaque, insensitive to light, spread without transitions or regard to neighbouring colours.

The outburst had been simmering for a number of years. Marquet dates the search for pure tones which he and Matisse had been conducting as far back as 1901. But Matisse had needed to experience the sunshine of the Midi with its sharp shadows and flood of light before he could release the full violence of the contrasts in his painting. It was he who dominated the autumn Salon of 1905 where the reds, yellows, greens and blues of Derain, Rouault, Vlaminck, Manguin and Friesz howled like Indians on the warpath. 'The shock to the senses', as Matisse called it, was intended. The public reaction was also foreseen. One art critic, noticing a small bronze in the Florentine manner amongst the strident canvases, cried out, 'Ah! Donatello amongst the wild beasts!' But, as so often in art history, the insult was accepted as a compliment by those at whom it was directed, and the artists grouped round Matisse were thenceforward proud to call themselves 'Les Fauves'.

One picture in particular at the Salon, Matisse's *Woman with Hat*, provoked an outcry. Some people howled with laughter, others tried to deface the canvas. To Gertrude Stein both indignation and mockery seemed totally out of place. It had taken her some time to get used to the portrait by Cézanne, but Matisse was so obviously right in her eyes that she could not understand the public's failure to appreciate him. Eventually she bought the picture and the artist became her firm friend.

It was at Gertrude Stein's that Picasso first met Matisse. The contradiction between them was at once apparent. In Matisse's own words, they were 'North Pole and South Pole'. Their relationship was always to be one of watchful curiosity, an attitude more pronounced on Matisse's part than Picasso's. To the end of his days Matisse would ask every visitor who had stopped off at Vallauris, 'What is Picasso doing?' Sometimes he would also drop in at the Antibes Museum with a sketching pad in his hand—'Not to copy me,' Picasso hastens to add, 'but to keep in touch with what I had been trying to do.'

Matisse was one of those artists who, according to Courthion, 'restored to the intelligence (which had been more or less excluded from the profession since Delacroix) its part in the creation of a picture'. He installed himself in his art, allowing himself no distractions, avoiding emotional entanglements and everything which might disturb his own serenity and that of his work. Courthion described him at the end of his life as a stern judge of others and of himself, always the visited, never the visitor.

He had been so from his early days. Whereas Picasso had believed in his youth that suffering was the sole source of all art, Matisse strove, in his own words, 'to create an art which should be a sort of cerebral sedative for the spectator, whatever his circumstances, affording a pleasant sense of certitude and hence peace and tranquillity'. Whereas Picasso watched, often in spite of himself, every change on the face of humanity and kept his finger on the pulse of his time, Matisse remained impervious to events as though he denied the march of history. Picasso welcomed, almost cultivated his creative torment: Matisse at an early age felt sure of himself and the world. With the frankness which people would accept only from her, Gertrude Stein once said to him: 'There are no conflicts in you'—this in reply to the suggestion that her friendship with Picasso was unworthy of a person with her qualities. Thus, when the two artists met at her house their relations remained outwardly correct, but she sensed both hostility and mutual respect between them.

The return to colour, the development taking place in Picasso at the time of the 'wild beast' scandal, might have drawn him into the orbit of the artists who now called themselves 'Les Fauves' and encouraged him to take part in their experiments. But though they, like his meeting with Matisse, were to have their influence on him in due course, he held aloof and even expressed the instinctive hostility between himself and Matisse by going to the opposite extreme. To the Fauves's orgy in colour Picasso replied with an increasing stress on monochrome. He ringed his figures in brown, as though they were in stained glass, to prevent them dissolving into a background of the same tonality. But this monochrome was no longer a night blue. The *Boy leading a Horse* (Museum of Modern Art, New York) is painted in a clear rose colour, his slim naked body barely stands out against an even more roseate sand-dune, the horse he leads is a transparent silver-grey and the sky is a slightly more bluish grey. The juxtaposition of slim naked adolescent bodies and the large masses of horses' chests and rumps had great attraction for Picasso at this time: he varied the theme in drawings and sketches, in oil or gouache.

In these pictures the Rose period finally triumphed over the Blue, and the effect of joyousness did not merely exist in the luminous colouring. The youthful bodies, the unbridled horses, the high undulating horizons all conveyed a pagan *joie de vivre*. Picasso never came closer than in these pictures to Matisse's dictum that a work of art should act as a cerebral sedative and afford peace and tranquillity.

This new serenity was accompanied by a formal change, the appearance of a new physical type in Picasso's paintings. The excessive elongation of the bodies and the faces disappeared, the latter no longer ending in a pointed chin, but in a square jaw. A new relationship was also established between the bodies and the surrounding space: closed blocks confronting a hostile void were replaced by loosened limbs and open movements. Finally, the features slowly underwent a change. Now they were traced in brown strokes while the eyes, which had formerly been wide open and fixedly gazing, narrowed down to slits of warm shadow.

In this year of 1905, Gertrude Stein was very conscious of the change that had taken place in Picasso. She believed that he had only recently become completely assimilated into French life. 'He has let himself go,' she said, 'living in the gay spirit of what he sees around him, of French sentimentality.' After years of withdrawal, she noted that 'the Harlequin or Rose period was one of enormous productivity', and she attributed this to the 'gaiety of France'. In this period of intense creative activity Picasso conceived a major work which never came to fruition. A preliminary sketch in gouache (Max Pellequer Collection) entitled *Naked Adolescents and Women* shows the figures either recumbent or crouching with hand-written notes in Spanish for colours or accessories, such as a bowl of fruit. This composition, too, was abandoned in its primitive form, but no doubt contains the germ of an idea which took shape later on.

Instead, the great work of this period became the *Family of Saltimbanques* (Chester Dale Collection, National Gallery of Art, Washington). In this painting, measuring 83¾ by 90½ inches, are assembled all the characters of that *commedia dell'arte* which he had invented for his

67

personal use. To this picture, too, best applies the qualification which Gertrude Stein made to her remarks quoted above: 'When I say that the Rose period was clear and happy, that is purely relative. The "gay" themes were, in fact, rather sad; the harlequin families were down-at-heel, but from Picasso's point of view the period was light, happy and gay.' The composition of the picture, or rather the absence of it, was no doubt intentional. The characters string out in space, drawn from everywhere and nowhere. They seem to have temporarily stopped walking, that is all: a fat clown, a harlequin in his checkered costume, a little girl trailing a basket of flowers, an adolescent boy wearing a slip, his young brother with a coat that is too large for him—and in the extreme right-hand corner of the picture without any connection with the other figures a seated woman from Majorca of whom Picasso had made a separate study (Moscow Museum of Modern Art). There are two main colours: an intense blue and a pinkish ochre. Though, with the exception of the woman, these are all familiar circus figures, there is something unreal about the way they are placed. It has the incoherence of a dream or of an interrupted story of which the end will never be known. In the First World War, when Rainer Maria Rilke, terribly distressed by the conflict, took refuge for a while with Frau Hertha von König in Munich, the picture was in her flat. 'The great, the magnificent Picasso', he called it, and when he left he wrote a poem beginning with these lines: 'But tell me, who are these wanderers more fugitive even than ourselves. . . ?'

CHAPTER VI 1906-1907

The Great Divide

IN 1905, Picasso met a brilliant young poet of part Polish and part Italian origin who was to provide an important stimulus for the development of his art. Guillaume Apollinaire, as the poet was known, had chosen this name for himself. He was the son of an unmarried mother whose family—the Kostrowitzkys—came from the lesser, but ancient Polish nobility. The identity of his father has always been a mystery, but he is thought to have come from an Italian patrician family. Soon after Guillaume's birth this anonymous parent disappeared and mother and child experienced changes of fortune that would have been worthy of a Greek tragedy. They moved to Monaco where the mother, a woman of charm and resource, received secret subsidies from an ecclesiastical source, possibly from the priestly brother of her vanished lover. Later, a rich young Jew from Alsace supported her. But between spasms of luxury there were periods of near-destitution and the child grew up against a baffling background of alternate pretension and penury, insult and servility, order and chaos.

Having suffered or enjoyed a cosmopolitan education from which his imaginative mind had acquired a knowledge of languages and an amazing smattering of diverse cultures, at the age of nineteen the young Guillaume came to Paris, alone and penniless. After working in a bank which soon after his arrival was forced to close its doors he tried his hand as editor of a financial journal. At the same time he was contributing articles and reviews to various newspapers. With André Salmon and Jean Mollet he also founded a short-lived literary review. It was at this stage in his career that Mollet introduced Picasso to him in a bar near the Gare Saint-Lazare.

Although he was on visiting terms with Vlaminck and Derain, Apollinaire had as yet small knowledge of art, but he made up for this by a mind that was unusually open to all that was new, strange or sensational. He would be the first to champion any novel idea, though he did not entirely believe in it himself, the first to uphold some artistic notion that he had barely assimilated, and the most eager to smooth a path for currents of whose destination he was only dimly aware. He was one of those men who by their undiscriminating enthusiasm tend to gain an ascendancy among their friends.

When Apollinaire saw the canvases of Picasso's Blue period he was immediately impressed and soon after, almost in spite of himself, he became the interpreter and prophet of this new school. In May, 1905, Picasso read this highly eulogistic comment over the signature of his new friend in *La Plume*: 'That discernment, that ease, that substance and that sinew in which Michelangelo saw the qualities of good painting will be admired in the pictures of Pablo Picasso.' It may be that Picasso in his proud self-confidence had no need of such support, at any rate he needed it less than most creative artists, but this superlative praise from a man like Apollinaire must certainly have encouraged him to pursue his chosen path. The two men saw a lot of each other and were on familiar terms from their very first meeting.

Fernande found Apollinaire something of a paradox: forceful and theatrical, at the same time simple and naïve. He looked like a Roman emperor with a narrow forehead, close-set eyes, a long curving nose and a small, rather precious mouth revealing vanity and a need for affection. He talked a great deal and enjoyed the sound of his own voice. 'Guillaume was extraordinarily brilliant,' Gertrude Stein recalls. 'No matter what subject was touched upon, whether he knew something about it or not, he quickly saw its significance, elaborated it in his mind and imagination and carried it further even than those who knew more about it than himself—and strangely enough his views were usually sound.'

Apollinaire had scarcely familiarized himself with Picasso's work and embroidered the themes of the Blue period with his lyrical effusions, than he divined the artist's intentions in his rose canvases. 'There is an admirable calm in them,' he wrote, 'and one feels in the more recent ones that the artist who conceived so much grave and youthful grace is already progressing towards the most objective forms of art in order to raise them to the sublime.' Beneath the somewhat vague lyricism of this remark there is at least the realization that Picasso was now in a period of transition.

In his canvases the proportions of the bodies were in process of changing: they were becoming thick-set, the heads shorter and more square, the eyes sightless and full of brown shadow. The features also were delineated in brown. One of the figures in the *Adolescents* (Chester Dale Collection, New York), the one facing the spectator, corresponds to this new physical type. The colour in this canvas has become uniformly rose verging on brick-red. The bodies with their brown contours seem pulled out of an almost monochrome background. The same colour scheme is in the *Femme nue à la chevelure*: the rose background is more accentuated than the amber-toned flesh with its rose reflections, the copper-brown of the hair stands out against the uniform warmth of a dawn-coloured background. The *Femme nue debout* (Gertrude Stein Collection) is standing on brownish soil the same colour as her hair. Her slender body with sloping shoulders and large square head barely stands out, with its rosy amber flesh, from a very vivid rose background. The uniformity of colouring makes the relief appear very flat, but despite the large planes underlined by strokes of brown, a rigour of treatment is evident, akin to wood carving.

The composition in these canvases was also changing. Open forms leaving plenty of air around them were succeeded by a tightening of the contours or of the figures which were now grouped in squat, superimposed sculptural blocks with full rounded angles, very different from the curves and sharp ridges in the compositions of the Blue period. *La Coiffure* (Metropolitan Museum, New York), painted between the end of 1905 and the beginning of 1906, reveals this new tendency in Picasso's art with its compact forms, its pyramidal composition built up in blocks, and the folds of the skirt as though carved in wood. The colouring of the flesh and the background, also, looks like clean wood.

It was at this point in his work that Picasso painted the portrait of Gertrude Stein. From their first meeting he had wanted to produce his own interpretation of her strong handsome head. 'Charmed by the physical personality of the woman, even before knowing her better he had suggested painting her portrait,' Fernande recalls. In fact, in a fit of timidity he had got Sagot to ask her if she would sit for him. She agreed at once. Picasso had quickly become a *habitué* at the Steins and a friendship sprang up between him and Gertrude which became a kind of intimate confederacy. On one of his first visits, Leo insisted on showing him his collection of Japanese prints. Always on the lookout for something new and original, he did not seem to realize that his hobby was becoming out of date. So as not to offend his host who, after all, was a client, Picasso solemnly inspected one print after another and listened patiently to the proud owner's comments. But to Gertrude Stein he whispered in exasperation: 'Your brother is very nice, but like all Americans he shows you Japanese prints: I don't happen to like them!'

Almost every afternoon Gertrude was now going to Picasso's studio for a sitting, travelling up the hill in the horse-bus that connected the Left Bank with Montmartre and returning home on foot. She posed sitting in the single rickety armchair. Opposite her Picasso planted himself on a small kitchen chair, sitting very close to the canvas set on a large easel and using, as Gertrude recalls, a very small palette on which there was a great deal of brown mixed with brownish grey. On Saturday evenings when she went home Picasso would go with her and dine.

The sketch made on the first day was striking. When the two Stein brothers arrived in the Rue Ravignan at the end of the sitting, bringing a friend with them, the latter begged Picasso to leave the portrait in this preliminary state. But Picasso obstinately refused and continued his work. Gertrude Stein reports that there were eighty to ninety sittings in all and that from the ideas exchanged during these long tête-à-têtes a number of artistic ideas emerged. Picasso caught her in a characteristic pose, her contours made even more massive by a huge cloak with wide sleeves and many folds, leaning forward with her hands on her knees in an attitude of concentrated attention. The pose seems to illustrate a remark she herself was fond of making that the characteristic of genius was the faculty to talk and listen at the same time, and the whole picture bears out John Brown's comment on Gertrude Stein: 'She imposes her authority not only by her work but most powerfully by her presence. Some people claim that she has consciously created this personality and that it is her greatest success. However that may be, the personality is there, with a density rare in this inconsistent age.'

But despite the rapidity of the first sketch, or perhaps because of it, Picasso did not succeed immediately in capturing Gertrude Stein. The portrait and the long conversations that took place during the sittings had a great importance for him of which perhaps at the time he was only dimly aware, and in the portrait he tried to catch something of the bold processes of her thought. 'She could look like a Roman emperor or a Buddha,' Sutherland said of her, 'but her truest expression was that beautiful, magnificently irrelevant smile of ancient Greek statues.'

The sittings continued into the spring, but Picasso believed he had failed in his efforts. One day, in a violent rage, he suddenly painted out the head. 'I can't see you any more when I look at you,' he complained in exasperation. So for the time being the portrait remained unfinished. 'No one remembers being particularly disappointed or particularly annoyed at this end to a long series of sittings,' remarks Gertrude Stein.

During the course of the previous winter Picasso's material position had begun to improve. For a long time Papa Soulier had been his sheet anchor. Berthe Weill relates: 'On one occasion, Apollinaire was very keen to have a good bouillabaisse and so were Max Jacob and Picasso, so they all went down to the junk-merchant with some ten or twelve of Picasso's paintings and drawings and came back with 40 francs, enough to buy the food.' But the Steins were already buying big canvases from Picasso and they urged their American friends to do the same. Picasso did not like the young Americans he met at their house: 'They are not men, they are not women, they are Americans,' he said. But Gertrude Stein succeeded in interesting one of her girl-friends from her Baltimore youth in Picasso. When the painter was nearly broke, she urged her friend to buy 100 francs' worth of his drawings. The young lady obliged, as an act of 'romantic charity'. . . .

Vollard also was beginning to take an interest in him, was finding him not quite so mad and was no longer complaining at his crooked belfries. No doubt the Rose period seemed to him to have more commercial possibilities than the Blue, and the harlequin themes were also more intelligible to the general public. At any rate, Picasso was no longer out of step with the times and was even about to enjoy a considerable commercial success. One day, Vollard arrived unexpectedly at the studio and made a bulk purchase, paying 2,000 francs for thirty or so canvases of varying dimensions. To Fernande this seemed a fabulous sum. It enabled Picasso to realize a dream which had been plaguing him for some time: a trip to Spain. 'The atmosphere of his native country was a necessity to him,' writes Fernande. 'I have never known a foreigner less suited to the life in Paris. He seemed to be irked and stifled there, not at his ease.' Fernande was thrilled at the idea of the trip, took an enormous amount of luggage with her, but on reaching Spain she was surprised to find a very different Picasso from the one she had known in Paris: 'Gay, less wild, more brilliant, animated, taking a calm and self-confident interest in things—at ease, in fact. He radiated happiness.'

Picasso did not spend much time seeing his relatives and the friends of his youth in Barcelona, but quickly set out for the small village of Gosol, above the valley of Andorra in the foothills of the Pyrenees. There, in the depths of the country, amid the warm scent of thyme and rosemary, he could find the peace he needed. The village could only be reached on mules and exuded a timeless atmosphere. Fernande with as much astonishment as her natural indolence permitted watched her friend adapt himself to life at least a century behind modern times. 'In that wild and grandiose scenery, those mountains with paths bordered with cypresses, he no longer seemed, as he had in Paris, a person apart, outside society.'

In Gosol, Picasso lived with the peasants, went hunting with them, climbed the mountain pathways familiar to a population of smugglers, listened to their age-old legends, drank with them, played games with them and 'enjoyed himself like a child'. He worked with tenfold enthusiasm, drawing local characters and scenes of daily life as though reality was his only inspiration. He painted in gouache the *Vacher au petit panier* (Columbus Gallery of Fine Arts, Columbus, Ohio), a cowherd with the erect and easy gait of the mountaineer, the strong column of his neck supporting a small head.

But for him reality was only a spring-board for a flight whose trajectory he could not as yet foresee. The *Vacher au petit panier* contained the germ of a picture which he probably painted on his return to Paris and to whose subject he himself gave the vague title of *Composition* (Barnes Foundation, Merion, Pennsylvania). For the same picture he also used a pen-and-ink drawing of perhaps more ancient date called *Peasants*, in which a blind man carrying a bundle on his back is leaning with one hand on a little girl holding a bouquet of flowers. This drawing and the gouache are very instructive in helping one detect how Picasso combined the various elements of the seen and the imagined in a new pictorial vision which he was developing at that time. The two cows and the cowherd are still in the picture, but the latter has now acquired a load on his back from the blind man in the drawing and is leaning on the little girl. The influence of El Greco is both very literal and very garbled. The cowherd has the receding forehead, the head flattened at the back and the long forearms of El Greco's angels, the little girl has their asymmetrical features and their slender body and both figures show the same excessive elongation. But the dissolution of the forms is achieved by means different from those employed by El Greco, not by the use of light which breaks up the contours and displaces the features, but by a division into interior planes, by spots of colour mostly of lozenge or triangular shape.

One of the most significant works painted at Gosol is *La Porteuse de pain* (Museum of Art, Philadelphia). The theme might be drawn simply from folklore. The picture shows a woman of the people carrying, after the manner of her country, two enormous flat round loaves on a small cushion which is placed on her head and held in position with a white scarf. Through the anecdotal theme appears a new conception of the human face and a vigorous, sculptural modelling. The eyes, of which one is filled with shadow, are slightly unequal, the mouth is a little asymmetrical. The features appear to be immobile, but a fleeting smile passes across them, like the strange smile of an Etruscan mask.

In Gosol, drawing his inspiration from Greek sculpture, Picasso also painted a fine picture prosaically entitled, *La Toilette* (Fine Arts Academy, Allbright Art Gallery, Buffalo). Some Venus of the classical age might have served as model for the nude body of the young woman raising her arms above her head to fix her hair. The woman in profile who is holding a mirror for her might have escaped from a Greek vase with her straight nose, draped robe and mass of curly hair. Attic grace which had occasionally appeared in his drawings here takes possession of a picture for the first time. It was later to mark a whole period of his work. *La Toilette* was the forerunner of this future triumph, but for the time it remained an experiment as isolated as the *Composition* in another genre.

The months spent at Gosol in rediscovery of Spanish surroundings seem to have been a period of arduous quest for Picasso. His turn to sculpture was like a man aiming at one of the cardinal points without knowing precisely how he is going to reach it, for classical sculpture was not, in fact, his goal. The *Femme au peigne* (former collection of Paul Guillaume) was one of the signposts on his road. The woman's head, framed by a heavy mass of hair, is too long and too large for her slender body which is treated in superimposed planes. The same head appears in the *Deux Femmes nues se tenant* (Fleischmann Collection, Zürich), where it reveals its origin in the long heads and slim, stiff

75

bodies of the wooden statuettes in Iberian sculpture. The woman standing beside her is more explicit still. The long face with the low forehead,
the flat top to the head, the slit-eyes and the stony smile go back a very
long way in time, nearer to Egypt than to Athens. Her slim torso
rests on strong, straight thighs and the calves are too short and too
prominent.

On Picasso's return to Paris these trends were to culminate in the
deforming vision of the *Two Nudes* (Silberman, New York), a pair of
hideous, thick-set female giants confronting one another with enormous
buttocks, short calves, flat feet and jutting breasts. The faces are masks
sculpted—or rather clumsily hewn—out of tough wood. The orbits of
the eyes are high beneath an accentuated curve of the eyebrows, the
noses V-shaped, the cheeks steep, the chins pointed.

From his solitary experiments in Gosol, Picasso brought back not
only a change in form but also in colour. The rose tone, his rose tinged
with purplish blue, still persists here and there, as in the *Deux Femmes
nues se tenant*, but the bodies are of a copper-toned monochrome, like
wood polished to a satin finish by long use.

At this turning point, Picasso realized clearly that in order to achieve
purity of plastic vision his art would have to acquire complete independence from emotional suggestions, anecdote and even from subject-
matter. One day, a friend, Henri Mahaut, heard him dismiss his
previous work with the contemptuous remark: 'All that is sentiment.'
In October of that year 1906, Picasso, though only twenty-five years
old, seemed to have run through a whole cycle of artistic creation and
with a curious lucidity he felt his whole past fall away from him. He
then set out to find a genuine pictorial autonomy.

It remains to ask what provoked this change. Was it at Gosol that he
became aware of the pictorial value of purely ornamental art, like
Moorish decoration or Hebraic calligraphy? Was it by a Catalan
primitive, and if so by whom, that he was inspired to give his nudes
the archaic rigidity of statues? The vision to which he was turning to
find his own personal mode of expression represented a rupture with
the traditional idea of beauty. Gertrude Stein said one day: 'Every
masterpiece has come into the world with a dose of ugliness in it. This
ugliness is a sign of the creator's struggle to say something new in a
new way.' In Picasso's case the ugliness of the *Two Nudes* represented
this sign.

The stay at Gosol ended abruptly. The innkeeper's daughter caught typhoid and Picasso, who has a terror of illness in any form, took flight. He wanted to return direct to Paris and scorning the transport difficulties in Spain, which were considerable, he and Fernande set off at dawn from Gosol and spent twelve hours on mule tracks before finally reaching a village where they could obtain a horse-drawn conveyance.

After these adventures it was a relief to Picasso to find firm ground under his feet in Paris. The unfinished portrait of Gertrude Stein was still in his studio and on the very day he returned he resumed work on it. Without seeing her again he repainted from memory the head which he had effaced, treating it in a different style from the subtly modelled hands, the cloak with its realistic folds and the careful detail of the frill of the blouse held in place with a brooch. He built up the face in large planes with severe modelling which emphasized the rise of the forehead, the shape of the eye-sockets, the eyelids and the taut, sinuous line of the upper lip. The face has the same mask-like appearance as the *Porteuse de pain*, but despite or perhaps because of its rigidity it conveys very well the impression of concentrated attention which was one of Gertrude Stein's outstanding qualities. The eyes are unequal, the left one is smaller and more narrowed, and it is this quizzical gaze which reveals so well Gertrude Stein's ability to listen, to take possession of things and to dissect them. The portrait was not at all flattering. It was a surprise to the sitter and she wondered whether it was like her. Picasso was reassuring. 'You will come to look like it,' he said and at times indeed her friends were struck by the resemblance. She herself quickly became used to the mask which Picasso gave her, and the portrait looked so definitive in its final form (Metropolitan Museum of Art, New York) that neither of them could remember what it had looked like before. But they were the only ones to appreciate it.

In due course, this portrait became a kind of link between them. One day, Gertrude Stein cut her hair which she had been in the habit of wearing in a plaited crown. Though she had a hat on, Picasso noticed the difference at once. 'What is it?' he said. 'What's happened?' He seemed so agitated, she asked him what the matter was. He gazed at her attentively. Finally, 'What about my portrait?' he said in a severe tone. But another glance reassured him and he added: 'Oh well, it's all there still.'

Years later, a rich collector noticed the portrait at Gertrude Stein's and asked her what she had paid for it. 'Nothing,' she said. The man was amazed. 'Nothing, because of course he gave it to me.' When he was told of this conversation, Picasso smiled and said: 'The fellow didn't realize there wasn't much difference in those days between a gift and a sale.'

Gertrude Stein stated that the Rose period ended with her portrait. After her death in 1946 it passed to the Metropolitan Museum of New York to which she had bequeathed it in her will. When the work was about to leave France for ever, Alice Toklas, her faithful friend, collected one or two people to say their last farewells. Picasso came alone and looked at his pictures on the walls in the Rue Christine. To start with, he did not pay much attention to the portrait of his dead friend, but talked in his usual way, alternately attentive and absent-minded. Suddenly, he got up with a jump and, on the point of leaving, gazed at it for a long time in silence, drinking it in with his eyes. Then he turned to Alice Toklas and, with a display of emotion unusual for him, kissed her. He, too, was saying farewell to a part of his life.

On his return from Gosol, Picasso also painted a self-portrait (Museum of Art, Philadelphia), of all those that he painted no doubt the one that resembled him the least. It shows Picasso in a white shirt with a wide neck revealing a broad chest with the right sleeve turned back over a powerful forearm. The right fist is clenched; in the left he holds a palette. The head with receding forehead and close-cropped hair is too small for the massive body. The chin is too short, the cheeks are too flat. The eye-sockets are firmly drawn as in the last pictures he painted at Gosol. The eyebrows—which are too long—curve away towards the temples and in the unequal eyes there is a strange hypnotized look of naked fear.

In 1907 a new phase began in Picasso's art which has been called the Negro period because he is alleged to have discovered negro art at this time. But the story of its influence has in fact never been completely elucidated. Vlaminck later claimed to have been captivated by negro masks as early as 1904 and to have interested Derain in them. Such masks were to be found everywhere and aroused vague curiosity among people with a taste for the exotic, representing a new stimulus amidst outworn subjects. They could be picked up for very little at Saint-Ouen or in the Rue Mouffetard. In his novel, La Négresse du Sacré-Coeur, André Salmon mentions having bought a fetish from Dahomey at the end of 1905 for 4 francs. Such objects could be found in plenty of dusty junk-shops, but a man named Heymann had made a speciality of them in his shop in the Rue de Rennes. Matisse recalled visiting it one day: 'There were some negro statuettes in the shop-window. I was struck by their character and the purity of their lines. They were as beautiful as Egyptian art. I bought one and showed it to Gertrude Stein, on whom I was calling that day. Then Picasso turned up and was at once full of enthusiasm. From then on, everyone began looking for negro statuettes. They could be found quite easily in those days.' Gertrude Stein confirmed this story and stated that Matisse's visit took place after Picasso's return from Gosol.

It is on the basis of this gossip that Picasso has been saddled with a 'Negro period'. But when a journalist asked him one day to define the influence of negro art on his work he gave the bad-tempered reply: 'Negro art? Don't know it.' In fact, a change in his plastic vision was already taking place when he came across specimens of primitive art and even without them his work would have assumed new forms of expression. Some years later, with the birth of cubism, Picasso was to show his independence of all outside influences. The African fetishes did determine some aspects of the new art when it first made its appearance, but Picasso's decision to break with the past was independent of their popularity.

Adolphe Basler has traced what he calls the 'cerebralization' of modern painting to Cézanne. 'Up to the beginning of the century, the artist used to paint more or less as he saw; since then he has begun to paint as he conceives.' Picasso was destined to complete the cerebralization of art in his time. His friend Manolo, who was a purely instinctive artist, was quite right when he said one day to Mahaut: 'For Picasso, you see, painting is incidental.'

If Picasso had not been there to bring about this change, the history of art in the last half-century would not have been what it is. There were other painters beside himself who possessed the same, or almost the same, means of expression. Excellent painters like Derain, authentic creators like Matisse felt the same need for a renewal of art and received the same stimuli as he, but it was given to Picasso to release his age from its fetters.

Among all those who have studied and still do study the enigma of his solitary creative effort, among all the varied discussions and interpretations, it was Gertrude Stein in her biography of Picasso who most clearly extracted its significance. 'It must never be forgotten that the reality of the twentieth century was not at all the reality of the nine-teenth, and Picasso has been the only one to have felt this in painting, really the only one. The struggle to express it became increasingly intense. Matisse and all the others saw the twentieth century with their eyes, but the reality they saw was that of the nineteenth century.' Picasso has denied having consciously sought what Gertrude Stein calls the 'reality of the twentieth century'. The mere word 'to seek' repels him. As he said one day to Florent Fels: 'Nobody can be in-terested in following a man who keeps his eyes on the ground in case fate should have dropped a wallet in his path.' For him a work of art derives from 'spontaneous generation' and 'there will never be an art which is not in the present'. In the same conversation with Fels he made this key-remark about himself: 'I have always painted for my time.'

Creative audacity does not explain everything in Picasso. There is also the audacity of the man, his horror of concessions. When recogni-tion and financial success came to him, and came to stay, he was accused of being daring for its own sake, of being deliberately un-intelligible, of performing antics for the sole purpose of causing shock and surprise. If some people have seen him as the great magician of our time, others have called him the biggest humbug of the century.

In reality, the rejection of all compromise was in Picasso from the start. Fernande recalls how one day, 'at a time of great distress', he was invited and energetically refused to do some drawings for a certain newspaper for which he would have been paid seven or eight hundred francs. At the moment when he embarked on his great creative adven-ture he had nothing to gain from a radical change and everything to lose. Abject poverty was not so far behind him that he had lost all memory of it. Success had come to him with the harlequins of the Rose period. Among his most devoted friends Mahaut knew some who would always be secretly attached to that period and in his opinion, 'Anyone but Picasso would have persisted in that course and exploited it.'

Picasso was no longer running after Papa Soulier, the ex-clown Sagot or other exploiters of artists. Though Vollard was the only one among the great French dealers to take an interest in him, foreigners were following his work with great attention and believed firmly in his future. One day, Picasso received a call from a young man who was destined to play a great part in his life. This was a young German who possessed that curiosity for new things, that urge to be in the forefront of ideas which turned Germany—before and after the First World War—into a vast battlefield of intellectual experiment. He also owed to his native country faculties of logic, perseverance and organizing ability. But Kahnweiler was also one of those who emigrated as though they felt themselves threatened in advance by a brutal force hostile to their particular form of sensibility, and who gave the best of themselves to a foreign country. He was barely twenty-two when he set up in Paris as a picture dealer. He had first come to the city at the age of eighteen and had stayed three years, trying, as he said, 'to see clearly what was happening in painting'. After two years in London he returned to Paris knowing no one, but with confidence in his own judgment. Slim, reserved and elegant, he was struck on his first meeting with Picasso by the young artist's unkempt appearance, his threadbare clothing and his dirty shoes. In the Rue Vignon, Kahnweiler had opened a small gallery as discreet as himself, hung with grey velvet and holland cloth. With the caution necessary to his calling he combined a taste for taking risks and this made him take a chance on Picasso. His system, as he explained to me one day, consisted in signing up contracts that were usually valid for two years. In this way he assured himself of Picasso's output during an exceptionally important period.

Soon Picasso was to have his devotees among the great foreign collectors. One day, Matisse brought one of his best clients to see him, a very rich collector from Moscow by name Serge Stchoukine. This man was to acquire about a dozen Cézannes, numerous Gauguins, some Van Goghs, some Derains, some Marquets and about forty pictures by Matisse. He was to be one of Picasso's best purchasers. Fernande has described him as an ugly little man afflicted by a horrible stutter with a large head and a pale face. But she also remembers that on that first visit he bought two canvases at a very high price for those times.

Easy circumstances were such a new thing for Picasso that he looked on his sudden good fortune with a kind of peasant suspicion. He stuffed the bank notes paid to him in a wallet until it became so crammed he did not dare leave it at home, but carried it about on his person in an inner pocket secured with a safety-pin. But affluence was bought at a price: he loathed parting with his own pictures. 'Picasso was always distraught at having to sell his paintings,' reports Fernande. In view of the speed at which he produced them—one or two in a day or a night, according to his friends—this seems surprising. But Picasso's relation to his work was always a peculiar one. Even in the case of pictures that dealt with the same subject and were painted consecutively he never believed he could replace them. At an early stage he started investing in himself. 'Later, when he became rich,' writes Gertrude Stein, 'Picasso began to buy pictures—but they were his own.' But in the days before he could afford not to sell his pictures, Picasso, according to Fernande, used to despair after a dealer's or a collector's visit and was put off his work for days. This attachment to his work seems in flagrant contradiction to the ease with which he abandoned one manner and assumed another, as though he were putting on a new skin. According to Zervos, as soon as he became successful he got rid of his past 'as though he did not know what to do with it'.

Towards the great change that was to take place in Picasso's art two paintings represent intermediate stages, though they contain little suggestion of the revolution that was to come. One was the *Man's Head* (Gertrude Stein Collection), looking like an elongated egg with a protruding nose, almost totally lacking in chin, one ear placed too high and the features painted with wide strokes. The other was the *Dancing Girl* (property of Picasso), done in large clearly defined planes.

The *Dancing Girl* was stowed away for some time with a pile of other pictures behind some junk in a corner of the studio in the Rue des Grands-Augustins. One day, Picasso pulled it out. It was in a white frame covered with dust and the glass was askew. But it was not the picture he wanted to show me, it was the frame. 'It used to belong to Degas,' he said proudly. 'He used to have them made specially for him. I managed to get hold of it.' It was a wide, slightly convex frame and the white was lightly tinted with rose. Having dusted it and adjusted the glass, Picasso lovingly passed his hand over the gently curving wood. It was indeed the ideal frame for the rosy figures dancing in the footlights that Degas was so fond of. But Picasso's dancing girl, with her joints and movements dislocated by planes of discordant colour, struggled inside the frame as though she wanted to burst it asunder. She clashed appallingly with its elegant form and tender colouring. But Picasso gazed at her, seemingly unaware of the incongruity.

In the spring of 1907 Picasso summoned his creative energies for a great work. He made very careful preparations as though he knew in advance that it was to be important. For the composition alone he made seventeen sketches in charcoal, pencil, pastel, water-colour and oil on canvas or on wood. For the figures, too, he made innumerable sketches, varying the detail continually, from small drawings jotted on a pad to elaborate pictures. The picture took its origin from a youthful memory which his stay in Barcelona had perhaps revived and there was a flagrant, almost absurd disparity between the importance the picture assumed and the futility of the subject which gave birth to it, between the profound seriousness with which Picasso summoned all his powers for the task and the licentious atmosphere which suggested the theme— just as there is a striking contrast between the hostility which the picture has provoked and the ribald laughter with which his friends first greeted it. A murky atmosphere of sensuality, of that sexual excitement which Picasso needs in order to create, surrounds the inception of the picture. To start with, it was called *Le Bordel d'Avignon*, an Avignon which had nothing to do with the former city of the Popes but referred to a street in Barcelona where there was a well-known brothel. 'Avignon,' Picasso told Kahnweiler, 'has always been a name in my life. I lived two steps from the Carrer d'Avinyo, the street where I used to buy my paper and watercolours.' When this name cropped up for the first time, Max Jacob reminded Picasso that his grandmother came from Avignon and later one of the figures in the picture was jokingly called 'Max's grandma'.

In the first idea for the painting, a student was seen approaching some *filles de joie* with a skull in his hand. This reminder of the vanity of all things, this *memento mori* was well in the Spanish tradition and would almost naturally have occurred to Picasso in contrast to the display of naked flesh. But it was also no doubt too sentimental for him and too symbolical for Max Jacob's taste. Probably based on an actual memory, Picasso then introduced a sailor into the picture—a typical figure in such a context. In one of the first sketches for the composition (pencil and pastel, property of Picasso) the sailor crouching in the midst of naked women, flowers and fruit is the central character. 'The women were in the act of eating,' Picasso explained later. 'Hence the basket of fruit which has been retained in the picture.'

In another sketch (oil on wood, property of Picasso) a naked man has taken the place of the crouching sailor. In yet another, in water-colour (Museum of Art, Philadelphia), the student moving into the room is replaced by a woman drawing a curtain. Throughout these sketches the composition becomes more and more severe, the anecdote disappears and only lingers in Picasso's memory as the initial stimulus.

Among the preparatory drawings for the composition as a whole (Picasso collection) there is a sketch for an interior showing a lightly-decorated section of wall and a curtain with deep folds. In another study this interior is visible only in the background where two figures are dancing in silhouette. In another sketch there is only one dancer in the centre of the background while a nude woman seen from the back stands on the right. This idea of a dancing girl in the background held Picasso's attention for a time and he repeated it in several drawings. A whole series is devoted to the placing of the characters in space, both in depth and horizontally. To start with, in most of the sketches there are six characters, then these are reduced to five.

The sailor is retained for some time in the detailed studies. There is a *Sailor's Head* in oil (Gertrude Stein Collection), a *Sailor rolling a Cigarette* (drawing and gouache, Yvonne Zervos Collection), a *Sailor with a Beret* (drawing, Picasso Collection) and a *Man with prominent Cheek-bones*—and with a gorilla jaw—also in Picasso's collection.

In these innumerable sketches Picasso was seeking to define the physical types of his characters, and the work he was planning was still so much in the melting pot that these types were still not decided upon when he began to paint the final picture. In the result, two of the female figures would be very akin to those that suddenly cropped up after his return from Gosol: a very irregular oval to the face, large Egyptian eyes, asymmetrical nose, a low mouth and ears placed too high. Another clearly Egyptian feature: the woman on the extreme left of the picture, in profile with one eye full-face.

But it would be idle to try and determine the exact influences which affected Picasso in the production of this picture. The result was of such startling novelty that research of that kind can only have a secondary interest. Moreover, the influence of negro masks is only apparent in the features of the two characters on the right-hand side, while it is in the picture as a whole that the new spirit is revealed.

The painting was finally called *Les Demoiselles d'Avignon*. 'How that title annoys me,' said Picasso one day. 'It was Salmon who invented it.' Indeed, the romantic title with its suggestion of a medieval tapestry could not have been more ill chosen, for the rupture with Western art —and it was the Western tradition in particular that Picasso was defying—was apparent in a number of aspects, but primarily in the abandonment of relief. This was not in itself a new departure. A division of the picture into flat surfaces and outlined planes had been one of Gauguin's objects and of all those who were influenced by the Japanese print. Abandonment of relief also involved the problem of integrating human figures or objects in space and here the background was brought forward until it was on a level with the figures in the foreground. But depth could not be eluded. Though the background vanished, this method of transcription did not suffice to detach flat bodies or objects from it. Picasso was one day to supply the solution to this problem through the calligraphy of curves. But in order to bring about a complete rupture with the traditional vision, in this year of 1907 he eliminated, or almost eliminated the curves as well. In his great picture —which was a transitional work—these curves coexist (for instance, in the calves of the second woman on the left or the thighs of the woman on the extreme right) with the new division of the bodies into geometric forms.

The curved line disappeared with the progressive abandonment of relief, that is of the method of detaching a light-coloured body from the background by means of graduated shadows. Henceforth the human body was built up of geometric planes fitting one into another and almost imperceptibly separated by a white or a darker border. But their relation with space was defined by a different colouring of the latter and also by a fringe of shadow outlining the bodies. On the right of the picture, the thrust of the figures towards the foreground is achieved by the hatching on the breasts of the woman standing upright and by the heavily shadowed outline of the concave nose.

Thus relief lost its previous function which, in its most extreme form, amounted to *trompe-l'oeil* and was now used to stress individual elements as part of a new way of presenting the human body. Objects were subjected to this same law of construction, the folds of the curtain, for instance, in the *Demoiselles d'Avignon* looking like facets which are given the appearance of crystal prisms by the use of shadowy blue and white highlights.

Picasso's new geometry with its rectangular or triangular breasts, waists or knees was not a plane geometry. In 1908, with full awareness of what he was doing, he told his friend Gonzalez who was a sculptor in wrought-iron: 'As the colours in these pictures in the last resort merely indicate different perspectives, planes inclined in one direction or another, all you would have to do to produce a sculpture out of them would be to cut them up and then assemble them in the way indicated by the colours.'

In fact, he was so preoccupied at that time in devising new means to give a plastic effect that he started to sculpture himself. He made a mask in bronze, hollowed a human head out of a round stone and in particular tried his hand at sculpture in wood, leaving the surface still rough and painting it in bright colours. A nude woman with a body as though composed of cactus leaves and a man standing upright with an enormous square head suggest primitive totems.

Thanks to this new plastic vision which Picasso tried to compress within the framework of a picture, the *Demoiselles d'Avignon* is a prelude to the revolution of the future: cubism. The colouring went through the same transitional stages as the break-up of the bodies or the physical type. The pale rose tinged with purple of the Harlequin period continues in the women's bodies beside an ochre dating from Gosol, which colour predominates in the woman drawing aside the curtain on the right. Finally, becoming increasingly aware of the revolutionary quality of his picture, Picasso underlined this by abandoning the misty sky-blue he had previously used and introducing a pure ultramarine.

The *Demoiselles d'Avignon* marked a Great Divide. All previous efforts to break with the existing tradition—and the need was widely felt—now looked like an attempt to redecorate a wall that nobody had dared to break down. From 1907 onwards, painting underwent a radical change and the rupture was to be unique in the history of art. Compared with the revolutionary character of the *Demoiselles d'Avignon*, no firm frontier, but only a fluid line seems to separate the end of the Middle Ages, for instance, from the beginning of the Renaissance.

This new era was not only without precedent, it was also the work of one man, and it was done in complete isolation. Picasso's friends joked as they watched him paint. They failed to understand the picture and, worse, they thought it gratuitous. They called it 'The Philosophical Brothel'. Kahnweiler, who saw Picasso at work during the spring of 1907, said later: 'I was a witness to the horrible moral loneliness in which he painted the picture.'

Another unique characteristic of this revolution was that it was complete. Like Christian churches which were built with stones from pagan temples, the different periods of art supplied materials to those which defied them, each period being in part foster-parent to the one which followed. But Picasso made a clean sweep, and was perfectly aware that he was demolishing from the ground up, completely. He said one day to Zervos: 'A picture used to be a sum of additions. With me, a picture is a sum of destructions.'

Another characteristic of the *Demoiselles d'Avignon* is that it was a fully conscious and deliberate work. It is difficult to imagine any former architect, painter or sculptor telling himself that at a precise moment, at a certain time he would set about creating a new style. But that is what Picasso did. It was his intention to free himself from the past, to 'destroy' it, as he says, in order to create a new vision in its place at the moment when he confronted the great bare canvas. He did not yet know what his picture would become, but he knew what it would not be: a continuation of the past. 'A picture,' as he has said, 'is not planned and fixed in advance, it follows the mobility of one's thought,' and in fact the pictorial revolution took place during the course of his work. It was then that memories of things seen crowded in on him, that certain influences more or less consciously played a part and that these all combined in a mysterious and unexpected fashion. If the picture had originated merely in the desire to destroy and in a lucid vision of the goal to be achieved, if there had not been this element of mystery, the result would have been a mathematical diagram without any vitality in it. But Picasso is conscious of his mental processes as few creators have been and he is aware that there is an inexplicable element in each one of his works. As he said to Zervos: 'A picture comes to me from far away, who can say how far? I have sensed it, I have seen it, I have painted it, and yet next day I myself cannot see what I have done. How can my dreams, my instincts, my desires, my thoughts which have taken so long to mature and reach the light of day be analysed, and how can you deduce from this what I have put into my work perhaps against my will?' And to me, referring to the *Demoiselles*, Picasso said: 'I had done half the picture and I felt: that's not it. I did the other half and I wondered if I should repaint the whole. Then I told myself, "No, people will understand what I intended." '

The revolutionary character of the picture is also in part due to the sheer dynamic violence which Picasso put into it, to his deliberate assassination of the beautiful and the pleasant. 'When you begin a picture,' he has said, 'you often find some pretty things. You have got to resist them, destroy your picture' (he often speaks of 'destruction') 'and repaint it several times.' The *Demoiselles d'Avignon* was the first and no doubt the most spectacular illustration of what someone has

G

called 'rejected brainwaves', and the identical process was to be repeated several times in future works. But this first proof of his visual autonomy was the most pregnant with consequences and also the most dangerous. Later, when he could risk anything with impunity, Picasso was accused of arbitrary changes of style, of extravagances for their own sake and of deliberately trying to be different. But this young man of twenty-six was not yet established and he had never yet experienced what was later to be called the magic of his success. He was completely alone in his great adventure and having only recently escaped penury he was running a great financial risk. 'I hadn't a sou!' he recalls. 'My earlier pictures were selling, but nobody wanted the new ones. I provoked an absolute storm, an incredible flood of abuse.' Stchoukine wrote: 'Is it true that Picasso has gone mad?' Even his most fervent admirers deserted him, Leo Stein, for instance, who called one day at the studio and gazed at the great picture in stupefaction. It completely baffled him. It was a joke, he thought. Still, he made an effort to understand and suddenly he burst out laughing. 'Oh, I see! Now I see what you've been trying to do. You've been trying to paint the fourth dimension—how amusing!' In telling this story, Picasso imitated the braying laugh which resounded in his studio. Leo Stein, he said, 'was holding his sides, doubled up; he, too, thought I was mad.'

'Yes,' said Picasso after a moment, 'I knew well enough what I was laying myself open to.' But I could not help asking him: 'How could you be so sure of what you were doing, how could you know that you were right?' 'I didn't know,' he replied. 'But I could not do otherwise. Later, when it was all over, Braque said to me: "It had to happen like that." '

For a long time the painting which was ultimately to acquire a legendary reputation remained a doubtful venture for Picasso. Kahnweiler, who bought all the preparatory studies for the *Demoiselles* and also Picasso's subsequent works, now states: 'The only reason why I did not buy the great picture itself was that Picasso did not consider it finished and refused to sell it.' The work remained very little known among the general public; only Picasso's personal friends saw it in his studio. It was seldom reproduced, for the first time with its present title in 1925 in *La Révolution Surrealiste*. In 1920, it had been bought by Jacques Doucet who gave it a prominent place in his collection. Today, it is one of the most famous pictures in the Museum of Modern Art in New York (Lillie P. Bliss Bequest), but it has only three times been shown in Europe, once at the World Exhibition in Paris in 1937 and, for the second and third times, in London in 1949 and 1960 by the Institute of Contemporary Arts and at the Tate Gallery. But by then the battle was over—and won.

CHAPTER VII 1908-1909

Away with Perspective!

IN the preface to the catalogue of the exhibition of the *Cercle de l'Art Moderne* of Le Havre in June, 1908, in which works by Braque, Matisse, Derain and Dufy were shown, Apollinaire specified purity, unity and truth as the three plastic virtues which 'hold nature prostrate beneath their feet'. The meaning of this lyrical statement was not as clear as his further remarks: 'Only photographers make reproductions of nature,' and, preaching disrespect for tradition: 'You cannot carry your father's corpse with you everywhere. You leave it in the company of other dead men.' From the same year dates Apollinaire's violent criticism of impressionism, whose characteristics were, according to him, 'ignorance and frenzy'.

Perhaps Apollinaire was secretly shocked by an art as revolutionary as Picasso's. Cocteau said of him that 'having opened a flood-gate, he came to revile the flood on the excuse that he had opened the flood-gate as a joke'. But in fact Apollinaire opened no gate at all in pictorial art; at the most, he was the lock-keeper who explained the reasons for the flood to the public. He himself stressed that Picasso had worked stubbornly and in solitude. Max Jacob also notes that at this decisive period he received no confidences from his friend. He speaks of the figures 'with the nose attached to the eye' which Picasso painted during those years, describes him absorbed 'in profound meditation, simplifying things animate and inanimate and achieving at a single stroke the kind of drawings which recall those of prehistoric caves', and he adds: 'I doubt whether there are any of them left now.' For his part, engrossed in the new world he had just created, Picasso kept his friends at a distance: 'Go and amuse yourselves,' he would tell them, as though determined that he was going to be the only one to indulge in solitary labour.

To some of his critics the pictures which followed the *Demoiselles d'Avignon* seemed to mark a 'retreat' from the audacity of that work, and in fact he was seeking the purification of form by various means and a short cut to the sign language of his future art. In this transitional period a number of women's faces were painted, shaped like Gothic arches, pointed eggs or slim leaves, with bodies built up in lozenges, like the *Danseuse jaune* (René Gaffé Collection, Brussels), the *Tête de femme* resting on a raised arm (Georges Salles Collection) or the *Nu à la draperie* (Moscow) where the relief is obtained by hatching or cross-hatching. Strong contours produce a rigorous isolation of each form; arms and legs shaped like lozenges or cactus leaves fit into flat, tri-angular bodies. The same novelty of form is seen in the *Fleurs sur une table* (Collection of Mr. and Mrs. Ralph F. Collin, New York) where the mass of leaves and flowers consists of heavily hachured rectangles and triangles. The dominant colours of this period are a bright lemon-yellow contrasting with a vivid blue and one or two touches of mauve or violet-brown.

In the still-lifes, hatchings rapidly yield to a direct presentation of objects in the round. A picture one would imagine to have been painted in the previous year—*Nature morte à l'entonnoir* (Museum of Modern Art, Moscow)—dates in fact from 1908. By their very simplicity the objects collected on the table anticipate the reign of humble daily life which was soon to prevail in art: glasses, bowls and bottles seen from above. The objects have acquired a new solidity, they seem to be turned in wood, even those which their colour reveals to consist of metal or glass. They form a compact mass, obscuring one another as though to prevent the air from circulating.

The *Fruits et Verre* of 1908 (private collection) represents a much clearer concession to convention and is a hark-back to the retrospective Cézanne exhibition of the previous year. With its apples and pears on a red table it is almost a pastiche. The new presentation of mass and the abandonment of hatching was accompanied by a total change of colouring. The dominating tone of most of the still-lifes is wood or brick and also of human bodies treated in large masses, like mechanisms loosely fitted together from pieces of roughly hewn wood. *L'Amitié* (Moscow Museum), for which Picasso did two preparatory studies in gouache during the winter of 1907-8, is halfway between the *Demoi-selles d'Avignon* and his search for a new plastic vision. The two nude figures form a criss-cross of light-coloured planes ringed with shadows or dark brown brush-strokes. On the other hand, the *Femme assise*

(Moscow), with her barrel thighs and her triangular legs contained within the framework of her folded arms, initiates the large, flat, chaotic picture, thrust—one might almost say catapulted—as she is from the background into the third dimension. Picasso's assertion that he had seen no negro masks before completing the *Demoiselles d'Avignon* seems to be borne out by the *Femme à l'éventail* (Moscow), the woman sitting in her chair like a barbaric idol, thrusting towards the spectator in inhuman splendour, the forehead and the angle of the nose roughly planed, bursting out of the shadows with a forcefulness rarely equalled. This forcefulness was not a chance success; it had been carefully prepared for in two preliminary studies.

In the summer of 1908, perhaps feeling exhausted by his efforts, Picasso did not undertake the usual journey to Spain. Instead, he moved in the autumn to the outskirts of Paris. He was not fond of the French countryside and disliked the damp soil of the forests which, no doubt thinking of the warm, dry odours of his native country, he said 'smelt of mushrooms'. He selected a little hamlet near Creil with the picturesque name of La Rue des Bois, renting a detached farm-cottage with two rooms with a bed in each. 'We used to eat in a room that smelt like a stable,' Fernande recalls, but Picasso quickly got used to the rural discomfort. Accompanied by a dog and a cat that was about to have kittens, he and Fernande stuck to their habits, getting up late, which no doubt shocked the inhabitants but failed to destroy the goodwill of the farmer's wife. He was soon at work again, catching, as he said later, 'indigestion' from the green of the trees and the grass which surrounded him: he had never liked an aquatic light. Green invaded his canvases, a dark green saturated with gold and harmonizing with the warm, russet tone which he was using.

Again, a series of landscapes were the prelude to a pictorial transformation. In those which he painted in the Forêt d'Halatte a few isolated tree-trunks and some outsize leaves are enough to suggest the density of a thick forest with soft mauve reflections gliding along the trunks (Museum of Modern Art, Moscow). Sometimes a single forked branch against a background of green suggests the heart of an impenetrable thicket (*Paysage*, Gertrude Stein Collection). Another picture, *Nu dans une forêt*, which is difficult to make out, is painted almost entirely in shadowy tones of ochre and green, and the human figures merge with the tree-trunks in a way which suggests the dissolution of form which Picasso was later to achieve.

While he was working at Rue des Bois, Picasso was progressing towards a new manner. He painted the *Maisonette dans un jardin* and the *Maisonette et arbres* (Museum of Modern Art, Moscow) where the building is a bare cube surmounted by a triangle of roof against a background of trees reduced to totem-like forms. Human forms, reduced in the same manner, acquire a brutal force akin to primitive savagery. On two occasions Picasso painted the farmer's wife with whom he lodged (*Fermière*, Museum of Modern Art, Moscow). In a half-length portrait, a bullet head, in which the sightless eyes are barely indicated and the mouth is lacking entirely, rests directly on massive shoulders. Reduced though she is to these simple contours, one senses a powerful woman whose tanned and reddened skin catches the warm daylight. In the picture which shows her seated her knees are raised, touching her heavy breasts, her hands hang massively at her sides and enormous, protruding biceps are visible. In her blue dress she looks like a block of wood draped with folds. Her face is in shadow. The purplish skin stands out against a purple and green background. She seems immutable, impossible to uproot, the spirit of the soil personified.

Cézanne's maxim in a letter to Émile Bernard that 'the cylinder, the sphere, the cone' must be seen in nature has often been quoted as the prelude to Picasso's new plastic vision, but even if he knew of the maxim it would not apply to his own aims, except in so far as it was the principle of constructivism. The pictures which he painted in that winter of 1908 represent an attempt to break up human bodies into broad, sharp-edged facets in perfect balance with one another. Minute preparations, including a drawing, a watercolour, four gouaches on paper and a large oil painting, were made for the *Trois Femmes* now in the Museum of Modern Art in Moscow. (The painting originally belonged to Stchoukine who had continued to buy Picasso's works after recovering from the first shock of surprise.) The *Trois Femmes*, of whom two are in frenzied movement, are less a variation than a logical continuation of the *Demoiselles d'Avignon*.

It is a characteristic of Picasso that each new act of daring makes the preceding one seem almost timorous. The left-hand group of three women in the *Demoiselles d'Avignon*, for instance, seems almost conventional compared with the *Trois Femmes* of Moscow. The *Trois Femmes* consists of a compact block of struggling stereometric forms, and even the body of the crouching woman which has been broken down into long, sharp-pointed triangles suggests strength temporarily at rest. Against a monochrome background of beige a single splash of green stands out, and this is so characteristic of his work at that time that to all the epithets—Negro, or Proto-Cubist —which have been applied to it, that of 'the Green period' has been added.

The curious picture, *Famille d'Arlequin* (E. von der Heydt Collection, Ascona), is a signpost towards Picasso's new plastic vision. Here he returns to a familiar theme as though it were the most suitable field of experiment for carrying out a work of what might be called self-destruction. One of the permanent conductors of Picasso's creativity has been the harlequin theme. In this picture the same skinny harlequins appear as occurred at the beginning of the Blue period in their characteristic attitude with hunched and pointed shoulders. The green harlequin has a hollowed block of wood instead of a face. The woman, with a single small breast, is built up of rectangles with such sharp edges that they appear to be made of metal. The colouring shows an innovation: instead of ochres and brick-reds, a pearl grey is introduced which was shortly to dominate his palette.

Another attempt to interpret the same plastic vision, but in a different genre, is represented by the *Baigneuse* (private collection, Switzerland). Of this subject Picasso also made a pen-and-ink drawing. This time, the breakdown of the human body is achieved with round-shaped segments, clearly differentiated and with almost visible joints, as though they were made of wood. This approach was soon to be abandoned, but as nothing is lost in Picasso's production, nothing occurs in complete isolation and the *Baigneuse* of 1908 was to recur twenty years later in a modified form in the *Baigneuses* of Dinard.

Being free of material worries at this time, Picasso was better able to devote himself to his artistic problems. He had rented a studio at the bottom of an old garden in the Rue Cortot and here he shut himself up from two in the afternoon until nightfall. When he emerged he usually wore a grim expression and sometimes his friends asked him whether he was worried or felt unwell. 'No, not at all,' he replied, 'I am thinking of my work.'

All the same, his exacting tasks were a considerable strain and sometimes he felt a touch of envy for more conventional artists. Walking in later years with Sabartés he would stop occasionally at the windows of the more prosperous picture dealers and gaze at some landscape or other representing a sunset with cows, lakes and tree-tops reflected in the water. 'How it would amuse me to paint like that! You can't think how it would amuse me!' But though amusements of this kind were not for him and he seemed absorbed in a solitary struggle with his problems, his own difficulties seemed to increase rather than diminish his sensibility and he was more than ever alive to the artistic efforts of others.

One day in 1908 he stopped at Papa Soulier's shop in front of a large portrait of a woman. 'It is not expensive,' said the old man. 'You can have it for five francs and repaint the canvas.' In the picture Picasso detected a logical but slightly grotesque effort at simplification which interested him. He asked about the artist. The man was not, as Soulier supposed, completely unknown. Searching as ever for talent, Uhde had discovered in the previous year a large picture serving as a fire-screen in a laundry. It showed a little woman in red walking in the forest in springtime. Because of its utilitarian use he was asked to pay 40 francs for it. At that time, the artist, Henri Rousseau, was considered a figure of fun. But in 1925 this same picture was sold for 300,000 francs.

From time to time Rousseau had sent some of his pictures to the Salon des Indépendents; then in 1907 Wilhelm Uhde had organized a special exhibition for him in Paris. Later, a friend lent him a shop in Montparnasse where he offered huge pictures by Marie Laurencin and Rousseau for sale. Rousseau himself supervised the hanging and soon the small shop was full to bursting with his canvases. But no one came to the varnishing: Uhde, the slap-happy amateur, had forgotten to inform his friends. At that time Henri Rousseau was sixty-four. He had fought in the war of 1870 and claimed in explanation of the exotic nature of his canvases that he had also taken part in the Mexican campaign—but this he was never able to prove. He was, in fact, an employee of the *octroi* or City Toll, a customs-house officer whose imagination regularly became peopled with the fauna and flora of the tropics while he went about his mundane duties.

The little man with the goatee beard, slightly bent now and completely indistinguishable from the small tradesmen and *petits bourgeois* with whom he lived, possessed, in fact, a kind of dual personality. He led the same humble and busy life as they, painting their portraits—first measuring his models with a ruler—their weddings, their family reunions and their Sunday excursions. His pictures were not expensive

—no more costly or appreciated by his customers, in fact, than the photographs which they had taken on solemn occasions—but Rousseau, and this was an advantage, would accept payment in kind. He also painted the Paris that he knew and loved and the suburb where he lived, transforming reality into a reflection of his dreams. In the background of the picture which Picasso bought, a window opens on to high mountains and fortifications. . . . Rousseau knew he was a great painter and he had retired early in life, at the age of forty, so as to devote himself entirely to art. The high quality of his pictures was not due to chance, but to a process of profound thought. A man of such vast culture and subtle intelligence as Uhde has written: 'I have never discussed his pictures with any artist more profitably or more seriously than with Henri Rousseau—the different artistic points of view, the way to obtain such and such a balance, the choice of this colour or that.'

The artist in Rousseau took charge of him with elemental force. 'It is not I who paint,' he told a friend, 'but another who holds my hand.' Sometimes this other Rousseau threatened to burst his frame. Then, when painting a tiger hunt, for instance, he would be seized with sudden terror or the onset of some fantastic vision would send him gasping for air to the window of his small studio to let out the heavy scent of the jungle and the odour of wild animals.

With his taste for the unusual, Apollinaire had unearthed the little man and got an invitation to what Rousseau solemnly called his 'soirées'. He took Picasso and Fernande with him. As the room was small Rousseau had arranged the chairs in serried ranks and asked his guests to sit down as soon as they arrived. Apollinaire and his friends found Rousseau's neighbours already installed: butchers, bakers and grocers sitting bolt-upright in their Sunday best, interspersed with one or two artists like Delaunay, Max Jacob and Duhamel. Rousseau opened the proceedings with a little air on the violin, then asked his guests to contribute something. Songs were sung and monologues recited. Rousseau was enchanted, Fernande recalls, and kept on saying how well the evening was going, and indeed it was some feat to reproduce in the heart of Paris the provincial atmosphere of long ago. Rousseau was a tender-hearted gentleman, overflowing with courtesy and consideration. He had been twice married, had buried both wives and though he had never known conjugal bliss his one thought was to marry again. 'At my age you can still love without making yourself ridiculous,' he said to Fernande. 'At my age you have a greater need to warm your heart and to know that you will not die alone and that perhaps another old heart will help you to pass to the other side.' He was, indeed, already engaged and pouring out on his fiancée the rich store of affection that was in him. But she would not marry him without her father's consent and the old man, aged eighty-three, thought Rousseau was too old for her, though she herself was already fifty-nine. This *petit bourgeois* cussedness was too much for Rousseau. Rejected and spurned, he lost interest in life and in art and died, as he was afraid he would, alone in hospital in 1910.

For a long time even connoisseurs failed to appreciate the value of Rousseau's art, no doubt owing to the chaotic, grotesque element which sometimes crept into his pictures. For a posthumous exhibition organized by Uhde a French art-critic wrote: 'It seems that Henri Rousseau is highly esteemed in Germany and Russia. That may be so. But happily we are in France and are Frenchmen.' This note of xenophobia which recurs from time to time in France at moments of confusion seems particularly incongruous when applied to a man who personified the French *petit bourgeois*. Uhde reports: 'Anyone defending him or Picasso compromised his honour and his name and was taken for an idiot or an impostor.'

But before his death the solitary old man had his brief moment of glory. A banquet was organized for him by Picasso and Apollinaire with the mixed motive of honouring him and at the same time pulling his leg. Immense care was taken in the preparations. Foliage was draped over the beams and walls of Picasso's studio. Garlands were suspended from the ceiling. A long trestle table was set up with, at one end, a kind of packing case for the guest of honour against a background of curtains and Chinese lanterns. A large banner proclaimed: 'Honour to Rousseau.' Emerging from her customary indolence, Fernande flung herself into the role of hostess, cooking a vast quantity of rice *à la Valencienne* and ordering a series of dishes from a caterer. Chairs, glass, cutlery and plates were hired in imposing quantities. The guests foregathered at a bar in the Rue Ravignan and included the artist Marie Laurencin, Leo and Gertrude Stein and a young female friend of Gertrude's who had just arrived from the United States, Alice Toklas. While waiting for Apollinaire who had gone off to fetch Rousseau, the company started the festivities by making Marie Laurencin tight—not a difficult task in view of her youth and inexperience. Soon, under the influence of aperitifs, she was performing a kind of rhythmic dance which entailed much staggering about and waving of arms. Then suddenly Fernande burst into the room in hectic gloom: the caterers had failed to deliver the dinner. Telephone the shop, suggested Alice Toklas, briskly practical. A search was made, at length a telephone was found—they were scarce in those days—but when Fernande finally got the number there was no reply.

Odds and ends of food were then bought from small shops in the neighbourhood. Added to Fernande's mountains of rice they would prevent anyone from starving. The company now moved off to the studio, supporting Marie Laurencin who could no longer walk and collapsed into a tray of jam tarts as soon as she arrived. Rousseau then made a solemn entry beside Apollinaire, tears rising to his eyes at sight of the preparations made in his honour. Dinner was served, wine circulated, voices were raised. Soon, the whole neighbourhood knew that a party was in progress. Frédé arrived with his faithful donkey, some Italian street-singers tried to gate-crash and Fernande had to summon her most stalwart guests to eject them. But pressure was maintained and soon 'almost the whole of Montmartre', as she later recalled, was winding its way through the studio, pocketing delicacies under the outraged glances of the hostess. Rousseau, meanwhile, had fallen into a gently inebriated sleep. When the last of the intruders had gone, events took a more artistic turn. Rousseau was roused and persuaded to play a piece on his violin which of course he had brought with him. As encore he sang his favourite song: 'Aïe, aïe, que j'ai mal aux dents'. Marie Laurencin, sobered by the food, then sang—something about Normandy. Then the great moment of the evening arrived. André Salmon jumped on the rickety table, recited a poem and proposed a toast in honour of Rousseau, draining his glass at a gulp. That finished him: the next moment he became violently aggressive and had to be removed to a neighbouring room to cool off with the ladies' cloaks. Next morning he was found peacefully asleep on the divan surrounded by the remains of a box of matches and by a brand-new hat of Alice Toklas's of which he had chewed the trimmings.

The wax in the Chinese lanterns was beginning to melt and drip in great burning tears on to Rousseau's bald head, but he remained oblivious, or stoical, until the drips formed a little pile like a clown's hat. Someone then began to intone:

*C'est la peinture
de ce Rousseau
qui dompte la nature
avec son magnifique pinceau.*

The company took this up, singing in chorus. More toasts. More poems. Apollinaire recited verses which he swore were impromptu, but had obviously been composed for the occasion. And all, all in honour of Rousseau. The Bateau-Lavoir was positively quivering with the re-echoed noise, and the old man was weeping with emotion. Still clutching his violin, he fell asleep again, then began to snore, then woke up, bitterly regretting every second he had missed of these unforgettable hours. At dawn, with the Chinese lantern bursting into flames above his head, he at last decided it was time to go, and the Steins escorted a blissful but exhausted Rousseau back to his distant home.

The banquet at Picasso's was talked of for a long time to come. Some people were indignant, thinking Rousseau unworthy of the tribute, but he himself never doubted Picasso's good faith. One would have thought his talents would have led him to admire Bouguereau, but it was in Picasso that he recognized an equal, saying to him one day with naïve and touching pride: 'We are the greatest painters of our time, you in the Egyptian style, I in the modern.'

The Rousseau interlude had been Picasso's last effort at sociability. From now on he was more and more averse to seeing crowds of people at the studio. In his early years he had of course felt the need of appreciation, but he now accepted admiration as something which was due to him and quickly tired of it. At the same time, celebrity in the eyes of connoisseurs and initiates brought him a certain popular fame, at first confined to the area in which he lived. One day, a number of young German artists recognized him at the Lapin Agile and insisted on carrying him on their shoulders in triumph to the Place du Tertre. Getting bored and finally exasperated with the ovation, Picasso drew the revolver which he always carried on him and fired it into the air. The crowd rapidly dispersed!

This surly humour was aggravated by fear of illness. He was always worrying about his health. The slightest thing could arouse his anxiety, a smoker's cough, for instance, which convinced him that he was suffering from chest disease and made him anxiously observe whether he was spitting blood. One night when he burst a small blood-vessel he sent for the doctor in terror and despite the latter's efforts refused to be reassured. A genuine kidney complaint made him take to a strict diet— no salt, bland foods consisting of vegetables, fish or rice cooked in milk and nothing to drink except milk or mineral water. 'Perhaps it was this diet which made him so gloomy,' suggested Fernande enjoying chronic good health. More charitably Max Jacob called him a stoic.

In this same year of 1908 Apollinaire introduced him to Georges Braque, and the meeting was to be of great importance to him. Braque was one year younger than Picasso and was described by Fernande as looking like a 'white negro' with a powerful head, a boxer's neck and shoulders, a very dark complexion, curly black hair and a short moustache. He looked a tough customer and enjoyed acting the part with brutal gestures and harsh inflexions to his voice. But Braque was a more cautious artist than Picasso, was averse to excess in any form, and at first he was not inclined to follow him. He had exhibited with the Fauves in the Salon in 1905, perhaps more out of friendship for his friend Othon Friesz than from any enjoyment of extravagance. He was, in fact, more subtle than his friends and he was to find it easier to cut adrift from the prevailing current. At one time he had been apprenticed to an interior decorator and he possessed a craftsman's caution which enabled him to build his pictorial revolution on a solid basis. He accepted Picasso's *optique* with considerable reservations, being revolted by the deformation of features in the *Demoiselles d'Avignon* and in particular by the angular protuberances stuck on the faces of the two women on the right of the picture. Picasso protested, 'A nose is like that!' but Braque was not convinced and told him: 'For all your explanations your painting gives me the feeling you want us to eat tow or drink paraffin so as to set us on fire.'

But Braque was generous with his approval once he was convinced and his feelings had been aroused. In the previous year in the strong sunlight of the Midi he had painted a picture strongly influenced by Cézanne. On the other hand, the picture he sent to the Salon des Indépendents was the first important canvas shown to the general public which had been influenced by Picasso's *Demoiselles d'Avignon*. According to Fernande the picture seems to have been painted in secret and Braque told no one, not even Picasso, either of his work or his intention to exhibit it. 'Picasso was a trifle indignant,' notes Fernande and Max Jacob's memoirs reveal the passing distress which this incident caused: 'It was Braque who was called upon to exhibit the first cubist painting for reasons which I will not go into.' In a comment published in the *Revue des Lettres et des Arts* on 1st May, 1908, the future herald of the new art, Apollinaire, noted cautiously: 'M. Georges Braque's great composition seems to me the most novel effort in this Salon. . . . The art of construction faces the artist with many problems which have not yet been resolved. M. Braque tackles some of them courageously.'

During the summer of 1908, while Picasso was interpreting after his own fashion the green masses in the Forest of Halatte, Braque returned to the Midi and looked at the familiar countryside with new eyes. Of six pictures which he sent on his return to the autumn Salon, two were rejected by the committee. Braque then indignantly withdrew the others. About this time, according to Uhde, Max Jacob said in his presence to Picasso, referring to a small landscape of Braque's: 'Haven't you noticed how Braque has been introducing cubes into his pictures recently?' Kahnweiler says that Louis Vauxcelles was the first to write publicly of 'cubes' in his review of the Braque exhibition held at the gallery in the Rue Vignon in November, 1908 and of 'Peruvian cubism' in connection with the picture sent by Braque to the Indépendents in 1909. Like many sensational innovations, cubism became accepted so slowly by the public that contemporary witnesses contradict one another in all good faith. However, it seems certain, as Kahnweiler says, that the name was invented by an adversary and he notes shrewdly, referring to synthetism, futurism, 'Les Nabis', etc.: 'Movements which choose their own names reveal either their artificial character or their dominance by an ambitious chief.'

Though Picasso's intimates speak of a certain amount of friction, his friendship with Braque was to develop into close collaboration. This was all the more important for Picasso in that, despite his growing reputation, he had remained very much alone in his artistic aims. The pictures he painted during the winter of 1908 and the spring of 1909 accentuated the simplification of forms and their reduction to geometric planes. From still-lifes not dissimilar from those painted by the primitive masters he passed to the *Chocolatière* of the spring of 1909 (private collection), in which round objects are broken down into acute angles. In the *Nature morte aux pains* (private collection, Paris) the depiction of forms in rhomboidal shapes is even more marked.

But this was not Picasso's only line of advance. In the spring of 1909

101

he painted several *Natures mortes au compotier* where the plasticity of forms was obtained by modelling in curves, such as the picture in the Museum of Modern Art in Moscow. There were even frank returns to an earlier style as in the *Bouquet de fleurs* (Moscow) where the half-open drawer of a table is painted almost in realistic style and there are curves and arabesques in the surface.

In the treatment of the human body the rupture with the past was more evident as though no half-measures were possible in this sphere, for instance in the *Reine Isabeau* (Moscow Museum), where the simplification is made more striking by the archaic costume. The picture seems to have borrowed from medieval tapestries their two-dimensional portrayal of forms, and it was this perhaps which decided Picasso to take his inspiration from an archaic subject. The abolition of perspective was, indeed, the dominating characteristic and the aim of cubism in its final form. Perhaps Picasso and Braque are still seeking to reach the stage where objects will cease to exist in depth, as they have done since the Renaissance, and exist instead simultaneously in time in the diversity of their successive aspects. But to achieve this aim it was first necessary to break with deeply rooted traditions and with centuries-old pictorial habits. The break took place in more or less brief stages during the course of that year 1909. *La Reine Isabeau* emerges from a flat background with an egg-shaped head in which the features are barely indicated. In the rich colouring—a legacy from the past—a flamboyant green dominates, combined with a warm ochre and a delicate grey.

In the *Femme jouant de la mandoline* (Museum of Modern Art, Moscow) a purple curtain provides a background for a chair and a dress painted in a complementary green. The picture was doubtless painted after the *Reine Isabeau*. The deformation of the human body is even more accentuated. The ball-shaped head with the face sliced off it in a flat plane is bare of features, except for oblique eyelids and the faintest suggestion of a mouth, but these cursory signs suffice to give the face an expression of sorrowful intensity. The picture is curious for the persistence of a double vision. The face, the hands, the body and the musical instrument are treated in large sculptural masses, but the right background, consisting of book shelves as well as the details of the Renaissance chair with its straight back, introduce a realistic note—even the spines of the books are reproduced with their multicoloured backs. The mandolin which the young woman is playing is a new

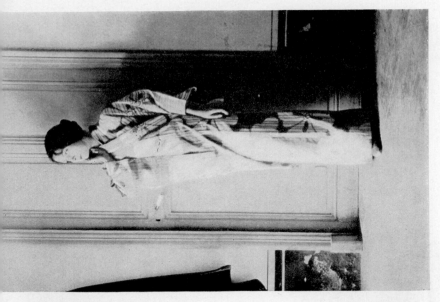

7 Éva in 1912

8 Self portrait, 1912

9   Picasso in Rue Schoelcher

10   Picasso in Rome, 1917

feature. Braque was the first to introduce musical instruments into his pictures at a time when no one was painting them. According to Juan Gris, the guitar was for the cubists what the Madonna was for the Primitives.

The harmony established between Picasso and Braque was far-reaching, for the adventure on which they now embarked was treated from the start as a collective effort. Between 1908 and 1914 they only signed their canvases on the back, as though to preserve their anonymity and the time was to come when in fact it was difficult to distinguish their individual contributions. Braque, who once declared, 'I like to correct emotions with rules,' gave Picasso a sense of unshakeable certainty and this was no doubt valuable as Picasso's friends had been unpleasantly surprised by his latest pictures. 'His studio,' writes Mahaut, 'became a kind of laboratory where he constructed and created creatures which to start with, while they were still identifiable, looked like monsters. I myself can remember in the early stages of this process gazing with nostalgia at the portrait of a young woman which he had painted with all the ambiguous and affecting charm of da Vinci and which still hung on a wall of his studio.' Manolo, forthright and outraged, demanded: 'And what would you say if your parents met you on Barcelona station with faces like that?' Picasso was just about to set off for Spain. Sensing perhaps that he would have to revisit the past in order to abandon it the more completely, he renewed acquaintance with his childhood friend Pallarès at La Horta de San Juan. There he was best able to break down and reconstruct the landscape, perhaps because it was so familiar to him. There was also the brilliant sunlight which enabled him to arrange what he saw in compact masses, the same light which enabled Cézanne to seize the essentials of a landscape at the expense of its momentary aspects. The particular conformation of the Spanish soil was also favourable with its superimposed planes and primitive, cube-like buildings of Arab origin. Even the economy of colouring—the pale horizon and the ochre soil—suited his needs.

As though anxious not to carry his divorce with reality too far, Picasso brought back some photographs of the villages he had painted taken by himself and Fernande, giving them to Gertrude Stein who bought three of his landscapes. The *Réservoir* has all the starkness of an industrial scene and consists of superimposed cubes arranged in depth. The colouring is almost monochrome and an insistent background makes the heavy masses look transparent. The *Usine* (Museum of

Modern Art, Moscow) is presented in shimmering facets, each radiating its own inherent light. The *Maisons sur la colline* shows tiers of houses rising like some mineral formation in slate or bronze-coloured crystal facets above the arch of a bridge towards a burning sky.

When Gertrude Stein first hung these canvases on the walls of her home everyone was scandalized and wondered where the landscape had got to in this agglomeration of superimposed cubes. She showed the photographs and said laughing: 'If you found the pictures too realistic I could understand your objection.' She knew in fact that here was the onset of a new pictorial vision and she called it later 'the real beginning of cubism'.

Though it was landscape which enabled Picasso to evolve the essential features of his new vision, it was in the latter's application to the human body that the change was most striking. One of the first portraits where the face was dissolved into sharp-edged facets was that of *Fernande* (Museum of Modern Art, New York). The face looks like a mass of crystals of fortuitous shape that have been assembled into a single block. In the *Femme en vert* (Roland Penrose Collection, London), painted in the winter of 1909, the bluish green which had persisted in Picasso's palette since the landscapes of the Rue des Bois alternates with shades of ochre, and this colouring helps to give the facets of which the forms are composed a crystalline transparency, as though one were looking into the depths of some strange mineral kingdom. But the curious fact is that, despite this break-down, the face is still a human one and even resembles the model.

Picasso worked relentlessly during his stay in La Horta. What other people called 'holidays' were for him a period of intense productivity. Apart from a series of landscapes, he painted a large number of heads and half-length portraits of women—pictures in which his style became firmer and more precise and, in doing so, ready to be superseded.

On his return, during the winter, the facets with which he had started to construct faces and human bodies ceased to form a compact, immutable block and began to coalesce and dissolve before the spectator's eyes. Thus in the *Femme et pot de moutarde* (Rosengart Gallery, Lucerne) the mouth which has slipped to the bottom of the face and the dissolving facets give an air of mournful oppression which is accentuated by the predominating greys and browns with a green curtain providing the only patch of colour.

This picture is very close to Picasso's only work of sculpture known to have been created in this period: a woman's head with deep hollows and sharp edges where the distribution of light and shade gives a striking effect of raddled flesh. At this time, when he was attempting to express his new vision, Picasso tried all sorts of experiments, but despite a certain amount of success, sculpture failed to satisfy him and he abandoned it for several years.

In his pictorial experiments the disintegration of forms took place at such a speed that it is difficult to follow it. In the *Femme nue* (Moscow Museum), painted in the same year as the *Reine Isabeau*, the green of the chair seems the only link between the two canvases. The crumbling facets of the face now involve the features as well, displacing them both upwards and downwards. Ochres turn to brick-red and the mauve-tinted greys are closely allied to some of the mannered tints in the La Horta landscapes. With the *Femme assise* (Georges Salles Collection) the period of transition came to an end. Henceforth the cubes and facets into which the human body was cut or sliced gave it a sense of violent movement, as though seen under a kaleidoscope. A new pictorial aesthetic had been born. Picasso still returned sometimes to his former manner and partially at least to the old 'legibility', but soon the word itself became a term of abuse when he applied it to other painters. The rupture with the direct representation of reality was now virtually complete, as was seen in the portrait of Georges Braque painted that same winter (Frank Crowninshield Collection, New York).

Picasso was now able to afford a more spacious home and he moved with few regrets from the squalor and confusion of the Bateau-Lavoir to an apartment at 11, Boulevard de Clichy, with windows looking towards the south and a large studio with a northern aspect. He and Fernande decided to employ a resident maid, but the furniture which they brought with them—a box-mattress without legs, a round folding table which they had used for meals and a linen cupboard—was barely enough to furnish her room, let alone the rest of the flat. Picasso's parents sent him one or two good pieces of furniture in Italian marquetry, and he soon discovered a passion for buying odds and ends himself: a low bedstead with heavy brass bars, a large antique cherry-wood sideboard which took up the whole of one wall in the small dining-room, several pieces in mahogany, besides china, copper and pewter utensils bought from junk-shops. The practical value of some of these objects was doubtful. Some were bought for their colour, others for their shape and a small mahogany organ (which no one played) because it emitted a pleasing odour of incense when the bellows were worked. Soon the pieces of furniture acquired a kind of squatter's right to stay where they were put—and stay they did until in due course Picasso moved house again. It seemed as though there was a strong conservative streak in Picasso's make-up, at any rate when applied to his surroundings. He lavished on objects an affection which perhaps he was unable to bestow on human beings. Fernande recalls an old hat-box stuffed with ties of every possible material and colour which he refused to get rid of for years.

Fernande also notes that his revolutionary ideas in art seemed to unfold best in solid and stolid surroundings. He felt the need, she suggests, for something normal amid the abnormality of his life—and perhaps also for a minimum of security. Hence the maid in cap and apron in the new apartment, and a piano which was completely useless to a man who admitted he understood nothing about music. The atmosphere in the Boulevard de Clichy was one of reassuring conformism, at least in some respects. Picasso's studio remained his personal kingdom. No one went in without his permission, even to sweep the floor, and this was seldom done. The result, according to Fernande, was dust flying everywhere and Picasso in a rage to see it sticking to his freshly painted canvases. Personal possessions littered the room: negro masks and scraps of tapestry on the walls, guitars and mandolins lying about—the same instruments of which Picasso said that he had painted them first and bought and looked at them afterwards.

Animals were as essential to Picasso as female companionship. In his new home he had his dog Frika, three Siamese cats and a long-tailed monkey, Monina. He could unbend with animals in a way which he never found possible with human beings, and to discover the true Picasso one would have perhaps to listen to the conversations he holds with his domestic pets.

Two snaps taken of Picasso at a few months' interval show him as he was at this time. In one of them he is dressed in a French army sergeant's uniform which he had borrowed from Braque who had come to see him during his period of military training. Perhaps Picasso wanted to see what it felt like to lose his individuality. As a Spaniard, he himself never performed military service or wore uniform at any time. In the other photograph he is sitting on a plush sofa with his Siamese cat in his hands. Both cat and Picasso look extraordinarily, unusually pleased with themselves, and the picture seems to immortalize the artist who had finally arrived. But it was at this moment nevertheless, installed in unaccustomed ease and conventional security, in a setting which promised to be permanent, that Picasso embarked on great adventures in his art and in his private life.

CHAPTER VIII 1910–1913

Cubism and Collage

'IT is forbidden to talk to the pilot,' the exasperated Picasso once replied to a painter who was pestering him with questions about the sources of cubist inspiration. 'When we went in for cubism,' he said later, 'it was not cubism we were after, but expressing what was in us.' The defenders and theoreticians of cubism used to be fond of quoting Cézanne to justify its most flagrant audacities. But Cézanne's influence stopped short of the point where the cubists shattered reality and it was, according to Malraux, when they ceased to take possession of the world and started to question it that Picasso 'succeeded' Cézanne.

Through cubism plastic vision assumed a new significance and took possession of a world so different from everything that had preceded it that modern painters have never quite found their way back to the old approach. Moreover, the reasons which determined the choice of this particular form of expression are still obscure. Waldemar George stressed this in his prefatory remarks to an exhibition of works deriving from what was later called the 'heroic period' of cubism: 'Almost half a century has passed since its birth, but it still eludes all definition and its origins are still controversial. For a long time it was considered an arbitrary choice springing from a deliberate desire to scandalize. A contemporary criticism reads: 'The cubists are these young jokers, disciples of Picasso who was once a gifted colourist and is now an equally gifted leg-puller.' The most serious art-critics asked with Vauxcelles: 'What is this cubist movement aiming at? Are these the obscure beginnings of something or is this—as I personally believe—a miscarriage?'

Those who attacked cubism were not choosy in their weapons—Picasso's foreign origins were exploited and those of his admirers. Paul Sérusier, for instance, the theoretician of the Nabis, wrote at the beginning of 1915: 'Now that the cubist fraud is about to collapse I believe we may be allowed to do some simple plane geometry in a straightforward spirit of Christian and French clarity.'

But even when the eddies provoked by cubism had died down and it was recognized as a chapter in the history of art, hostility was not disarmed. Jules Romains asserts that 'Picasso's activities were nothing but an imposture and his cubism offended us with its illusions'. With his instinctive classicism Paul Valéry has stigmatized, without naming Picasso, the curious habit we have contracted of considering any artist a poor one who does not begin by shocking us and by being himself sufficiently abused and mocked. Of Picasso's last Paris exhibition in the summer of 1955 François Mauriac writes: 'Confronted with Picasso I have never been able to escape the contradictory evidence of genius and imposture. . . . There is always this impression of being present at a murder attempted by an artful sorcerer with an almost supernatural hatred for the human face and more, for the soul which the human face reflects.'

But René Huyghe had long since written: 'Happy are those simple souls who imagine that a practical joke can suffice to nourish the spiritual life of artists many of whom possess the most brilliant gifts of our time.'

Some cubist painters have denied that Picasso was pilot of the movement and, like Albert Gleize, have stressed the independent efforts of their own group to achieve the same pictorial transformation. But Picasso was in the van of the fight and it was he who was the target for the concentrated attacks which resumed with full ferocity, accusing him of imposture, whenever he changed his manner.

It was his sense of humour which enabled him to cope with the permanent doubts cast on the seriousness of his efforts. Cocteau reports a savoury example. One day in 1919, a young American girl, naïvely avid for instruction and already learning 'all sorts of things' in Paris, asked him to take her to Picasso's studio so that she could be initiated into cubism. Cocteau refused, knowing, he says, how much Picasso disliked random visitors and the sort of reception he usually gave them, being well aware that explanations would be useless and receiving them with a kind of venomous amiability, returning tit-for-tat the ruderies which 'our elegant ladies never fail to bestow on artists'. But shortly afterwards the fair American told Cocteau triumphantly that she had been taken to Picasso's by Zuloaga. Well? 'Well,' she said, 'Zuloaga is one of his very greatest friends and to a friend of course he could let his hair down. He admitted everything.' 'Admitted what?' Cocteau inquired. 'Admitted that his cubism is a joke. I had asked him if it was, and he said he didn't want to make fun any longer of a person as beautiful and intelligent as I was. . . .'

At the opposite pole to frivolity and scepticism were the interpretations offered by those, most of them Picasso's fervent admirers, who sought to provide a scientific basis for his work. According to them, an actuary employed by an insurance company, a man by the name of Princet who also lived at the Bateau-Lavoir, was the spiritual father of cubism and inspired Picasso in his search for a new conception of the universe.

But Picasso has always protested vehemently against any explanations founded on elements extraneous to his art. It is repugnant to him to see cubism reduced to a laboratory experiment, for, as he said in 1923: 'Mathematics, trigonometry, chemistry, psycho-analysis, music and what-have-you have been brought in conjunction with cubism as offering an easier interpretation. But all this is mere literature, not to say nonsense and it has had bad results because people have been blinded by theories.'

Contemporary witnesses agree in ascribing the initial misunderstanding to Guillaume Apollinaire who, according to Kahnweiler, had listened, not at Picasso's but in bars and elsewhere, to lesser cubist painters commenting more or less soundly on the rare pronouncements of their chief who himself seldom entered into a discussion and never wrote anything at this time. According to Zervos, Apollinaire also got some of his ideas from Juan Gris who was attracted to mathematics and had set himself the task of studying art scientifically with an aesthetic object in view. But in Picasso's opinion intellectual interpretations did not take instinct sufficiently into account, and his own memory of this period, beginning in 1910 when cubism as we know it first began to emerge, was one of continual effort: 'We worked with enthusiasm and that was the main thing, putting much more into our efforts than usual, for we were involved in them body and soul.'

This was one of the rare periods in Picasso's life—perhaps the only one—when he could say 'we' in speaking of a creative effort. His deliberate self-effacement suggests the degree of intensity with which he was pursuing the dissection of reality to arrive at what he called 'pure truth without pretension, tricks or malice'. The state of tension in which he and Braque produced their joint work made them feel cut off from the rest of the world like explorers of new continents and very conscious of what was happening to them and of their own integrity. Quite apart from their visual novelty, there is a rarefied atmosphere, a climate of austerity about the cubist pictures painted at this time. 'We had moved so far from all hitherto known and appreciated modes of expression,' said Picasso later, 'that we felt we were secure against any suspicion of ulterior motive.' According to Zervos, their communal effort was so intense that later they were barely able to identify their own contributions. But though they tried through self-discipline to sink their basic differences of temperament, these were still clearly apparent to initiates. 'While to the layman the results of their work were so similar as to be indistinguishable,' wrote Uhde, 'I could see clearly that their personalities were aiming at different ends. Braque's temperament was straightforward, balanced, bourgeois; Picasso's was sombre, extravagant, revolutionary.' One day, still far distant, these fundamental differences were to lead to a quarrel.

The history of cubism can best be traced in the great portraits which Picasso painted in this year of 1910, for the real purport of his experiments is revealed in his treatment of the human face. In the spring he painted the portrait of Wilhelm Uhde (Roland Penrose Collection, London). At first sight the whole canvas seems to be covered with nothing but a shower of prisms, but curiously enough the portrait which emerges from them is an extraordinarily good likeness, not only physically, for all those who knew Uhde, but in the revelation of character suggested by the long head, the close-set eyes and the line of the mouth, so faint yet so exact in its suggestion of preciosity. The distinction of the man is clearly conveyed—even his pale skin by the use of dull greys and yellows.

This portrait, which Picasso gave to Uhde, was in payment of a debt of gratitude which he owed to a fervent admirer who had been the first to speak of him abroad and had put him in touch with German purchasers like the great Berlin art dealer, Alfred Flechtheim. Another cubist portrait painted in the same year was that of Ambroise Vollard (Museum of Modern Art, Moscow). This too was a striking likeness, the facets of the prisms seeming to convey a direct insight into the agitation behind the high, bumpy forehead, the secrets beneath the sleepy eyelids and a sense of sullen watchfulness in the face with its massive cheeks, Mongolian nose and straight, broad mouth—the whole bathed in an artificial light of ochres and greys which gave the strange countenance its true relief.

Picasso spent the summer of 1910 with his friends the Pichots at Cadaquès in Spain, the holiday season and contact with his native soil seeming to have the usual effect on him of clarifying his intentions. The disintegration of form continued, the whole pictorial space, including the features, being split up methodically. There is a charcoal drawing dating from the previous spring anticipating the series of nudes which he painted at Cadaquès with superimposed rectangles and triangles cascading down the whole length of the long canvas, as in the picture belonging to Mrs. Meric Callery, like tiles on a roof. This drawing, in which the body of a nude woman is constructed in geometrical planes, was to be exhibited in April, 1911, together with eighty other Picasso drawings and engravings, by Alfred Stieglitz, the dynamic promoter of the new art in the United States, in his New York gallery. This first one-man exhibition of Picasso's provoked a scandal in America, indignation and mockery being concentrated particularly on this drawing which was dubbed 'The Fire-escape'.

A picture which still retains some resemblance to 'real' life is the *Jeune Fille à la mandoline* (Roland Penrose Collection, London). Feminine grace, the curve of a youthful breast can still be detected amidst the sharp prisms and geometrical forms.

But in the works painted at Cadaquès Picasso finally broke with facile pictorial representation. In the *Joueur de guitare* (André Lefèvre Collection, Paris) the shapes are split up and redistributed with such vigour that nothing remains of their familiar aspect and no intelligible whole can be reconstructed. Only one or two figurative attributes, a few revealing touches remain to supply a key to the puzzle.

In the autumn, on his return from Cadaquès, Picasso painted a portrait of Kahnweiler (Mrs. Charles B. Goodspeed Collection, Chicago). Compared with the portraits of Vollard and Uhde this represents a rapid advance on the road to total disintegration: the shimmering facets submerge and displace the features, dragging them down the whole length of the canvas. And yet this portrait, in which the only remnants of human features are the hair with its parting, a neat moustache and an eyelid looking like the slit of a half-open drawer, resulted from a laborious study of the model. Kahnweiler recalls that he gave about twenty sittings.

In fact, cubist painters claimed that they were conveying a new vision of reality—reality as it really was in the multiplicity of its aspects, not fixed and monolithic as it appeared to the human eye. Many years were to pass before literature discovered this simultaneous technique, though it was obviously easier to convey in words successive perceptions of the same object in space than it was to transfer them to a canvas. The conception underlying cubist portraits is very close to that other means of expression employed in modern literature: the interior monologue. The cubists convey the diversity of forms which coexist in the human being; the writer, the diversity of his mental life which consists of simultaneous emotions, visual impressions, memories and mental associations. The new means of pictorial expression which revealed the underlying cubist or prismatic structure of a curved object made it very difficult to distinguish its simultaneous aspects. Juan Gris, whose completely intellectual conception of cubism was often to supply a theoretical prop to the new art, called this simultaneous presentation of an object (from above, from below, in transverse section or from the inside) 'Analytical Cubism'—and the expression has stuck.

The difficulty of interpretation is increased by the way in which the fragments of the object seen are scattered over the whole canvas, as though an explosion had taken place in the middle of the picture and pieces were being flung towards its edges. The force of the explosion was determined by Picasso's urge to impart rhythm to the picture and to burst its bounds. He considered various means to achieve this and to convey the centrifugal force of his visions. 'Long before Calder,' said Kahnweiler, 'Picasso had thought of sculptures which some mechanism would set in movement, pictures which would shift when a button was pressed like targets in shooting galleries at fairs.' Being unable to impart real movement to his pictures, Picasso had to be content with interior movement, with rhythmic disintegration.

With the abandonment of the direct representation of nature, colour, too, was abandoned. In Picasso's case particularly violent colouring disappeared as soon as stress was laid on a new conception of form, as though he did not wish to distract the spectator's attention from the essence of what he was trying to communicate. His greatest works are almost always in monochrome. The pale and silvered tones with light green shadows which still prevailed in the *Jeune Fille à la mandoline* yielded increasingly to dull greys, pale yellows and opaque beige.

By refusing colour Picasso not only rejected a means of charming the spectator but also deprived him of facility of access to an increasingly hermetic art. But he denied that his painting had become unintelligible. 'I cannot understand English,' he said, 'but why should I blame anyone but myself if I can't understand what I am ignorant of?' In this connection Zervos reports a significant incident. 'One day when I was discussing with Picasso the reproach frequently levelled at him that he had suppressed reality in his painting, he picked up from my table several photographic reproductions of his works and drew in the margins stroke by stroke the objects which they represented. . . . All the elements of reality had been scrupulously preserved when they had been transposed to the pictures.'

But analysis in cubist painting became increasingly rigorous, and like the manifestations of some new religion the works of this period possess a fanatical austerity. Purged of colour, of all formal attraction, of any suggestion that they are based on reality, these canvases preserve nothing but an interior rhythm marked by vertical lines or later by triangles. They still possess titles, but these bear no relation to the purified, geometrical, almost anonymous shapes which they present. The last trace of sensuality is banished, for instance, from canvases called *Femme couchée sur un divan* (private collection) which Picasso painted during the winter following his return from Cadaquès and where the curve of a thigh or a breast barely emerges between interlocking rectangles. Yet Picasso denied any desire to abandon the representation of humanity, just as later he condemned non-figurative art. Indeed, he claimed to have emotional ties even with his most abstract-seeming pictures. 'To my misfortune and perhaps to my joy,' he said one day, 'I value things according to the degree of love I have for them.' This affective link between the object represented and the painter seemed to him so important that he said very characteristically to Kahnweiler one day: 'I think it is monstrous that a woman should paint pipes when she does not smoke a pipe.'

To facilitate understanding of pictures increasingly remote from the objects they represented, the cubists turned to still-life, choosing the simplest and most familiar objects for their experiments and always the same ones so that the spectator eventually became used to them. Thanks to them, the most commonplace things in daily life made their triumphal entry into art: a box of matches, a packet of tobacco, a glass, a plate, an apple or a book.

Jean Metzinger, another cubist theoretician, wrote later: 'Before us no painter had ever bothered to handle the objects he painted.'

Though cubism continued to provoke scandal, it also, like all militant religions, attracted fanatical converts. Braque and Picasso were no longer isolated in their anonymous efforts, but were joined by a young compatriot of Picasso's who was six years younger than himself. Juan Victoriano Gonzalez had studied at the school of Arts and Crafts in Madrid and had left the country at the age of nineteen, evading military service. Posted as an absentee because he was unable to afford the substitution tax, he was embarrassed throughout his life by the lack of a passport. He landed in Paris with 16 francs in his pocket, but also with Picasso's address. He was one of the first to call him 'cher maître' which, according to Gertrude Stein, annoyed Picasso greatly—in revenge he began to call Braque 'cher maître'. The sworn enemy of all solemnity, even at the pinnacle of fame Picasso retains his dislike of adulation and even today he will cut short a too respectful 'cher maître' with a brief gesture and an amused smile: 'I am not such a master as all that. . . .'

But though the exaggerated deference of his compatriot, who now took the name of Juan Gris, exasperated him, Picasso remembered his own early struggles too vividly to leave the young man in distress. He helped Juan Gris who, according to Fernande, even had his own corner of a napkin at meal-times—she explains that they were so short of table-linen at that time that the four of them, including Apollinaire, had to share one napkin, each of them using a corner. This arrangement inspired Apollinaire to write a story called 'La Serviette des poètes'.

Juan Gris was handsome in a masculine way with a very dark skin and large sombre eyes. He was a very skilful draughtsman, had worked in Madrid for comic papers and contributed in Paris to the *Assiette au beurre*, the *Cri de Paris* and the *Charivari*. He now tried his hand at painting, producing in 1910 a number of large realistic watercolours. Lucid in his aims and very conscious of the importance of what he was doing, one day he said to Max Jacob: 'I never stroke a dog except with my left hand, so that if it bit me I should still have my right hand for painting.' After his death, when looking at one of his pictures, Picasso said to Kahnweiler: 'There is a painter who knew what he wanted.' But during his lifetime, his very lucidity, allied to shyness, sensitivity and inordinate ambition aggravated Picasso. Gertrude Stein took an interest in the young Spaniard as soon as he attempted cubism, professing to detect in him exactitude combined with mysticism. Later, Picasso asked her: 'Tell me, why do you defend his work so much? You know very well that you don't like it.' But Gertrude Stein was silent because she had a real affection for Juan Gris as a man. He grew up as an artist under the shadow of Picasso and the first picture he exhibited at the Salon des Indépendants was entitled *Homage to Picasso*. 'This portrait is supremely idiotic,' wrote Vauxcelles at the time. From 1912, Kahnweiler was interested in Juan Gris and bought his entire production.

Adherents to cubism became increasingly numerous, for, as Waldemar George pointed out, it favoured the growth and development of the most varied personalities. Yet however divergent these personalities might be they had this in common: they were consummate masters of their craft. An art preaching the disintegration of forms might have attracted artists uncertain of their own gifts, those least sure of being able to establish themselves in a normal sphere, but the opposite was the case. It was the 'mystical exactitude' of Juan Gris which led him to cubism and it was the exceptional draughtsmanship of Louis Marcoussis which made him follow the same path. Apollinaire noticed this characteristic when in 1913 he wrote, in *Les Peintres cubistes*, that cubism was a revolution which 'restores order and craftsmanship to a place of honour'.

Two years younger than Picasso, Louis Marcous had been born in Warsaw and come to Paris in 1903. He was one of Max Jacob's oldest friends and it was Apollinaire, who was always very ingenious in such matters, who had given him the name of Marcoussis, which was that of a village near Paris. His mastery of the portrait either drawn or engraved was second only to Picasso's. At the time when cubism arrived he had been earning a good living by doing pleasantly frivolous drawings for *La Vie Parisienne*, and from a material point of view he had everything to lose and nothing to gain by joining the cubists. André Salmon records how his adherence to the movement convinced him that the cubists had something serious to say.

Collaboration with Marcoussis was also to entail consequences for Picasso in the personal sphere. Marcoussis was living with a charming young lady by the name of Marcelle Humbert. Sure of her own beauty or too indolent to listen to the promptings of instinct, it was Fernande who first made friends with her. Physically, Marcelle was the exact opposite of Fernande; she was also charmingly unpredictable and possessed great liveliness of mind. When the four of them dined at her house Gertrude Stein found her '*petite* and perfect' and well understood

Fernande's protective affection. At this time Picasso discovered that he could not work so well in his studio in the Boulevard de Clichy as at the Bateau-Lavoir and, as he could not rent his old apartment, he took another in the same place. He started to go out at night again, often visiting the Medrano Circus or the Café de l'Ermitage.

Accompanied by Braque, Picasso spent the summer of 1911 at Céret in the eastern Pyrenees. Max Jacob who came to visit him there two years later gave Apollinaire this description of the place: 'Céret—a pretty little town at the foot of the Karpathian or Carpathian Mountains. The population is roughly between 500 and 10,000 inhabitants. This small number of inhabitants is no doubt due to the large number of pederasts and ether-maniacs who spend their lives in the local cafés. Situated amongst orchards rich in fruit-trees and in bricks, the town regretfully sees itself by-passed by a mountain stream which seems to harbour an aversion for it. . . . It seems that the mountains are fragrant with thyme, rosemary, lavender and dew, but I never go near them.' As always on his holidays, Picasso worked hard, exploring new possibilities as though the change of scene had opened up new horizons.

The interior rhythm which he had given to his canvases led him to use musicians as a theme with increasing frequency. At Céret he painted *L'Accordéoniste* (Solomon R. Guggenheim Museum, New York). His 'hermetic' period was then at its height. The picture which bore the word 'Céret' on the back of the canvas was for a long time considered by its former owners to be a local landscape. But close examination of the superimposed and dovetailing prisms reveals a bowed head, the curved arms of a chair and a suggestion of bellows and keys.

The *Joueur de clarinette* (Douglas Cooper Collection, Château de Castille, Gard), painted during the winter of 1911–12, is governed by the same triangular composition, the lightening of the prisms towards the top, through a vigorous upward movement of diagonals. With Picasso this seemed to be a purely instinctive form of composition, but like many styles which he adopted and then abandoned, this one was to give birth to a movement which assumed the title, 'La Section d'Or'. Pyramidal composition was in fact an achievement of the Renaissance at its height and it runs through the work of Leonardo da Vinci, particularly from the start of his Milanese period.

Like every movement which includes divergent personalities, the growing numbers of cubists were searching for a programme and on Sunday afternoons they used to foregather in Jacques Villon's studio in

Puteaux. Villon's real name was Gaston Duchamp, but he had chosen his favourite poet's name as a pseudonym. Like Juan Gris and Marcoussis he had joined cubism in that year of 1911, leaving a secure job which gave him his independence as illustrator for humorous or satirical journals. He was followed by his whole family, his sister Suzanne Duchamp, and his two brothers, the sculptor Raymond Duchamp-Villon and the painter Marcel Duchamp. Jacques Villon realized what disciplinary and organizational power were latent in cubism and he set about expressing these elements through an ideology and a programme. Painters like Albert Gleizes and his friends Metzinger, Delaunay, Léger, La Fresnaye and others wished to become independent of Picasso, but they also desired to pursue common aims. From their discussions the group united under the name 'La Section d'Or' was formed. Its exhibition in the autumn of 1912 was to be an important event in the history of art.

Gertrude Stein shared their difficulties with her artist friends and she has also recorded their triumph. 'Life among the cubists became very gay. . . . Everyone was gay. There were more and more cubists, and as a joke people talked of someone as the youngest of the cubists. From now on, cubism was sufficiently accepted for it to be possible to talk of the youngest of the cubists; after all, cubism existed and everyone was gay.'

Several new elements appeared in Picasso's pictures which he painted at Céret. He and Braque chose a shape for their canvases which had long since fallen into disuse as being associated with purely decorative art: the oval. It seems curious that an art as austere as cubism with its geometrical forms should revive the oval and abandon the strictly rectangular frame. Perhaps the contrast between the content and the surrounding curve was intentional. Braque said later that it was thanks to the oval that he had 'rediscovered the sense of the horizontal and the vertical'. It was probably the centrifugal rhythm, which started from the centre of the picture and in a rectangular frame had to come to a dead stop at the corners, which led the cubists to economize the painted surface in this way.

The catalogue of the Picasso exhibition at the Arts Décoratifs in the summer of 1955 mentions about thirty-five oval pictures painted mostly between 1911 and 1913. One of the earliest was *L'Homme à la pipe*, painted at Céret (private collection). The focus of the picture, the sort of nail from which the cascading shapes are suspended, consists of

11 Picasso and Paulo

12 Picasso's house at Céret

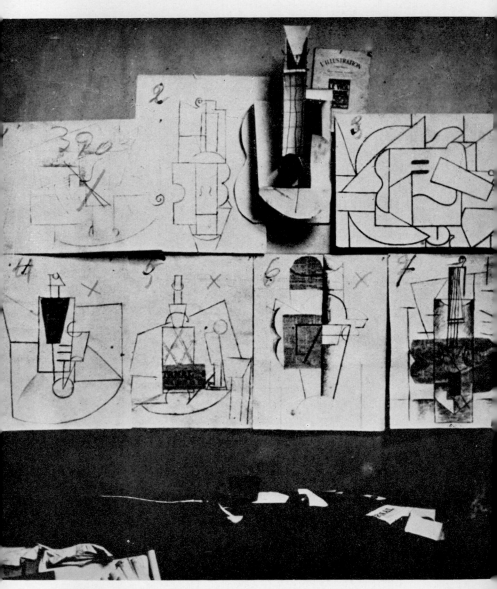

13   Picasso's studio in Boulevard Raspail

the pipe, a corner of a mouth and the half of a large bristling moustache. In the same canvas some printed letters are faintly traced. These had already appeared in the still-lifes and, like the moustache, were to be used again with increasing frequency. Kahnweiler uses a German word difficult to translate to describe this insertion of a real-life detail as the nodal point of a picture. He calls it *Hineinsehung*, which implies that, thanks to this familiar detail, the spectator can 'see into' and understand the picture. Stressing the value of the prosaic, Picasso said one day: 'Pictures are made like princes make their children: with shepherd-girls.' A wad of tobacco, an old chair, a tumble-down shack in the Midi were the raw materials for art, not the Parthenon or Louis XV furniture.

Among the pictures which he painted at Céret was one of a fan (former collection of Paul Guillaume), another of a fan with glasses and a violin (former collection of Alphonse Kann) and *La Clarinette* (Vincenc Kramar Collection, Prague) with a glass, a pipe, some playing cards and a newspaper also featuring in the picture. When Picasso left Céret he had reached the end of a phase and was ready for a fresh departure.

But the autumn of 1911 had a distressing adventure in store for him which nearly took a tragic turn. It sprang from Apollinaire's taste for picturesque people who lived in the margin of society. At the time when his mother had faced him with the necessity of earning his own living and he was running *The Stockholder's Guide* with a total lack of success, he came across a man who greatly attracted him, one of those who do not attempt to storm the citadel of society, but leave it voluntarily. Géry Piéret, the son of a Belgian magistrate, had chosen a life of adventure and possessed a rich fund of stories which delighted Apollinaire and which he was able to use as the raw material for his literary work. In 1907, to give proof of his daring or because he wanted some money, Géry Piéret stole some Hispano-Roman statuettes from the Louvre and sold two of them to Picasso, or, according to Fernande, gave them to him without saying where they came from, but advising him, all the same, not to display them too prominently. Later, Apollinaire told a girl with whom he was in love and whom he wanted, therefore, to impress, that he had warned Picasso that the statues came from the Louvre and had urged him to return them, suggesting that he stage a newspaper stunt and take them to the *Matin*, claiming that they had been stolen to prove how badly the nation's treasures were guarded.

But Picasso insisted on keeping the statues—then he confessed that he had 'broken them up in order to discover the secrets of the art, both ancient and barbarian, from which they had come'. According to André Billy, Apollinaire himself had one of the stolen statues in his possession and instead of following his own advice to Picasso was exhibiting it on his mantelpiece.

Géry Piéret, meanwhile, went to America. In 1910 he returned having made a fortune, but quickly lost all his money at the races and in May, 1911, he stole another statue from the Louvre. Eternally quixotic, Apollinaire put Piéret up at his home and employed him as secretary, urging him, it seems, to return the statue at once. Then, on 21st August, the *Gioconda* was stolen from the Louvre, and this provoked a world-wide sensation. This time, as it happened, Piéret was not the culprit. But a thirst for notoriety coupled probably with a vague hope that some money could be made now persuaded Piéret to take the last statue he had stolen to another newspaper, the *Paris-Journal*. Nothing loth, the editor published an article on the inadequacy of the security arrangements at the great national museum and displayed the statue for a while before returning it. Piéret then prudently took to his heels.

Meanwhile, police inquiries had started for the missing *Gioconda*. Apollinaire believed that Piéret had stolen it, but he knew that he, too, was under suspicion. According to Fernande, Picasso, now returned from Céret, met Apollinaire by chance one evening to find him terrified by the thought that he was a wanted man. According to Apollinaire, on the other hand, he went at once to Picasso to warn him of the awkward consequences that might ensue from his destruction of the two statues that had been in his possession. Thereupon, the horrified Picasso confessed that he had lied—the statues were still intact.

The story is continued by Fernande. It was early evening, she says, and the two men were like terrified children. They even thought of escaping abroad. Then they decided to put the statuettes in a suitcase and throw them into the Seine—at midnight when there would be less people about. Meanwhile, they had to wait for several hours. The police had already called at Apollinaire's home. At this very moment they were probably on his tracks. At any moment they might burst into the house. It was necessary to keep calm—calmness above all. . . . So the two men started to play cards: the greenest detective could have seen that they knew nothing about the game. But they played with intense earnestness until at midnight they set off on foot with the suit-case. Two hours later they returned in a state of collapse, stil lcarrying the suitcase with the statuettes still inside: they had wandered up an down the banks of the Seine, but had thought they were being followed and had not dared get rid of their burden.

Apollinaire spent the night at Picasso's. Next day, he—or according to Apollinaire, Picasso—went to the offices of the *Paris-Journal* with the idea of returning the statues anonymously to the Louvre through the newspaper which could make good publicity out of it. The newspaper accepted them, but the police were not amused and the following day, after they had searched his house, Apollinaire was arrested, sharply interrogated by an examining magistrate and thrown into prison at the Santé. Abruptly the underworld lost its picturesque attractions for him as he found himself caught up in an implacable judiciary machine. He had never dreamt that it could be so harsh. Wishing to cover his ex-secretary and his friends he had denied everything at the first interroga-tion, but two days of the prison régime were enough to make him tell all he knew. Picasso was now involved and brought at dawn before the magistrate. Deluged with questions and confronted with the pale, haggard, unshaven, dishevelled Apollinaire—so different from his usual debonair self—he was considerably shaken, but managed not to incriminate himself and was let off with a warning to be available for further questioning. All this time, Géry Piéret, full of his new-found importance, was writing letters to the newspapers and also a letter to the magistrate attempting to exonerate his former employer.

In the midst of this resounding scandal Apollinaire's faithful friends organized a petition for his release, and thanks to their initiative his imprisonment did not last long—his 'feeble reason' was already begin-ning to totter. But he was not finally cleared until January, 1912. His experiences, however, and Picasso's stalwart denial of any association with him did not disturb their friendship. According to Philippe Soupault, Apollinaire's affection for Picasso was so strong that nothing could shake it. A feeling of solidarity in misfortune also united them, for they felt they were under observation for some time to come.

But the sordid episode left a certain stigma on both of them and on Apollinaire it conferred the reputation of a somewhat dubious adven-turer of which he was painfully conscious. The desire to rehabilitate himself perhaps played a part in his later decision to enlist voluntarily in the army.

121

This affair was the last major incident in Fernande's life with Picasso. One day, Gertrude Stein came to see him at his studio in the Rue Ravignan. He was out and as a joke she left her visiting card at the door. When she returned he was painting a picture on which he had written 'Ma jolie' and stuck the visiting card at the bottom. 'Fernande is certainly not "ma jolie",' she said to Alice Toklas. 'I wonder who it can be.'

No one at that time knew the identity of 'ma jolie', but she was, in fact, Marcelle Humbert, or 'Éva', as Picasso liked to call her, signifying that for him, in spite of his varied love life, she was the first woman in creation. At the time when she had been living with Marcoussis, the four of them had often gone with their friends to the cabaret where a popular song was fashionable which ran: O *Manon ma jolie, mon coeur te dit bonjour.*

Every woman who enters Picasso's life is like the first he has ever loved. He acquires a new sensibility and becomes as sentimental as a schoolboy. The refrain became associated with the delightful little creature. Like all passionate lovers, he felt the need to cry his happiness from the roof-tops. A clandestine adventure could not satisfy him. Each broke their attachments and they set off together one day— suddenly, to avoid explanations.

Fernande showed great dignity in this situation which in fact brought her emotional life to an end. In her memoirs she merely states: 'Marcoussis was above all a wit and on the basis of the amorous disappointment which Picasso caused him he produced a drawing for *La Vie Parisienne*: I can still see him hopping joyfully to see Picasso loaded with chains.'

But Picasso was relishing his happiness as though he had never tasted it before. The two lovers set off for Avignon, but meeting friends there, did not stay long. After trying Céret where they also found too many friends and too many memories of the past, they finally settled in Sorgues-sur-l'Ouvèze (Vaucluse) and spent the summer there. Kahnweiler, in their absence, was commissioned to make a clean sweep of their former existence, transferring the contents of the studio in the Rue Ravignan to the Boulevard Raspail. Thither Picasso returned in the autumn. 'The gaiety of France had once more seduced him,' wrote Gertrude Stein. 'He was working enormously.'

This new phase in his life was also, not by coincidence but by the relation of cause to effect, a dividing line in his art. With Picasso a sentimental change is always accompanied by a creative change. The theoreticians of cubism have called the second period which then began 'synthetic cubism' to distinguish it from 'analytical cubism'. Picasso has always dissociated himself from theories and, just as he left it to others to affix names to his pictures, so he allowed them to attach the label to his art.

Apollinaire (who by instinct, according to Billy, was closer to Bouguereau) called the result of Picasso's ruminations at this time 'conceptual painting', as though the passage from analytical to synthetic cubism was a deliberate, premeditated and calculated act. In fact, a limit had been reached in the simplification of forms which Picasso was unable to exceed.

In *The Cubist Painters*, which Apollinaire published in 1913 and his friends considered to be the gospel of the new painting, he spoke of the 'assassination' of anatomy which Picasso had performed with the skill of a great surgeon. In the *Femme à la guitare* (Museum of Modern Art, New York), which probably dates from the end of 1911, this dissection is performed with absolute rigour for the benefit of a triangular construction, a mechanism of interlocking prisms with ever-larger facets and particularly sharp edges.

Dutch constructivists like Piet Mondrian were to draw their inspiration from works of this kind, and it was from them that the movement started which was in full flood in 1920 and made a profound impression on all the arts: architecture, interior decoration, posters and even printing. Daily life took on a new appearance. 'But when one looks back on all that the thousands of artists and designers who were influenced by cubism have achieved,' wrote Alfred Barr, 'it is difficult to find a work superior in quality to the series of canvases and drawings produced by Picasso and Braque in the years 1910, 1911 and 1912.' Picasso himself was very conscious of the general application of his efforts to all spheres and he had in fact a structural intention when he painted such rigorously organized pictures. Towards 1911 he maintained that a picture should show objects in such a way that an engineer could have them constructed in three dimensions. Later, Juan Gris was to object vehemently that such an aim exceeded the bounds of pictorial art: 'If Picasso did utter that erroneous claptrap at some time or other, so much the worse for him.'

But it was this very excess, or at least its possibility, its application to all the arts, its generally valid aspect which conferred its growing influence on cubism. A quite extraordinary phenomenon occurred. The cubism of that time was particularly difficult to interpret and for many years to come it was to repel the most unprejudiced minds. And yet its general application could not have taken place if there had not been a conviction that its processes somehow produced a more convincing effect than mere copies of reality. The new plastic vision became popular in the same way as great intellectual movements, literary currents or philosophical systems. The main works from which they derive may remain unknown to the general public and the esoteric language of their theories make these equally inaccessible, but through newspaper articles and discussions at home or in public the main ideas gradually filter through and finally, with the aid of snobbery or fashion, become accepted even by those individuals who are the farthest removed from the fountain-head. In the same occult fashion one or two names reach the surface and become well known even to those who have never read a book or seen a picture by one of the authors or painters who are being most widely discussed. In the most obscure fashion this process lifted Picasso to fame or notoriety as though there were something in him which provoked praise or condemnation. One day, at the sight of some extravagant productions which professed to be inspired by him, he said angrily: 'Michelangelo was not responsible for Renaissance sideboards.'

The new development which then took place in the art of Picasso and Braque was, according to Kahnweiler, 'the frontier-stone in the history of art', and indeed it was impossible for disintegrated and reconstructed forms to convey a stronger impression of reality. Picasso and Braque had reached the end of a road and to avoid repeating themselves they felt what cubist theoreticians have called a desire to convey an idea of integral instead of disintegrated forms.

In this movement towards synthesis, printed letters which at first had been used as a key merely to the understanding of a work became an integral part of it, as in the oval picture framed in rope which Zervos dates from the winter of 1911–12: *Notre avenir est dans l'air*. The letters of these words, mutilated but easy to complete, are painted in relief beside a clearly identifiable pipe. An abbreviation of the same words occurs in the *Coquilles Saint-Jacques* (J. Muller Collection, Soleure, Switzerland) of 1912. One day, in front of one of these pictures representing shells Picasso said to Jean Cassou: 'I suddenly smelt all the odours of Barcelona harbour'—a statement revealing his adherence to reality even when he grossly deforms it.

Soon, printed letters were joined by other details of 'reality' as constituent elements of the picture. Braque (whom Picasso called Wilbur Wright) was the first to introduce a nail painted in *trompe-l'oeil* into one of his still-lifes and it was Braque also who, remembering his past as an interior decorator, conveyed illusions of marble, wood and wall-paper. He even used the special combs employed by decorators to imitate wood. Having been broken in, sometimes reluctantly, to the austerity of cubist geometry, the spectator was amazed to see realistic plaster mouldings suddenly appear before his eyes, or planks with the grain and the knots in the wood perfectly imitated as an integral part of what was still a prismatic vision. To this disturbance of the painted surface Picasso added a procedure of his own: the blistering of large planes with dots in relief, until the canvas seemed to be spattered with coarse confetti. By this same process—the massing of dark spots through which the light could filter—Seurat had built up the compact blocks of human figures and the solid masses in his landscapes. Picasso used it for the first time in a still-life in 1911, varying in the following years this pointillist technique which added the contrast of smoothness and roughness to planes diversified by light and shadow. Braque and Juan Gris also used pointillism and later, in agreement with them, Picasso tried to obtain the same effect by mixing sand or cinders with oil paint, thereby conveying an impression of shimmering light to the canvas.

But even these variations were not enough. The partial imitation of reality did not satisfy them and they began to introduce reality itself into their works, in fragments. The first picture of this kind was painted by Picasso in the winter of 1911–12: the real detail was a piece of oilcloth imitating the caning of a chair. In this *Nature morte à la chaise cannée* (property of Picasso), an oval picture framed with rope, the first three letters of the word 'Journal' appear, a glass, a pipe and an analytical version of a lemon—these contrasting strangely with the chair-caning which looks so real one could almost touch it. From now on, the most varied materials were included with increasing frequency in pictures painted by Picasso and Braque. In *La Lettre* (former collection of Paul Éluard), which dates from the same winter, an envelope addressed to Picasso is stuck on the canvas, just as Gertrude Stein's visiting card had been stuck on *Ma Jolie*. 'The ascetic, quasi-religious gravity of the cubist discipline,' wrote Frank Elgar, 'was replaced by irony, humour and the free-and-easy juxtaposition of materials which chance brought to hand.'

From the spring of 1912 date a large number of experiments in which the label from an aperitif bottle, strips of news-print, fragments of crinkled paper are stuck or pinned on to a sheet of drawing paper, as in the still-life: *Bouteille de vieux marc, verre, journal* (private collection, Paris) which was done at Céret. These stick-ons are accompanied by very severe drawings, like engineers' or architects' blueprints.

The same rigorous construction is found in the still-life which dates from the following spring: *Bouteille de Pernod et verre* (Museum of Modern Art, Moscow). Some of these novel experiments show a return to colour with mauve backgrounds and the warm colour of wood contrasting with the ethereal grey prisms of the glass and the bottle. During his short stay at Céret Picasso painted several still-lifes, portraits—like that of the Spaniard with the enormous moustache (P. Gaut Collection, Paris)—and landscapes, mostly drawings with fragments of papier collé. When Braque rejoined him at Sorgues they both perfected their communal technique of including different materials in painting. The vulgarity of these strips of newspaper, where you could still read news or advertisements, labels from bottles, tobacco packets or match-boxes provoked a scandal. The dignity of painting seemed to be attacked under the guise of a proud challenge: 'Look what works of art we are capable of producing with the contents of our wastepaper baskets!'

But these motives would not have sufficed to make Picasso or Braque pursue their papier collé experiments for several years. Their idea was evidently to enlarge the possibilities of art by including in their new plastic vision materials which were foreign to painting, but in such a way that they acquired a pictorial value. This was certainly the case with Picasso when he used broad strips of newspaper. He was also searching for a palpable contrast, trying, as it were, to get the feel of the materials in the same way as baroque painters gave an illusionist effect to angels painted on a ceiling by giving them plaster legs. The sense of shock was also intentional in order to heighten receptivity and the use of commonplace in preference to rare materials seemed to serve the same purpose—namely, to make the picture more intelligible—as the everyday objects which were actually painted on the canvas. Finally, the whole procedure was somewhat of a game, like the verbal malice of Apollinaire in his rhymes.

The papiers collés were in themselves too fragile to last, but the same technique was taken up, somewhat surprisingly, by sculptors like

Laurens and Arp and by the Italian futurists, while they served as a field of experiment for the surrealists at a time when their creators had long since abandoned them. What seemed to their contemporaries a joke, an infertile seed destined to perish, was to grow and bear fruit in the most distant places. Papier collé was also to give Matisse a kind of posthumous survival when, tortured with rheumatism and no longer able to paint, he found in its use a strikingly effective means of expression so that he felt that 'scissors can acquire more sensitivity than the pencil'.

Drawing the balance-sheet of these experiments, Frank Elgar concluded: 'What was at first no more than a minor innovation became an undeniable art, an autonomous art, an art in itself.' Very felicitously Tristan Tzara called Picasso's papiers collés 'proverbs in painting'. He stressed that they could be compared to the use in poetry of clichés and ready-made phrases, and Max Jacob was in fact taking a malicious pleasure at that time in using snatches of overheard conversation in his verses while Apollinaire and Blaise Cendrars were introducing clichés, proper names and place names into the flow of their poetry. Though at that time the evolution in poetry and painting were only parallel, later the papiers collés were to exert an influence on various poetic trends and be reflected in the work of Tzara, Breton, Aragon and Éluard. But in its contemporary manifestations, synthetic cubism, that 'conceptual' art as Apollinaire called it, seemed so cerebral that it was believed to have derived from the intellectuals of the time. Picasso expressed their relationship in their true proportions when he said: 'The poets followed our efforts closely, but they never dictated them.'

During his stay in Sorgues, Picasso continued to paint as well as pursue the new papier collé experiments. He painted his nostalgia for Spain in L'Aficionado (Museum of Art, Basle) into which he introduced the title of a bull-fighting magazine. He painted a number of still-lifes such as the Violon et Clarinette (Museum of Modern Art, Moscow) where the illusion of wood is achieved with a comb, the Oiseaux morts (Douglas Cooper Collection, Château de Castille, Gard) with clearly identifiable feathers and several guitars accompanied by glasses and bottles forming an iconography of café life.

But most of his paintings were inspired by his new love: nine are known with the inscription 'Ma jolie'. In June, 1912, he spoke of Éva in a letter to Kahnweiler, adding: 'And I love her very much and I shall put her into my pictures.' Two of his canvases in fact bear these words:

'J'aime Éva'. The *Violon posé sur la table* which he painted at Sorgues (private collection, Paris), with its realistic marble in the background, mouldings on the walls and realistic wooden table, wainscoting and door, contains a sheet of music with 'Jolie Éva' written on it as a title. At the bottom of the *Femme nue* (Columbus Gallery of Fine Arts) appear the faint letters 'Pablo-Éva'.

At Sorgues Picasso had rented a villa, 'Les Clochettes'. Temporarily out of canvases, he painted a still-life on the wall of one of the rooms: *Bouteille de Pernod, verre et feuille de musique*, and again on the sheet of music were the words 'Ma jolie'. But this time the picture was not abandoned to the demolition contractors like the one in Sabartés's studio. Picasso was no longer the unknown artist and when he left Sorgues Kahnweiler had the work removed from the wall by a qualified mason and sent to Paris in a special packing where it was remounted on a wooden panel (Gandarilles Collection, Paris).

But communicative as Picasso was and anxious to cry his love to the world, it is a curious fact that no portrait is known to exist by him of the girl he loved, and when efforts were made to include Éva in the gallery of women who have influenced his art, only a small snapshot of her could be found. The discipline which Picasso imposed on himself was so rigorous that he did not want to break the austerity of his cubist vision with a realistic study of the beautiful Éva.

Nevertheless, glimpses of objective reality recurred increasingly in the geometrical arrangement of his pictures. In the autmn of 1912, he and Braque spent a short time in Le Havre. He came back with an oval picture with the words 'Souvenir du Havre' (J. La Roche Collection, Paris) written on the bow of a ribbon, such as appears on Christmas cards and chocolate boxes. The organization of the picture is no longer triangular; it is constructed in vertical bands, the whole surface is filled with prisms on which printed letters, fragments of propellers, of ropes and of a life-belt are superimposed.

During the course of this winter Picasso perfected all that he had learnt in the previous months. It was a violin which appeared most frequently in his pictures, set in an oval frame, like the *Souvenir du Havre*, or in vertical bands painted in pale grey or beige with occasional blues and pinks, or it was accompanied by a bottle of Bass, a pipe or a glass. Picasso used all the techniques; several of these pictures are painted in pastel, probably for the sake of the sustained tone, while others are painted in oil on paper, like the *Bec à gaz et guitare* with its plaques of realistic marble and prominent mouldings (Dr. Vincenc Kramar Collection, Prague).

But the most numerous works of this winter were the papiers collés: the *Bouteille de Suze* (Philadelphia Museum) with strips of paper arranged in festoons, the *Violon et Compotier* (same museum) made of papers arranged over a background of a newspaper and completed by a painting in pastel and the *Bouteille, verre, violon* (Tristan Tzara Collection, Paris), a very loose composition in which the bottle is cut out of a piece of newspaper and stuck on the paper.

One of the papiers collés where the search for new pictorial elements is accompanied by a humorous touch is the cartoon *Au Bon Marché* (M. G. Bollag Collection, Zürich) which owes its title to the large label with old-fashioned characters stuck slantwise in the middle: 'Au Bon Marché. Lingerie. Broderie'. Beside many still-lifes, large numbers of the papiers collés are variants on the subject of men's and women's heads (several in the collections of Tristan Tzara, Paris, and of Roland Penrose, London). The drawing in these is schematic and deliberately flat, and the strips of news-print or coloured papers disturb rather than support it. 'Cubic forms,' wrote Gertrude Stein, 'were replaced by surfaces and lines. The lines were more important than anything else, they lived by and in themselves, and this tendency became more and more pronounced.'

The severity which Picasso was seeking led him to make experiments in semi-sculpture, or rather in papiers collés in relief. These pictures were made of extremely fragile materials and the only one which has survived is *L'Homme au livre* which he gave to Gertrude Stein and was immediately put under glass in a box. But Picasso asserts that papier collé lasts as long as paint and in any case all that matters is the legend created by a picture and not whether the picture itself survives. 'He was indifferent to what *did* happen to his pictures,' wrote Gertrude Stein, 'although what *might* happen to them affected him profoundly.'

With the move to Montparnasse a new phase began for Picasso. He was now materially secure and even well-off. He already had one contract with Kahnweiler and at the end of December, 1912, he drew up another with his own hand making him his exclusive agent. One of the clauses reveals Picasso's creative rhythm and the fact that he was fully conscious of it: 'You will refer to me to decide if a picture is finished.' This contract shows the degree of his fame and also of the movement of which he was the promoter.

The prospectus announcing Apollinaire's book appeared at the beginning of 1913 and stated that 'this movement of the cubist painters interests the whole of Europe'. It was planned to publish the book under the title *Aesthetic Meditations* with 'The Cubist Painters' as a sub-title, but it was no doubt the interest which had been aroused in a movement that was still violently attacked and sharply defended that decided the publisher to reverse the titles. Later in the year, however, when Apollinaire had become editor of *Soirées de Paris* and published five still-lifes by Picasso in the issue for 15th November, all but one of the forty subscribers showed their disapproval by withdrawing their support.

CHAPTER IX 1913–1918

First World War

DON José Ruiz Blasco died in Barcelona in May, 1913, at the age of seventy-two. Picasso had seen little of him in recent years, but he was strangely affected by the death of this self-effacing man. His friends had often heard him repeat cetain maxims of his father's as though he used them as a guide in his incredible creative adventure. He seemed to believe in that wisdom of the heart which some fatalists possess and like all those who take great risks he probably had need of it. At that time, Apollinaire was preaching the abandonment of all sentimental bonds: 'Above all, artists are men who want to become inhuman.' On principle Picasso probably agreed to this maxim, but apart from family feeling which is very strong with all Spaniards, he possessed a power of affection which he lavished on his friends. He had taken Max Jacob with him to Céret and the latter wrote to Apollinaire: 'Éva is a charming woman. Pablo is spoiling me.'

But if Picasso spoilt him, Max Jacob was able in return to distract his thoughts and relieve the depression which had descended on him when his father died. Max Jacob had already seen a vision of Christ on the wall of his cheap room in the Rue Ravignan. He had then immediately gone to a priest in the hope of being accepted into the Christian Faith, but the latter had been so badly impressed by the excitable little man who told him he had seen the Lord in a robe of yellow silk with blue facings that he had refused to baptize him. But in spite of this reverse and the piety which now descended on him, despite a recurrence of the vision:

> La première fois
> Tu vins dans ma maison
> Et la seconde fois
> Au cinématographe. . . .

Max Jacob preserved his good humour and his customary banter. Picasso had rented a large flat in Céret; according to Max Jacob he always preferred flats to studios, which were either too hot or too cold. The one in Céret had tall windows looking on to a park. To Max, the city-dweller, the countryside seemed very noisy: 'Frogs, toads and nightingales prevent us from sleeping.'

In Céret they met the friend of their youth, Manolo, and his American patron Frank Haviland, one of the porcelain manufacturers of Limoges. Haviland owned a small former monastery in Céret and Manolo, with whom Kahnweiler had made a contract assuring him a regular income, had settled in the neighbourhood. The one-time deserter from military service was delighted to be on the frontier of his own country and later, under a general amnesty following the fall of Alfonso XIII, he returned to Spain, settled in Barcelona and became quite a personage in the land of his birth.

In Céret Picasso was joined later by Braque and Juan Gris and immediately he took them over the frontier to a bull-fight. In a letter to Apollinaire, Max Jacob described their journey by bus across the Pyrenees in 'the charming company of cooks, engineers and courteous draper's assistants'. He also described his first impressions of the country: 'Spain is a land of squares and angles. The houses have no roofs and the aloes are bitter like the people.' It was a rainy summer, Éva fell ill, but in spite of everything Picasso resumed work with a frenzy which never ceased to amaze his friends.

At that time certain characteristics of his pictures became more marked. To vary his technique and, according to Kahnweiler, to 'avoid all virtuosity of execution' he, like Braque and Juan Gris, made increasing use of the 'solidification' of colour. In the *Verre et Bouteille de Bass* (S. R. Guggenheim Foundation, New York) papiers collés were used in combination with oil paint mixed with sawdust and the same search for tactile differences was apparent in the papier collé, *Étudiant avec la pipe* (Gertrude Stein Collection) where a beret in partially pleated paper breaks up the flat surface. The search for variety also extended to the subjects. In the *Femme à la guitare* which he painted during the winter of that year, Picasso introduced Russian letters at the bottom of the picture. Kahnweiler relates that he had sent some of Picasso's canvases to Russia for an exhibition organized by a society called 'The Knave of Diamonds', and that they had been returned carefully wrapped in Russian posters. 'Picasso saw them and found them so attractive that he took them away and used them in his still-lifes.'

At the same time, colour came powerfully into his work. In the *Violon au café* (Rosengart Gallery, Lucerne) bands of pure ultramarine stand out against a background of cream and pale bluish green, while the use of a decorator's comb to imitate wood introduces those tactile differences which Picasso was striving for at that time. These are heightened by red and green dots which look like confetti stuck on the canvas and provide a contrast between speckled and smooth surfaces.

Among previous subjects which Picasso revived at that time is the *Harlequin* (Rosengart Gallery, Lucerne) painted *en clair* in cream and grey and composed like the steps of a staircase. A clear turning-point in his art is represented by the *Femme en chemise dans un fauteuil* (Mlle Ingeborg Eichmann Collection, Zürich) painted during the course of that winter. In this picture reality insistently obtrudes, underlined by violent contrasts in colour. A mauve upholstered armchair with satin-like reflections and violet shadows stands out against a yellowish-grey background. With its broad plaited border and fringe the chair is one of those old-fashioned pieces which unexpectedly crop up in Picasso's work. The chemise in English embroidery with a scalloped edge is painted minutely, its folds resting against the pinkish-beige flesh. The ribs are painted schematically and jut out in the same deep flesh colour, while a violent pink underlines peculiar breasts which look as though they are nailed or rivetted to the chest.

Picasso was very conscious of the successive stages in his art and, knowing in advance that this picture would be important to him, he prepared it carefully with a watercolour in which only the scalloped chemise and the upholstery of the chair are missing. Later, because of its prevailing incoherence and the juxtaposition of the real and the abstract, the *Femme en chemise* came to be considered as a precursor of surrealism. In Picasso's work it marked the abandonment of geometrical rectangles, though these were continued with unabated rigour in certain still-lifes.

Many of his friends followed Picasso when he moved to Mont-parnasse, but according to Gertrude Stein life was not the same. 'He was not unhappy, but after he left Montmartre we did not hear his braying Spanish laughter any more.' Slowly the bonds of friendship with Braque loosened and in their work, too, they began to pursue separate paths. After 1914 they no longer signed their pictures on the back to preserve their anonymity. In his impetuous fashion Guillaume Apollinaire plunged into the adventure of pictorial art, setting himself up as the archpriest of the new religion and dreaming of reconciling futurism inspired by Marinetti with cubism to which the latter was violently hostile, so as to create in art and literature a single powerful *avant-garde* movement. A series of savage futurist manifestos attacking cubism did not prevent him therefore from drawing up a manifesto of his own in 1913 entitled 'The Futurist Anti-tradition', in which he offered the palm in the first place to Marinetti, in second place to Picasso and in third place to himself—all this with the object of bringing the two movements together.

The manifesto made a great stir, but merely aggravated the conflict, and when Marinetti refused to be reconciled to cubism Apollinaire tried to restrict its scope. Meanwhile in Italy the futurists were gaining ground and in Paris Picasso made friends of those who had settled there, like Gino Severini, or those who stayed for a time, like Ardengo Soffici. In the futurist exhibition in Paris in 1913, Severini scored the most striking success with his picture *Danse du Pan-pan au Monico* which was considered the most dazzling achievement of the group. It represented a deliberate attempt to capture the movement with violent colours, superimposed forms and a rain of luminous little rods revealing Seurat's influence.

The Italians felt particularly close to Picasso, Ardengo Soffici declaring that by nature, temperament and his way of thinking and feeling, he was 'one of us', 'a man from my country'. Picasso remained in contact with Soffici when the latter left Paris and asked him to make researches into his hypothetical ancestor, the Genoese painter Matteo Picasso. Some of the ideas which his futurist friends expressed in Picasso's presence were familiar to him or close to his own. Futurist sculptors, for instance, demanded the abolition of the 'finished line and of hermetic sculpture' of the 'purely literary and traditional alleged nobility of marble and bronze' and were thinking like him of wood or metal constructions to which some form of movement could be imparted.

Picasso's recent works had shown a return to colour. This became even more marked during the summer of 1914 which he spent with Éva at Avignon.

Towards the end of his stay in Avignon, Picasso, indignant no doubt at the bellicose language which was being spoken across the Rhine, painted the richest of his still-lifes: it has been called *Vive la France!* In front of wall-paper imitating tapestry, a curtain, and mouldings in strong relief, stands a bottle of rum in a straw jacket, glasses and playing cards, and on one glass there are two crossed tricolour flags surmounted by the inscription: 'Vive la . . .' The picture, painted after the outbreak of the First World War, reflects the pleasure of a life that would never return, it was like a farewell to a joy that no one yet realized had gone for ever.

A work characteristic of Picasso's new technique—his manner of thinning out forms like leaves from a tree and of enriching them with multicoloured stippling, the integration of geometric planes by means of a few realistic details painted in relief—was the *Femme assise dans un fauteuil devant une cheminée* (Georges Salles Collection, Paris). The most unexpected object in this picture is a feather boa surrounding the woman's shoulders. This is painted in little touches of white and is like the work of a miniaturist.

In the same 'rococo' vein is an isolated return, in the spring of this year, to sculpture: *Le Verre d'absinthe* of which Kahnweiler had six copies cast in bronze, each with a different finish. According to Barr, this glass surmounted by a spoon and a lump of sugar was 'a minor *tour de force*'. Among the less serious works of this summer are some experimental paintings in relief like the *Grappe de raisins* painted on a wooden panel and dusted with sand. There are also semi-sculptures done in the most varied materials: the *Guitare*, for instance, consisting of coloured paper with wires for strings. Though these varied constructions, almost all of which he kept, incidentally, in his own possession, did not seem to satisfy him as independent works of art, Gertrude Stein asserts that they did allow him later on to tackle stage design with confidence.

It was also at Avignon that Picasso began a series of seated men which marked the end of one period in his art and the beginning of another. One of these was the *Joueur de cartes* (Museum of Modern Art, New York). It is constructed of rigid and tightly interlocking planes rising like the steps of a staircase with one or two stippled rectangles. This stippling continued for a while in pictures with large, carefully balanced planes of pure colour in what came to be known as the Crystal period.

But this development was interrupted by outside events. On the declaration of war many of Picasso's friends had been called up, and he suddenly became conscious that he was a foreigner. As he said later: 'I took Braque and Derain to the station in Avignon. I never found them again.' He himself returned to Paris, a city where everything seemed upside-down and nothing was the same. Gertrude Stein had been surprised by the war in England where she had gone to see her publisher and for the moment she was unable to return. Long ago Picasso had tried to persuade Kahnweiler to become a naturalized Frenchman, but like so many Germans abroad, Kahnweiler and Uhde had been out of touch with feeling in their own country and had refused to believe in the possibility of war between Germany and France. Kahnweiler now took refuge in Switzerland. After the war his collection of paintings was sold and Uhde's dispersed as enemy property. Apollinaire, meanwhile, had lost his mistress, Marie Laurencin, who had married a German. He possessed the Russian nationality of his mother, but he had been born in Italy, which was still a neutral country, and his friends urged him to go there. But instead he applied to join the army. His application was refused. In despair over Marie Laurencin and seeing his world collapsing around him, he then sought oblivion in opium and amorous adventures. Tiring rapidly of these he again applied to join up and this time he was successful. Once in the army, the man who had never been on time for an appointment in his life found an unexpected pleasure in the harsh military discipline and he wrote: 'It seems to me that the profession of soldier is my true calling.'

While Apollinaire was training at Nîmes, Max Jacob was preparing for a great event. He had had another vision, this time the Virgin Mary had appeared to him in church, and he was making renewed efforts to be baptized. At last he found the Fathers of Notre-Dame-de-Sion, who specialized in the conversion of Jews and were ready to perform the rite. 'On 20th January, Pablo will be my godfather,' he wrote to Apollinaire, 'and Sylvette Filassier, of the Théâtre des Variétés, my godmother, if it please God.'

Picasso could not help teasing his friend about his neophyte's zeal. 'Pablo wants to call me Fiacre (the patron saint of gardeners),' groaned Max Jacob. 'The thought appals me.' They finally settled on the name of Cyprien, which was one of Picasso's. But despite his quips in these solemn circumstances Picasso was very fond of Max Jacob and all his affection is revealed in a portrait of his friend drawn with surprising and minute realism and constituting a sudden break with his contemporary manner. He had already shown Kahnweiler some realistic drawings which dated from the previous year. No doubt he was one of the few people to see Max Jacob without the mask. He drew a face with an expression of melancholy and disarming kindness and a thin smile on the broad lips which seems due solely to ingrained irony. Max Jacob wears a thick sweater, a soft collar and a creased jacket and trousers. His delicate hands are lying half open on his knees. Max Jacob was delighted with the portrait which he considered resembled his grandfather, an old Catalan peasant, and his mother.

Mahaut supplies an interesting explanation for this sudden return to realistic portraiture. 'In 1915, Picasso told me he wanted to see if he could draw like everyone else and he suddenly produced some pencil portraits of friends, so exact and so precise that they have been compared to drawings by Ingres.' No doubt Picasso's desire sprang from a sense of isolation as a man who was spared the horrors of a world in torment. All his friends had been called up, Braque was now serving as an officer in the front line. 'I see few people,' Picasso wrote at that time to an Italian friend.

To draw like everyone else, to attach himself to the realities of daily life offered a kind of security, though the comparison with Ingres is not applicable. In August, 1914, he drew a portrait of Ambroise Vollard in the most classical style with the painstaking virtuosity of a Holbein. The portrait shows a man with heavy eyelids, moujik's beard, a mouth both sulky and loquacious and small podgy hands. Confronted with these realistic drawings, some people were convinced —and said as much on a note of triumph—that Picasso had abandoned cubism as a dead-end into which he had strayed by mistake. But in fact he was still identifying himself with cubism and there is a picture dating from this time of a reclining woman in which he tried to combine cubist design with realistic detail: the body is foreshortened and constructed in geometric planes while the two enormous soles of her feet are painted realistically in the foreground.

When Gertrude Stein finally returned from England she invited Picasso and Éva to dine with her. After the meal they were taking a stroll along the Boulevard Raspail when an enormous lorry suddenly crossed the street. Picasso stopped dead in amazement. It was the first camouflaged vehicle he had seen. 'We did that!' he said.

He said one day to Cocteau: 'If they want to make an army invisible at a distance they only need to dress the men as harlequins.' This theme of the harlequin, which he had been fond of in his youth and to which he seemed to return particularly in troublous times, now reappeared in several watercolours transposed in rigorous cubist planes. The master-work of this kind is the *Harlequin* in the Museum of Modern Art, New York. The tall picture consists of broad superimposed planes inclined at different angles, coloured bright vermilion and ultramarine and standing out against a black background. The rectangular body is made up of multicoloured lozenges and the head is in the form of a stick with a black pommel. The gaiety of the colouring is all the more striking in that the construction is schematic in the extreme and all sign of con-ventional reality is excluded.

At the same time as Picasso was drawing realistic portraits his paint-ings revealed an increasing austerity of form and profusion of colour. Among his still-lifes one was placed in a window-frame, a motif which was often to recur in his work. On the whole and compared with his usual rhythm of production, Picasso painted little during the early years of the war and then mostly small watercolours. He seemed more affected than he was prepared to admit at being on the margin of great events and excluded from a national cause which demanded every sacrifice. But later, when the civil war broke out in Spain, he was to realize that his loyalties had not been entirely involved in the First World War.

Rumours and news of friends wounded at the front deepened the gulf between soldiers and civilians. In 1915, Braque was severely wounded and for a long time was unconscious. All hope of saving him was abandoned, but after a trepanning operation he was slowly restored to life.

Soldiers on leave in Paris became embittered to find it so unchanged. Apollinaire returned in February, 1916. He found 'feverish activity in painting and sculpture—cubism, of course', and added: 'They can sell anything at ridiculous prices.' But he noted that artists were sorry that Kahnweiler had gone; the poor fellow had only one fault—he was stingy with money.

Apollinaire had sent Picasso a ring from the front made out of metal from an enemy shell, but the packet got lost. During his short leave he also saw Max Jacob who predicted a thirty years' war and much greater carnage in 1916 than in 1915. Some years before, Max had told Apollinaire's fortune, saying that he would have a short life and glory after his death. Back in the front-line trenches amidst mud and slaughter Apollinaire remembered Max Jacob's reputation as a 'satanic sooth-sayer' and wrote him a long letter on the eve of going over the top. Three days later, a shell fragment pierced his helmet and entered his skull. He was evacuated to Paris, operated upon and nursed devotedly by Serge Férat who was a male nurse at the Italian hospital. Apollinaire recovered, but the severe wound left him with the conviction that his youth had gone 'like a withered garland'. During his convalescence his book of poems, *Le Poète Assassiné*, was published and his friends, chiefly Picasso, Max Jacob, Juan Gris and Cendrars, organized a banquet in his honour which all the big names in art and literature attended. Apollinaire felt hugely flattered and described the occasion as splendid, 'like a magnesium flare'. Picasso made a virtuoso drawing of him when he came out of hospital showing him in uniform, the Croix de Guerre pinned to his breast, with his head and one hand still bandaged.

At this time Picasso was producing an increasing number of realistic drawings: still-lifes—a dish of apples and bananas showing practically no deformation, or a sugar-bowl—and particularly harlequins, harlequins holding the slap-stick, or masked and playing the guitar or accompanied by an old gentleman in a top hat. Often the realistic drawings served merely as a basis for a cubist transformation in which the structure was simplified and the features redistributed.

But there was a human conflict underlying these artistic efforts: Picasso's distress as a foreigner in a country at war. At a time when hatred was the prevailing human emotion and French clarity and logic were felt to be at war with turgid Teutonic metaphysics, Uhde suggests that Picasso felt himself the butt of those who accused him of being in secret collusion with the 'enemy', and that his realistic drawings were an attempt perhaps to range himself on the specifically 'French' side.

However that may be, this conflict was now aggravated by private grief: Éva died. Each time that he is separated from a woman he has loved Picasso's reaction is the same: he draws a veil over the past by changing his surroundings, moving either to another house or another town. After Éva's death he left Montparnasse and took refuge in a small house in Montrouge. During the move most of the objects he had made of paper, tin or zinc were broken or lost. Then thieves broke into the new house and stole some linen. When he was still unknown,

Picasso had told Gertrude Stein that he thought it very unlikely that a professional thief would steal any of his pictures. Now, when his reputation was established, he seemed disappointed that a robber should prefer his linen to his art.

But now a new element entered his life in the shape of a slim young man with an expressive mouth, narrow face and watchful eyes. When he had first met Jean Cocteau, Picasso had asked him to pose for a harlequin picture, but its cubist organization had destroyed all personal features of the model; nevertheless to him Cocteau remained the incarnation of his favourite personage. When Cocteau was elected to the Académie Française in 1955 and asked Picasso for a design for his academician's sword, the latter sent him a series of astonishing drawings representing variations on the theme of a slim harlequin's silhouette with hat surmounted by a cock whose long tail fell down in a semi-circle to his feet to form the hilt of the sword. But in 1916 Picasso was suspicious of anything which suggested adventure in his material life, and all Cocteau's by no means inconsiderable powers of persuasion were needed to induce him to collaborate in a scheme which would involve emerging from his rut and the abandonment of his habits. Cocteau once wrote to me: 'My meeting with Picasso changed my whole life and I make bold to believe that I graced his with an anti-pedantic crown to which, alas, he was not accustomed.'

The idea which led to their collaboration had been conceived by Cocteau when on leave from the front in April, 1915. It took the form of a ballet based on a music-hall act in which the principal characters were a Chinaman, an acrobat and an American girl. These were to be announced by an anonymous voice repeating current advertising slogans through a megaphone. The idea appealed to the directors of the Russian ballet whom Cocteau approached through Diaghilev. They decided to go to Rome for rehearsals. For the costumes and setting of a ballet on this subject it seemed natural to invite the assistance of an artist who had painted so many harlequins, jugglers and acrobats, but it was a novel idea of Cocteau's to approach a man who had never designed a stage set, was not in the least interested in music and knew nothing about the Russian ballet which had performed in Paris in 1911 and 1913.

To Picasso's dislike of undertaking any journey were added the objections of his associates. 'I had to drag him to Rome,' states Cocteau not without pride. 'His friends refused to believe that he would follow me.' He recalls the intransigent artistic atmosphere of those times. 'A dictatorship weighed on Montmartre and Montparnasse. This was the austere period of cubism. The objects which could stand on a café table, and the Spanish guitar were the only permitted pleasures. To paint a stage set, particularly for the Russian ballet (those young people had never heard of Stravinsky) was a crime. The café "de la Rotonde" was scandalized when Picasso accepted my proposition.' And the cubists, whose 'code banned all journeys beyond the North-South line of the Métro', considered the trip to Rome a monstrous extravagance.

But, as always when his mind was made up, Picasso was adamant. He had made the models, including house-fronts, trees and a fairground booth, for the ballet, which was to be called *Parade*, and these he now carefully packed up. Before his departure he said his farewells to Gertrude Stein who had just come back from Spain. He went to see her with the slim and elegant Cocteau who leant one hand nonchalantly on his shoulder. 'This is Jean,' he said, 'and we are leaving for Italy.' She found him very excited at the idea and thought that he needed a change.

Picasso and Cocteau set off in holiday mood. Léonide Massine was the choreographer for *Parade*. Cocteau's idea opened up new possibilities. Serge Lifar wrote later that, though his inventions were certainly literary, a new choreographic style originated from them which has not yet been fully exploited. As in all important works of the theatre, the final result was due to a combination of chance, improvisation and mishap. The key figures of the ballet, the 'managers', did not exist in the first version and, according to Cocteau, it was Picasso's sketches which first suggested the idea of 'inhuman, superhuman figures which would combine to create a false scenic reality and reduce the real dancers to the proportions of puppets'. For the Chinese conjuror Picasso invented a costume which has become famous, consisting of red, yellow, black and white hatchings, rays and spirals representing a rising sun obscured by smoke. The acrobats came from Picasso's Rose period. 'We tried to dress them,' he says, 'in the melancholy of the Sunday evening circus.' The 'managers', on the other hand, were 'fierce, noisy, vulgar and uncouth, arousing the hatred, laughter and incomprehension of the audience by the strangeness of their appearance and their behaviour'. For them Picasso designed gigantic cubist structures which were like moving parts of the scenery and, far from seeming unreal, produced the intentional effect of reducing the flesh-

and-blood dancers to the status of marionettes. The French manager who introduced the Chinese conjuror was clothed with panels covered with signs, pipes and interlocking planes like an enormous enlargement of a cubist picture. The American manager who vaunted the merits of his small compatriot wore cow-boy boots and his structure ended in a sky-scraper.

The 'managers' were of pure cubist inspiration and clashed with the drop-curtain for the ballet which Picasso designed in his Montrouge studio. In this he revived figures from his Rose period, a female equestrian, harlequins and guitarists, but the colours were darker and more crude and the style was so laboured that the scene seemed like a parody of a popular spectacle.

All these features were to arouse disapproval on the first night in Paris, but it was Satie's music which turned it into a violent outcry. Cocteau had asked for a background of noise representing the sounds of an aeroplane, an express train, sirens and a morse signalling apparatus, but all these had to be abandoned on the first night because of the lack of compressed air, and the only sound which survived was the clicking of typewriters imitated by sticks being struck together.

But unaware of, or indifferent to the hostility they were about to unleash, Picasso and Cocteau plunged eagerly into their work in Rome and also found time to enjoy themselves. Picasso came across some artist friends among the 'gay futurists' and, apart from Massine who was directing the choreography, he got to know all the people connected with the Russian ballet: Diaghilev, Stravinsky (who was then composing the music for the *Feu d'Artifice*), Semenoff and Bakst. He drew their portraits and those of several other acquaintances, but among the large number of masterly sketches which he produced, not one is concerned with Rome either past or present, although he was seeing the city for the first time. Picasso, it seems, was concentrating all his faculties on the immediate task and was living in the Cave Taglioni, where rehearsals for the ballet were held, as though he were still in Montrouge. There is nothing to suggest that he had eyes for Greek or Roman statues, or for the Sistine Chapel and indeed according to Kahnweiler he did not see them at that time. But one can never know what Picasso's implaccable plastic vision has retained, for memories of things seen often occur to him in the most unexpected fashion and most frequently after an interval of time.

There is no record, either, in his work of his visit to Naples and

Pompeii, no trace of his journey to Florence or his meeting with the *Quattrocento*. But a time was to come after this Italian journey when his canvases were invaded by Venuses of triumphant sensuality, graceful Tanagra figurines and giantesses exuding imprisoned power like sisters of Michelangelo's athletes.

But to Picasso Rome did not merely signify febrile activity in a sphere hitherto unknown to him or meetings with new or former friends. 'We used to go for walks in the moonlight with the dancers,' recalls Cocteau. Among these ballet dancers was Olga Khoklova. She was not of the stuff of which stars are made. The daughter of a general, of good family, she took to dancing too late to aspire to leading roles. But she had pure, regular features, a smooth skin and a strongly feminine temperament, all of which appealed to Picasso powerfully. Strangely enough, she also possessed a kind of nostalgia for the bourgeois rigidity which she had abandoned, a sort of basic intransigence. It was these qualities which seem to have drawn Picasso most strongly to Olga Khoklova. He himself had thrown off all constraint at such an early age that he had perhaps forgotten how much it could oppress him. He had lived so long according to the laws of his own morality, indulgent to others and to himself, that to discover a girl of good family in the little Russian dancer seems to have moved him profoundly. She reminded him perhaps of the solid bourgeois foundations of his own family, and a longing for a former way of life suddenly rose up in the most unexpected fashion amidst the organized disorder of his existence.

Parade was produced at the Châtelet on 18th May, 1917. Apollinaire wrote the programme notes, seeing in the experiment a new spirit which would exert a radical influence on art and manners and coining, with his usual felicity of expression, a word destined to become famous: 'sur-realism'. But oblivious of these wider issues, the audience was incensed to the point of violence and the critics, too, were vitriolic in condemning the ballet. 'Each morning,' wrote Cocteau to a friend, 'new insults arrive, some of them from a great distance, for some critics are railing against us without having seen or heard the work.' He recalled later that Paul Souday was the only man who took it upon himself to write in 1917 and tell him that he, Picasso and Satie were neither Germans nor criminals.

Produced again three years later, the 'accursed *Parade*' achieved a striking success and Picasso's name remained linked to the ballet both in triumph and disaster, thereby coming before a wider public than the one which knew his pictures. Meanwhile, the failure of the ballet cast a shadow on a play of Apollinaire's, *Les Mamelles de Tirésias*, which was produced a month later. The play was noisily acclaimed by his friends, but provoked a scandal which the author had failed to foresee. It was clear that the hour of surrealism had not yet struck. As for Picasso, he was more accustomed to abuse than Apollinaire or Cocteau, he was used to waiting for public opinion to change and he was also too busy at this time with his personal adventure to be unduly worried.

During the summer of 1917 he took Olga Khoklova to Madrid and Barcelona. He was more serious about this new attachment than he had been over his previous adventures. He wanted to show the young woman his country and present her to his relatives. Perhaps also he wanted to reconcile or underline the affinities between the Slav and the Spanish elements, for he painted Olga with a Spanish mantilla over the heavy bandeaux of her hair curled into regular waves. The portrait is so realistic that it looks like a photograph. He left it as a gift for his mother, but it is now no longer among the pictures which his family possesses in Barcelona.

Despite the shortness of his stay in Spain, Picasso set to work in a studio which he borrowed from a friend, painting a composition in flat, fluid planes ringed with curves which reflected the brilliance of the Catalan summer. But with a mixture of realistic and cubist design he also painted a Spanish dancer with her blue-black hair caught up like a helmet and crowned with a tall comb and a mantilla. It seemed as though the return to familiar scenes revived a whole series of figures that had haunted his youth—*diseuses*, music-hall dancers and girls flaunting their charms—and, carried away by his memories, he revived a former manner: the face of the Spanish dancer stands out proudly against an explosive background of multicoloured rods such as he used in painting *La Naine*. Gertrude Stein was then in the South of France helping to administer the American fund for French wounded. From Barcelona Picasso sent her a delightful little picture representing a guitar. He wrote that he was intending to marry 'une vraie jeune fille' and enclosed a photo of Olga Khoklova's portrait.

After the end of the war, when Gertrude Stein was once more in Paris, Alice Toklas conceived the idea of using the guitar picture as the basis for a tapestry. Gertrude Stein told Picasso she had promised to transfer the design for her, but he insisted on doing it himself. The tapestry was one of the few of his 'works' which disappeared during the German occupation of Paris during the Second World War. Some years later, apparently about 1929, Alice Toklas again asked Picasso to trace some designs for her directly on to the canvas. On a grey background he painted some vivid splashes of red, yellow and brown with intertwining arabesques in black. On one canvas a white hand appeared on a grey background between undulating bands of green and black. The finished tapestries were then sent to an upholsterer to be fitted into the backs and seats of two small Louis XV chairs which had been repainted black. Alice Toklas relates that several of his customers wanted to buy the chairs and others the tapestries, but no one wanted the two together.

Picasso returned from Spain to find his studio in Montrouge flooded out. This, combined with the new life he was about to embark on, persuaded him to move house. But he did not go to the trouble of finding a new studio himself. Paul Rosenberg, a picture dealer who had replaced Kahnweiler, found him an apartment near his own gallery at 23, Rue La Boétie. Here Picasso installed himself with his fiancée like a man who has sown his wild oats and is ready to forget his turbulent past. For a brief while it seemed that his life might enter a more peaceful path leading to family happiness, official honours and academic recognition. The twin brass bedsteads were like those in adjoining bourgeois establishments. In his appearance Picasso, who was now comfortably off, seemed anxious to conform to accepted standards, dressing in elegant style—more elegant than he would ever be in his life again—with a watch-chain attached to his button-hole, well smarmed hair, a butterfly tie and a white fancy handkerchief in his vest pocket.

His civil marriage with Olga Khoklova was registered in Paris on 12th July, 1918, but the young woman was not content with this formality and what was to her the real marriage ceremony was celebrated according to the rites of the Orthodox Church, with all the customary pomp and obligatory length of service, in the Russian church in the Rue Daru. Among the witnesses were Cocteau, Max Jacob and Guillaume Apollinaire. A short time previously, on 2nd May, Picasso with Ambroise Vollard had himself attended Apollinaire's wedding which was again a religious ceremony to another 'vraie jeune fille', Jacqueline, called by her friends Ruby, who had nursed him after his severe wound and during a serious bout of pneumonia at the beginning of 1918. These ordeals had left Apollinaire a changed man. At thirty-eight he knew that his youth was finished and his love of adventure over. Like Picasso he felt the lure of domestic stability, particularly as he had undergone severe privations in his youth.

But this was not to be. Spanish 'flu held Paris in its grip and Apollinaire, with his constitution undermined, quickly succumbed. He fell into a coma. Picasso and his wife spent the evening with him. It was the night of 9–10 November, the eve of the Armistice. The long nightmare was almost over. It was a warm evening, the windows of the apartment were open and outside a delirious mob could be heard surging through the streets and demanding the Kaiser's abdication at the top of its lungs: '*A bas Guillaume. . . !*' On the dying man's face Olga Picasso thought she could detect spasms of distress at the sound of those hate-filled voices repeating his own name.

Picasso was in front of the bathroom mirror in a Paris hotel when he heard by telephone of the death of his friend. He looked at his face, saw the mouth drooping with shock and grief, saw fear creep into the eyes ringed with insomnia and realized all that the passing of Apollinaire meant for him and his friends. His loss closed the chapter of youthful struggles which they had shared.

Picasso has painted no self-portrait for many years. When I asked him the reason he said: 'If mirrors did not exist I would not know my age,' and held a hand to his heavily lined face in explanation. But many artists have preferred to paint themselves when age has left a strongly marked individuality in their faces. I asked Picasso the date of his last self-portrait. He replied without hesitation: 'The day when Guillaume Apollinaire died.'

CHAPTER X 1918-1923

Classical Frolic

'PICASSO is still doing nice things when he has time between a Russian ballet and a fashionable portrait,' wrote Juan Gris to Kahnweiler in August, 1919, not without a touch of bitterness, and when he himself a few years later was commissioned by Diaghilev to design the sets for a ballet he was disgusted by the atmosphere of eccentricity and jangled nerves and complained of an infernal existence where people lived in a state of perpetual misunderstanding.

But Picasso had stronger nerves, or rather he was better able to protect himself against unwelcome interference by his sense of humour and a built-in ability to disregard it. Despite the failure of *Parade* Diaghilev made another approach, but this time it was not to Picasso the Cubist. Having succeeded with great difficulty in keeping his company together, thanks to tours in North and South America, he began to realize that the public in Europe was beginning to tire of spectacles from Russian folklore and, seeking choreographic inspiration elsewhere, decided to mount *The Three-cornered Hat* with music by Manuel de Falla. The choice of a Spanish artist for the settings was clearly indicated. Picasso rediscovered the traditions of his native country and painted on the curtain an arena where a bull-fight was in progress with women in mantillas and men in capes and sombreros as spectators. On the backcloth he painted a small bridge with a large overhanging arch which seemed to recall the backgrounds of Goya's tapestries or perhaps was drawn from a common source of inspiration. The colours he gave to the whole—salmon pink and pale ochre against a starry blue sky— recalled his own Rose period and contributed to the triumph which *The Three-cornered Hat* achieved when it was produced for the first time at the Alhambra in London on 22nd July, 1919. Picasso put the

147

final touches to the costumes at the last moment in the wings, painting motifs of striking effect, as, for instance, for Karsavina, whose costume was finished just before he was due to go on stage. The one-time recluse of the Bateau-Lavoir was seeing London for the first time, but crowds and strange places no longer worried him and—temporarily—he had become a sociable individual. For his holidays he no longer sought out inaccessible villages in a fold of the mountains or the company of peasants, smugglers or 'outsiders' such as he himself had once been. He spent the summer of 1918 at Biarritz and that of 1919 at Saint-Raphaël. At that time he seems to have possessed a taste for serenity, for reconciliation, and this resulted in a truce with society and a return to traditional plastic values and intelligible subjects.

Among pictures revealing a return to the scrupulous technique of the past is a very small one which illustrates both this state of creative serenity and the strength of his emotional loyalites. Shortly after his return to Paris he turned up one day at Gertrude Stein's with this diminutive picture representing an apple—a single small apple, very firm and painted with a clarity of detail reminiscent of Dürer. At the time when he had first met her, Gertrude Stein had owned a picture by Cézanne of three small green apples. When her brother had left Paris before the war to live in Italy they had split up the collection of pictures which they had bought together, Leo Stein taking almost all the Matisses, while Gertrude had wanted to keep the Picassos. By mistake Cézanne's little apples had been included in Leo's share. Being very fond of them Gertrude tried to get the picture returned, but her very insistence revived her brother's interest in it and, even when she offered to pay for it, to her great disappointment he refused to let it go. Picasso's memory had faithfully recorded this disagreeable incident and when the war was over he brought his own small picture to his friend, saying with an expansive smile: 'It is to compensate you a little for your Cézanne apples.'

At this time, impressions he had received in Italy, among them those of the Mannerist period, bore belated fruit, in a masterly drawing, for instance, done in Biarritz of the *Baigneuses* (Fogg Art Museum, Harvard University) with its fluid contours of elongated nudes and its slightly troubled sensuality. Familiar subjects from the circus world were also treated in a new style. As early as 1917 in his Montrouge studio he had drawn a seated pierrot in indian ink with his capacious costume and conical felt hat. The *Pierrot assis* of 1918 (Museum of

Modern Art, New York) is a variation on the same theme, but here the classical Pierrot of the *Commedia dell' arte* is represented, a handsome, melancholy figure waiting, mask in hand, with a vague smile on his face for the arrival of Columbine. This is a pierrot of the theatre painted under harsh footlights which throw red, violet and green reflections on his long face and streak the folds of his white costume with the same contrasting colours. An open book lying on the red cloth of a table seems to be a collection of verses which he reads while he is waiting.

In his rediscovery of the world of the *Commedia dell' arte* Picasso was pursuing a parallel path to Diaghilev who was also thinking of reviving these traditional elements in a ballet, and to Stravinsky who was making free use of Pergolesi in his musical themes. This was a period when Picasso took pleasure in exploiting his realistic vein. He painted numerous portraits of his wife in deliberately conventional poses. In one of them, for instance, (property of the artist) an arm is flung over the back of a chair, a fan is held in the other hand, the face is pensive under heavy bandeaux which fall low over the forehead, and the gauze hem of the dress is painted transparently over the chest. This, to use Juan Gris's expression, is a fashionable portrait *par excellence*. But he also painted familiar objects in the same painstaking detail, such as the *Nature morte sur une commode* of 1919 (property of Picasso) with mouldings on a grey wall in the background, pears in a bowl and the stems of flowers painted in stylized arabesques, the whole given the appearance of an old-time engraving by hachured shadows.

The set for *Pulcinella*, which Diaghilev assigned to him, had the same charming old-fashioned appearance. As a framework for the ballet he designed the interior of an eighteenth-century theatre with much gold on white, a deep perspective, a ceiling with baroque ornamentation, boxes draped with red velvet and a crystal chandelier, a whole series of gouaches and drawings in indian ink or graphite bearing witness to his patient effort of reconstruction.

But in a sphere of activity where, according to Juan Gris, nothing was ever ready on time and confusion and backbiting ruled the day, the set and costumes so carefully evolved by Picasso were destined never to be seen by the public. Cocteau remembers that a mistake over dates and lack of liaison between the choreographer Massine and the scene-painters resulted in a situation where a ballet prepared in Rome was due to be presented in Paris in a space of two days. Thus Picasso was faced with the necessity of improvising costumes and simplifying the décor in the extreme. In place of sumptuous vistas he designed a severe frame for the diminutive scene with a background of a street leading down to the Bay of Naples. The houses were represented in cubist style. Beyond them the outline of Vesuvius was roughly sketched beneath a large moon and a sky spangled with stars. The set was painted in dark blues, greys and white. The one-act ballet was presented at the Opéra in Paris on 15th May. Picasso became rapidly famous. He was in close contact with all the celebrities of the day and he even had a salon where he received visitors. His apartment in the Rue La Boétie offered a suitable setting for receptions with its large dining-room with an immense, round extending table in the middle, and the sketch he made of it shows it completely free of the usual clutter of his existence. He also sketched his *Salon avec des visiteurs*. In front of the fire-place Madame Picasso is sitting in a relaxed attitude in a large armchair, while Cocteau stands beside her, his hair brushed up and his slim wrists escaping from his shirt-cuffs. Opposite them, Satie in heavy boots and spats stands somewhat awkwardly, contrasting with the graceful appearance of Cocteau.

Picasso did another portrait of Satie, one of those revealing drawings in which he excelled at that time. His portrait of Manuel de Falla showed exceptional virtuosity even for him, consisting of a single continuous line circling a head almost innocent of hair. He drew Stravinsky several times, reproducing the model's receding forehead, large fleshy mouth and heavy hands.

In post-war Paris several new currents were forcing a passage amid the general disorganization of life. One of them was a reviving interest in literature. Informing Kahnweiler of the changes that had taken place in his absence, Juan Gris wrote: 'The most surprising thing has been a subtle flowering of poets.' Cocteau discovered a youthful prodigy acclaimed by all his friends, Raymond Radiguet. Towards the end of 1920, Picasso drew his portrait which was reproduced as a frontispiece in the *Joues en feu*. He also did one of Paul Valéry which was curiously uninspired. Many of these portraits were reproduced by lithography, a process which he used for the first time in 1919. The ease and rapidity of the lithographic technique were particularly well suited to Picasso's fiery virtuosity and later the combination of the two was to produce some astonishing results.

Meanwhile, despite realistic portraits and stage-settings Picasso was far from renouncing his cubist past. In the same year as the realistic,

14 Boisgeloup

15 7, Rue des Grands-Augustins

16   Picasso in the Café de Flore, 1940

barely stylized work, *Nature morte sur le guéridon*, he painted at Saint-Raphaël another still-life with the same title (property of Picasso) and in the most severe, one could almost say orthodox cubist tradition. Planes that look as though they were cut out of plywood interlock to represent a table in front of an open window. At the top of one of these panels, against a beige background, some undulating lines appear, representing possibly a memory of reflections seen on a calm sea. An open window was one of his favourite motifs at this time. He often painted an open french window with blue shadows falling across a wrought-iron balcony on to a rose-coloured carpet, with luminous reflections from the sea and the sky streaked with fair-weather clouds (private collection, New York).

This motif dominated the exhibition of his work organized in Paris by Paul Rosenberg in October and November, 1919. The invitation card underlined this fact with a reproduction of a variant of the *Fenêtre à Saint-Raphaël*. This was Picasso's first attempt at lithography. But despite his return to realistic portraiture and still-lifes, it was as a cubist that Picasso was presented to the public. Cubism had now become almost respectable, but for that very reason perhaps a reaction was setting in against all excess. The post-war period, like all periods of comparative calm after storm, encouraged nostalgia for the past. Picasso with his particular sensibility had merely anticipated a tendency which now became generalized. The serenity which he had acquired became a universal aspiration. At the same time, a certain xenophobia became apparent in a country that was deeply scarred despite its victory. While new experiments in the fields of art and literature were multiplying in defeated Germany, in France a taste for permanent values was reviving. Just as people sought to forget the horrors of war and recover stability, so a return to classical traditions was demanded. With Picasso, classicism first appeared in his drawings of 1918 and 1919, just as it was through drawings that he had approached realistic portraiture. As Barr has pointed out, the drawing *Paysans endormis* was inspired by the *Bain turc* of Ingres, but it was an Ingres seen through the eyes of Michelangelo and from this drawing of 1919 dates a tendency to deform objects to colossal proportions.

In the pastel of the *Deux Femmes nues* (Douglas Cooper Collection, Château de Castille) Picasso found his own interpretation of a style which was to be called in his case 'antique'. The two women have short, thick-set bodies, their small round breasts are placed high, they

L

have thick necks, protruding calves and enormous hands with stubby fingers. The heads, which are too large for the small bodies, have regular features drawn with a fine brush in rose-pink flesh with mauve reflections. For Picasso this was a moment of experiment before his vision crystallized. He returned to the subject again and again as though he were kneading a lump of clay in impatient fingers to see what effect he could produce from it by distorting reality. The torment which Picasso imposed on female bodies, treating them like lumps of clay or half-filled sacks of bran, was like a vision of primitive cruelty and at that time it did not persist for long. Later however these excessive distortions were to appear again in a new and spectacular form. In their features Picasso's giant women are akin to the Delphic Sybil, but their arms and legs are excessively long and their firm flesh seems to imprison them in a great animal calm.

Picasso's new style provoked the most diverse reactions, from bitterness among the cubists who saw it as a sort of defection from their movement, to secret relief among those who had not dared to continue it to this logical conclusion. Matisse who, as always, was keeping a close watch on Picasso's activities seemed to treat the serenity which now prevailed in the art of a man eternally tormented as an incursion into his own domain.

At this time, Picasso found the soil and climate most favourable to his creativity. One by one he seemed to draw up the roots which he had anchored in the soil of Spain and transplant them to the shores of the Mediterranean. In the South of France the voluntary exile had found what was to be the permanent setting for his life.

When Picasso paints a landscape and lingers for a moment over the scene before his eyes, this is often a prelude to new adventures and also something of a stylistic exercise in a minor art. After the Rue des Bois and the great turning point which the landscapes painted at La Horta denoted, landscape disappeared from his work for over ten years. In the still-lifes of Saint-Raphaël, sea and sky entered incidentally into his pictures as a background for inanimate objects, mingling their reflections with the colours of his palette. Then, in the spring of 1920, he felt a sudden nostalgia for the sun and the sea and a glittering vision arose in his mind which he immediately fixed on canvas. He saw this imaginary landscape in real life when he arrived at Juan-les-Pins. He spoke of it cautiously: 'I don't want to pretend to clairvoyance, but really I was staggered: everything was there just as it was in the canvas which I had painted in Paris. Then I realized that this landscape was mine.'

Faced with the reality of his own dream, he was interested in everything he saw around him. He drew numerous sketches in his notebook of houses between palm trees, the sun above the hills, the view of an orchard, a farm behind cypresses, and on the large pages he sketched motifs as conventional as a commonplace church, an ordinary-looking house, a railing with palm trees and even a road lined with telegraph poles.

When painting a number of small gouaches in Juan-les-Pins culminating, as is often the case with him, in a large variant in oil, Picasso dated them from day to day, as though anxious to keep note of the breakneck rhythm of his work. Henceforth he continued to date his sketches and his small pictures, like those spendthrifts who force themselves to keep an account-book.

Men and women bathing being the most familiar sea-side scene, it was inevitable at Juan-les-Pins that Picasso should take them as his subject. Usually his women bathers have Olga Picasso's features, her splendid shoulders and her supple dancer's gestures. Towards the end of his stay Picasso drew and then painted in gouache an antique vision that might have been suggested by the shimmering of the sea. The picture was called *Le Rapt* (the Abduction) and represented a bearded centaur carrying off a magnificent female body. Of perfect purity of line, this was one of Picasso's first mythological drawings. But he also continued to paint cubist bathers in striped costumes or giant women frolicking in the water, hesitating sometimes between the appearance of a classical statue and that of a robot with arms of roughly hewn wood.

At this point in his work, when he was employing various styles, he painted *La Plage* (collection of Walter P. Chrysler Jr.), a picture which was the prelude to innumerable adventures in Picasso's art. A woman with an enormous, deformed body, a single gigantic foot and hand and an excessively small head is lying on the beach; another woman is standing with one leg inordinately long and the other short and small; a third woman is running along the edge of the sand with huge legs and her head and flipper-like arms reduced in size as though they were at an immense distance from the lower part of her body. The American critic J. T. Soby was the first to suggest the analogy of a snap-shot foreshortened by a badly focused lense. Picasso seems to have wanted to paint the successive stages of a movement just as they strike the retina: the feet of the running woman are recorded at the same time as the upper part of the body seen at a distance after a certain lapse of time. This fusion of time and space resulted in such a grotesque deformation of the three figures that some critics have seen the picture as a parody of the solemn bathing scenes of Renoir, Cézanne and Matisse.

But the most important new element acquired during that long summer's work at Juan-les-Pins was a definitive vision of the giant women that had long been haunting him. They seemed to rise up of themselves from the ochre sand, the sun-baked earth, the green Mediterranean sea, as though they were part of that cradle of ancient civilizations.

In Picasso's personal life, meanwhile, all was settled calm. On 4th February, 1921, his son Paulo was born. Like all Spaniards, to whom the birth of a child seems like a favour from heaven, Picasso was an enraptured father. Men of his virility who are unsentimental to a point bordering sometimes on brutality are all the more ready to be moved by a small, delicate and perfect specimen of humanity. The baby was only two weeks old when he drew it at its mother's breast and he was careful to date the drawing: '19:II:1921, at noon.' Thereafter he drew his son almost month by month, revealing the stages of his growth and also the father's amazement at what seemed to him, now forty years old, a miracle.

Picasso had always been attracted by the eternal mystery of child-birth and in his youth he had painted the sorrowful mothers and children of his Blue period. Now the theme of maternity again invaded his work and during 1921 and the following year he painted a dozen variations. His mothers were no longer anguished figures drawing their children towards them as though to protect them against a hostile world. The giantess sitting on a bench is a block of formidable flesh with hands so huge that the child on her knees seems a plaything. By degrees Picasso deprived his Maternities of all contact with reality. The *Mère assise dans un fauteuil* (property of Picasso) is a monument to the forces of fertility. She is akin to the solar myth of the fertilized earth, triumphant in its insensibility since the beginning of life on the globe. The woman's profile is Egyptian, her feet are enormous and her barely articulated arms and hands might be those of a granite statue standing at the threshold of a temple. There is no association between her and the child struggling in her lap. The colours with which Picasso painted these Maternities and other contemporary pictures stress the inhuman aspect of his goddesses. The oil paint is flat like distemper as though he deliberately refrained from giving lustre to the skin or highlights to the hair.

Picasso also tried his hand at this time at another theatrical setting, Diaghilev having invited him to design costumes and scenery for a ballet. The choice of a Spanish artist was once again indicated as the ballet was to consist of a series of Andalusian dances and songs for which Manuel de Falla had composed the music. As for *The Three-cornered Hat* Picasso chose the interior of a theatre as a setting for the ballet, but though he still possessed the almost finished sketches for the previous production, he decided this time against an eighteenth-century setting as unsuited to the new theme and chose instead the interior of a nineteenth-century theatre with a small stage surrounded by heavily draped boxes peopled with characters appropriate to the period. The ballet, entitled *Quadro Flamenco* was produced in Paris on 22nd May, 1921.

Picasso spent the summer of this year at Fontainebleau, having rented a villa there to avoid disturbing his wife and newly born son. Exploring the nearby forest, he drew a small pastel of a knotty tree and a path passing between farm buildings to lose itself in a field of corn. In another *Paysage* the trees take on a human aspect; the trunks are female bodies, the branches waving arms or raised hands. In the *Trois Femmes à la fontaine* (Museum of Modern Art, New York) the figure of the Mother reappears with a severe, straight profile, low forehead and globulous eye, one hand resting heavily on her knee with open palm, the other stretched towards a pitcher held by a woman on the left, while a third woman, seen half-length behind some rocks, pours water into an amphora.

Picasso took great pains with this picture, making several drawings of the subject and varying the composition in oil paintings and pastels. He ranged the three women on different planes, at first by the conventional means of a staircase. Then he scattered them throughout the landscape, thinking for a while of making this form part of the ensemble. Then he varied the position of the figures and drew them closer together, seeking with a persistence unusual for him to inter-relate the various elements as convincingly as possible. The importance which Picasso, like his classical predecessors, attaches to composition becomes evident when one follows his preparatory work for any ambitious picture. In this case he finally found his nodal point in the woman in the centre of the picture, who is leaning on her elbows behind the rock with arms stretched forward and lowered head. He took the same care in the elaboration of details, making several drawings in charcoal, sanguine and pastel of the women's shapeless hands with their stubby fingers.

The finished picture resembled a sort of bas-relief from barbaric art, simplification being obtained by the successive rejection of details added here and there in the preparatory sketches, many of them akin to the pretty-pretty style of the Pompeii frescoes. When he painted *La Source* Picasso took his inspiration from the most conventional Roman statuary. The picture shows a woman half reclining with an amphora from which water pours. The woman's face is like marble, empty of all expression. Her enormous thighs and deformed arms comprise a mass heavier than the rocks on which she is lying and seem to crush earth and sky.

Among the axioms which he had inherited from his father was one to which he was particularly attached: *Dans les mains on voit les mains*. With his acute observation he knew that hands can still speak even after the artist has succeeded in controlling the expression of a face. He looked at his own hands with great curiosity and even more intensely after he had ceased to paint self-portraits and no longer looked at himself in a mirror. A series of very expressive studies of hands were drawn in charcoal in 1919. In a pastel dated 14th September, 1921, he resumed the study, drawing his own hands with their powerful wrists and thick palms tensed so that the joints stand out.

The effort which Picasso put forth during that summer at Fontainebleau bordered indeed on the miraculous. Not content with exploiting the antique vein, he resumed a theme which had continually occupied his thoughts, in variations, during the preceding year. In the cubist field he worked with increasing intensity, exploring new possibilities of arranging coloured planes in space and of co-ordinating movements which he redistributed on the canvas. The harlequin with his motley costume was well suited to experiments of this kind and had always played an important role in what might be called the cubist mythology. In the same way the movements of a jumping-jack were useful in the search for increased dynamism and it was, in fact, as a piece of mechanism that Picasso painted the *Polichinelle lisant 'Le Populaire'* at

Juan-les-Pins besides three other paintings on the theme of the pierrot or harlequin.

These pictures suggested the motifs for a major work which was now undertaken. At Fontainebleau in the summer of 1921, as though possessed of herculean powers and confident that unlimited time and means were at his disposal, Picasso painted the vast canvas of the *Trois Masques musiciens* (Museum of Modern Art, New York). The subject captivated him to such an extent that he simultaneously painted a second version of almost equal size.

The vision which so delighted him was a strange one. Three masked figures are seated behind a small table: a pierrot, a harlequin and a monk, the first two with musical instruments and the monk with a musical score on his knees. Larger than nature, the figures are inscribed in a rectangular framework and composed of interlocking planes which give them the appearance of perpetual movement. They are painted flat against a warm brown background which throws whites, blues and the red and yellow lozenges of the harlequin's costume into stark relief. Unlike the matt surfaces of Picasso's giant women, the three musicians are painted in hard brilliant colours like enamel and this accentuates the character of the picture which is mournful despite its richness of colouring. Under the table—a strange companion for these impressive masked figures—a rough-coated dog is lying like an elongated shadow.

The second version painted simultaneously (Philadelphia Museum of Art) is more compact, richer in contrasts, gayer in colouring with a touch of the ornamental fantasy of the period which in Picasso's case was called his 'Rococo Cubism'. With the *Trois Masques musiciens* Picasso's cubist adventure reached its apogee, although he continued his cubist experiments for some years to come.

It might be thought that such pictures which demanded all his powers would leave Picasso empty and exhausted, but he himself supplied the key to his apparently inexhaustible creative urge when he quoted to Cocteau the device added by the Duc d'Olivarès to the arms of the King of Spain, which was inscribed on the rim of a well: 'The more that is taken from it, the larger it becomes.'

Among his new experiments the most striking feature was the humanization of his goddesses. In the *Mother and Child*, for instance, which he painted at this time (Alex Hillmann Collection, New York), the mother holding the child on her knee is still a giant and the fist which she raises in a playful gesture is as formidable as a club, but Picasso has given the woman his wife's features and the child with its protruding upper lip is also a portrait. The composition is particularly skilful in the way it fills the frame and co-ordinates the movements. The colouring is also carefully studied: the warm, uniform tint of the flesh and the grey-pink monochrome which dominates the picture. Picasso was now abandoning his extravagant visions and his fearsome mountains of flesh. His figures were becoming smaller and, instead of seeming turned in wood or chiselled in stone, their features were traced with a brush in sepia against a background of warm tones. In the *Femme et l'enfant* (Cone Collection, Baltimore Museum of Art), which is really a coloured drawing, the planes of colour with their acidulous pinks, russet purples, intense blues or luminous jades often overrun the contours traced, and this was a technique which Picasso was frequently to employ in the future. The picture was painted in the summer of 1922 which he spent with his family in Dinard.

He made several drawings of the landscape, but his eyes were fixed particularly on his son and he never wearied during this first year of the child's life of recording his features and attitudes in drawings and paintings, some of which are almost photographic in their detail. The company of his handsome wife and gracious child beside the sea, playing with a pigeon while the mother touched the trusting little head with her lips was a source of constant wonder to him.

The heavy triumph of satisfied flesh vanished from his new studies of mother and child to be replaced by a shadowless, weightless *joie de vivre*. Gertrude Stein called this a new Rose period, airy like the first, but an adult one from which all the uncertainties of a wandering life had been banished. His goddesses were resolutely pagan, with a kind of sensual grace, and mothers and children were no longer united by tenderness, but were more like Venus and Cupid conniving at a game. At this time, Picasso once more revived some of the memories of his stay in Italy, abandoning archaic goddesses and dreaming Junos to resuscitate the bodies of Roman goddesses with voluptuous curves. His classical frolic was a rapid one. Barely a year previously he had been painting his three weird women at the fountain; now he was seeking inspiration among the divinites of Pompeii. Soon his attenuated goddesses would be modelled on the fragile grace of Tanagra figurines. The summer of 1922 produced a number of small pictures whose charm varied between the intimacy of interior scenes and subjects familiar to antiquity. The time was past when beauty frightened him or grace seemed like a screen concealing the essentials of what he wanted to say. During the following winter he continued to paint Arcadian scenes until the art of antiquity became as familiar to him as though he had never had any other vision of the world.

The profundity of Picasso's knowledge is illustrated by a story which Cocteau has told. He himself had returned to classical subjects and had written a play on the theme of Antigone which was to be produced at the end of December, 1922. On the eve of the dress-rehearsal he asked Picasso to supply some details for the set and some antique masks. The actors, the author and Picasso had assembled in the auditorium facing the still unfinished set which contained openings on the right, and on the left, high up in the middle, a hole through which the chorus was to be declaimed through a megaphone. Around this hole were suspended the masks which Picasso had designed, and beneath the masks was a panel of unpainted scenery which had yet to be filled in. On this panel it was desired to paint some haphazard theme which should underline the purpose of the set, which was to convey the feeling of a hot day. Cocteau relates that Picasso paced up and down. 'He began by rubbing a stick of red chalk on the panel which, because of the unevenness of the wood, took on the appearance of marble. Then he took a bottle of ink and traced motifs of a masterly effect. Suddenly he blackened a few empty spaces and three columns appeared. The appearance of these columns was so sudden and unexpected that we burst into applause.'

Spellbound like all those who have been present at what has been called Picasso's 'magic', Cocteau asked him whether the appearance of the three columns had been calculated or whether he had himself been surprised. 'He replied that he had been surprised, but that the artist always calculates without knowing it, that the Doric column results, like the hexameter, from a conscious process and that he had perhaps invented this column in the same way as the Greeks had discovered it.'

The man who could evoke a Greek temple with a few strokes of the pen seemed finally to have returned to an antique world of grace and serenity and in fact Picasso seems at that time to have reached a rocky base, a granite bed on which the torrent of his inspiration could flow and even overflow tumultuously without leaving it altogether. Henceforth the Arcadian goddesses and nymphs with supple bodies and hair decked with flowers would never completely disappear from his work.

Even at times of greatest torment they would continue to plough a luminous furrow in his art; banished from his pictures, they would return victorious to his drawings, engravings and lithographs. But they were never to dominate his art; even in the years when beauty presented itself to him in its most smiling aspect Picasso painted the most stark of his cubist still-lifes.

This coexistence of two means of expression has been the most incomprehensible feature of his work and his temperament. It has earned him the reproach of versatility and even doubts in his sincerity as a creative artist. But if he showed himself capable of achieving the purest harmony in an accessible art, the simultaneous persistence of his cubist vision corresponded to a need for discipline and it was out of a taste for austerity that he chose its rigorous forms contrasting with his pagan enjoyment of the world.

At Dinard he painted giant Bacchantes pounding along the shore in a small gouache which was later to serve as model for the curtain of *Le Train bleu*, a Diaghilev ballet-operetta with libretto by Cocteau and music by Darius Milhaud which was produced at the Théâtre des Champs-Elysées on 20th June, 1924. Also at Dinard and during the following winter he painted thirty or so still-lifes, mostly of small size and of extremely simplified composition. Their salient characteristic is the persistence of rectilinear stripes, dark on a light background or vice versa and sometimes painted in relief. The only variation on customary themes—due to his stay by the sea—is the appearance of a fish either lying on newspaper or beside a bottle, a fruit bowl, a glass or a lemon. Many of these small still-lifes are painted in turpentine and graphite; they are mostly in monochrome.

Gertrude Stein recalls that Picasso 'took an immense pleasure in drawing during the year 1923, almost repeating the fecundity and felicity of his Rose period—everything was in rose', and in fact he indulged in an orgy of drawing, his pictures being mostly drawn with the brush with colour as a discreet accompaniment like clear notes on the harp or the harpsichord.

Picasso also drew portraits of his family with loving care. His mother had come to join him at Cap d'Antibes where he spent the summer, and he painted her portrait in a way that would please her with perfect mastery of the conventional style as a rather massive old lady with wavy hair carefully combed. In the amiable face with features softened by age two large dark eyes stand out with long protruding lashes—eyes which she seems to have bequeathed to her son—and at the junction of her lips there is a trace of irony. Picasso also painted his wife on several occasions, but above all he devoted himself to his son with his wide eyes, deep upper lip and dimple on his chin. He painted him in his white bonnet with fine black strokes and cyclamen-coloured flesh offset by an enamel-blue background. He painted him at the age of two sitting at a small table with his heavy head leaning over a sheet of paper. Another picture shows Paulo, somewhat unsteady on his small legs, taking a white lamb for a walk—and this portrait confirms him as the model for the Cupids in Picasso's classical scenes. In yet another picture the child, dressed in white clothing and bonnet, is sitting rather anxiously on a large donkey. The child is treated in large planes, but the donkey is painted with surprising attention to detail, including the rough hair on its back and the straps of the harness—and in fact Picasso was amusing himself by copying a photograph of his son. In flagrant contradiction to all his characteristics he seemed to be acquiring a curious taste for the conventional as though, having fled the commonplace for so long, he was now at moments finding a curious attraction in it.

But this was not the first time that Picasso had drawn from a photograph. One day, the photo of an unknown man fell into his hands. Among the sketches done in 1920 there is a scrupulously detailed drawing of this worthy personage leaning on a pedestal in a pose beloved of provincial photographers. Picasso seems to have devoted all his faculties to achieving the most commonplace style, but perhaps it was also a form of relaxation, like a crossword puzzle.

At this moment, when he was toying with all the possibilities that were open to him, the favourite themes of the past returned as though summoned by his prodigious facility. Starting in 1921, various drawings resumed the subject of the bull-fight. In a picture of 1923 which represents a corner of an arena with tiers of seats filled with spectators, Picasso painted a white horse on the point of collapse, its long neck stretched out and bared teeth rubbing in agony against the barrier. The stricken horse remained one of his permanent themes. Harlequins, too, resumed their place in his art, even creeping into his daily life. He painted his son at the age of three in a little costume of blue and yellow lozenges with a tulle ruff round his neck. The child is sitting, looking a trifle embarrassed, on a corner of a Louis-Philippe chair whose crushed velvet, braid and tassels often featured in pictures painted at that time.

161

The round, smooth face of the child with a fringe of reddish hair drawn in miniaturist style, the black eyes against the rose-pink flesh, the diminutive mouth of pale coral, are painted in exactly the same manner as Goya painted his grandson Mariano.

The glorified family circle which supplied him with his favourite themes also gave him his flower-crowned Venuses and his tender Cupids. In the course of innumerable drawings which he made in 1923, his nymphs acquire more ethereal grace, legs too short for long torsos resume their proportions, broad hips become more slender, brush-strokes become finer and Picasso's classical world rises up in perfect purity. At the same time the complementary personage of the faun made its appearance, representing animal lust confronting its object. With the *Flûte de Pan* and the *Trois Grâces* of the following year—themes prepared in innumerable drawings and engravings—Picasso reached the summit of his classical expression.

In this year of 1923 the refinement of colouring in his classical works was accompanied by an explosion of colour in his cubist paintings. The *Cage d'oiseaux* (collection of Mr. and Mrs. Victor S. Ganz, New York) is split up into small multicoloured planes ending in regular points like picot-edging on lacework, either light against a dark background or vice versa. The bars of the window, the branch and the bird are stylized after the fashion of popular embroidery and the whole has a curiously traditional air. Echoes of folklore often occur in Picasso's work, as though he had roots in every part of the world where a lively popular imagination has been active. *L'Homme à la guitare*, painted in the follow-year with brightly-coloured interlocking planes, has the same character.

A period in Picasso's art was drawing to a close and with him the abandonment of a manner; the end of a creative phase is as spectacular as a sunset. His extraordinary successes in the double sphere of cubism and classical antiquity necessarily led him to exhaust all their pos-sibilities. Gertrude Stein has explained this creative process: 'Picasso has always been obsessed with the need to empty himself, to empty himself completely, his whole life has been a repetition of this process of self-exhaustion. . . . Then people say that he has changed, but in fact this is not the case: he empties himself and at the moment he has finished emptying himself completely he has to start again, because he fills up again so quickly.'

CHAPTER XI 1923-1931

'Art is never Chaste'

THE curtain of the ballet *Mercure* was like an opening on a new world. Two of Picasso's familiar figures stood out against a twilight sky, a fat harlequin dressed in white and a red pierrot playing a game. But neither of them resembled their former counterparts. They were like phantoms of themselves, deformed silhouettes set vaguely within wide curves.

The ballet had been staged for the *Soirées de Paris* by the fashionable organizer, Count Étienne de Beaumont, but the entertainment presented to the public on 15th June, 1924, was less a ballet than a series of 'plastic poses' produced by Léonide Massine with music by Éric Satie. The preparatory studies for the costumes and the set had been conceived in the same style as the curtain, in shifting curves and contours which seemed to undulate under the eyes of the spectator, and it was this idea of movement which had primarily interested Picasso.

This was a period of revolt against all rigidity in art and literature. In its most spectacular form the revolt had originated during the war in neutral Switzerland under the inspiration of Romanian-born Tristan Tzara, a firebrand who concealed his energy beneath the gentle air of an absent-minded poet. Dadaism repudiated 'cubist and futurist academies, the laboratories of formal ideas'. In defeated Germany the movement tended to attract the hopes of those who had been disappointed by the revolution and aimed at social objectives, but in Cologne it assumed a special form under the impulse of the painter Max Ernst and preached the free use of the imagination without regard to subject-matter, the importance of the fortuitous and the exploration of the subconscious. After the war, Tzara transplanted dadaism to Paris and there other revolts were born of an anti-literary kind.

After a violent break with dadaism André Breton assumed the

leadership of a movement to which he gave the name invented by Apollinaire: surrealism. The violence, the scandals, the excesses, the powerful shocks inflicted on public apathy were to serve surrealism as they had served Dada. André Breton's aim was to liberate 'what lies unknown to man in the depths of his mind'. To release this material surrealism created zones of 'systematic dissociation' and had recourse to automatic writing and hypnotic sleep.

In 1924, André Breton launched his 'Surrealist Manifesto'. Picasso had met the writer at Cap d'Antibes in the previous year and had drawn a striking portrait of him of particularly subtle execution, showing his regular features, straight nose, long upper lip and fine head of hair. In this portrait Breton looked like a young god, with clear, hypnotic eyes such as Paul Éluard remembered when he called him 'one of the men who had most taught him to think'. But though Picasso got to know Breton and the other promoters of surrealism, the movement had no influence on his art. His own works featured in an exhibition organized by the surrealist painters in Paris in 1925, but purely by chance, having been lent by friendly owners. The lucidity which characterizes Picasso necessarily kept him aloof from a movement which glorified 'secondary states' and mental incoherence and was influenced by experiences undergone by Breton in a psychiatric clinic. As he himself has admitted, it was only much later that Picasso was tempted by the arbitrary quality of surrealist associations at a time when the painful circumstances of his private life opened the door to confusion.

The only influence derived from his contacts with the surrealists was also not revealed until later, and then not in his own proper sphere but in what was for him a minor exercise: his literary ventures. It was the surrealist poets and not the painters who influenced him, as though he found it easier to abandon a less important part of himself to contemporary pressures than his essential creativity.

Picasso's interest in calligraphy—which appeared in his work for *Mercure*—revived a permanent factor in his art, the Spanish element or, according to Gertrude Stein, his Moorish heritage. She has stressed the extent to which the taste for arabesque is linked in Spain, partly through the medium of Mudéjar art, with painting and sculpture. In Europe, she adds, written decorative embellishment is considered a minor creative activity, but for Picasso as a Spaniard 'the art of writing, that is, calligraphy, is an art'.

After the eclipse of Italian influences from which he profited to the maximum extent, the swing of the pendulum restored this permanent factor. 'The second Rose period,' wrote Gertrude Stein, 'finished naturally in the same way as the first, that is to say with the triumph of Spain.' The curtain and the set for *Mercure* showed the public the change in his style, the invasion of his art by simple penmanship. In his pictorial work it was revealed in still-life variations on the same theme. The choice of a new form of expression took place in him with such speed, and the old rectilinear composition was so close to the flowing curves that were now adopted that it was often used simultaneously. In 1924, the period of Picasso's most sumptuous still-lifes began. The forms acquired no depth, but they lost all rigidity, their contours became ill-defined and they began to overflow with luminous haloes, festooned shadows and fleeting arabesques, as in the *Nature morte* of 1924 (Saidenberg Gallery, New York).

The still-life *Guitare, Verre et Compotier avec fruits* (Kunsthaus, Zürich) also plays with explosions of light around objects which seem like phantoms of themselves. In the last days of 1924 he painted the sumptuous *Nature morte à la tranche de melon* (collection of Miss Micheline Rosenberg, New York) in which, perhaps for the first time, an element appeared which was to recur frequently in later pictures: a pedestal topped by a black classical head, standing on a red carpet.

Picasso at this time seems to have been eager for movement and the urge appeared suddenly in the large picture of *La Danse* (property of Picasso) of 1925. He had spent the spring of that year in Monte-Carlo where he had watched the Russian ballet in rehearsal, this time as a spectator. He made many drawings during the course of rehearsals of the graceful, sexless dancers with young muscular bodies and excessively small heads, depicting them in movement or at rest with a very pure continuous line and conveying shadow or relief with delicate pointillism in indian ink.

But in *La Danse* nothing remains of these young classical gods in the three dislocated silhouettes which stand out against an intense blue beyond an open french window: here the human body in movement is conveyed merely by signs, by fragments of reality glimpsed through a whirlwind. The dancer in the middle, with her mauve-pink body and a spot of white light on the raised breast, seems drawn out indefinitely as though the laws ruling the consistency of matter were abolished in her case. The neck and the junction of the arms with the body are elongated and thinned out like stretched elastic, while the knee and the biceps are squared off at an angle. The face, which is cursorily drawn in a rectangle, is pitted with one enormous vertical eye—a precursor of transformations to come in Picasso's manner. The brown and white silhouette on the right is constructed of slats of wood like the cubist harlequins. As in the *Demoiselles d'Avignon* the new element is only introduced into part of the picture. Compared with the dancer on the left the most revolutionary of the *Demoiselles* appears only moderately daring. When Picasso departs from the intelligible or the beautiful he swings immediately to the opposite extreme: the enigmatic and the monstrous. With the left-hand figure in *La Danse* monsters erupt into his work. They do so noisily, accompanied by a fanfare of colour. Cold, warm and violent blues, bright reds, strident yellows, greens and violets are accompanied by stripes, saw-toothed edges and violent wall-paper motifs. Against a patch of red which has unexpectedly found its way into the blue of the window a black door-handle stands out; this motif was to play an increasingly important part in Picasso's still-lifes, as though symbolizing access to a changed world.

With *La Danse* post-war neo-classicism and cubism came to an end at the same time in Picasso's painting. But though classical inspiration disappeared from his painting, it flourished and reflourished in full flower and still lasts in his drawings and engravings.

The frenzy of *La Danse* opened the door to a new world for Picasso, but at the same moment as he was trembling on the threshold he allowed visual reality to return to his pictures, as though anxious to allay the spectator's fears. According to René Huyghe, the still-lifes which he painted in that summer are among the most masterly of his works, those 'in which the sovereignty of the master appears through the paradoxes of his doctrine'. Though he now took up a number of new themes and accessories, the theme of the table in front of an open window with contrasting objects placed in the foreground was now less frequently employed and finally vanished altogether from his pictures. In its place, and as though to fill the gap, the theme of the studio arose. On a studio table pushed against a window stands a black bust etched in the pictorial manner representing perhaps the head of Homer (Museum of Modern Art, Paris). This bearded head on the studio table had come to stay, and the theme of the sculptor or of the painter facing his model was to remain a favourite one.

These visions of a studio, of which Picasso painted many versions

17   Picasso's palette

Salon d'Automne de la Libération, 1944

19 Picasso in 1944

at that time suggesting the solitude of creative work—such as *Le Buste* (Stephen O. Clark Collection, New York)—make it seem probable that Picasso was then devoting considerable interest, perhaps not unmixed with anxiety, to the problems of creation. This period of his life seems to have been particularly fraught with hesitation and his notebooks reflect the uneven rhythm of his anxiety. His stroke has become nervous and even when he was drawing a nude woman at rest his lines suggest a body tense with expectation. But beside these drawings, curious linear compositions appeared in his work at that time, all carefully dated and drawn with charcoal or a brush, and consisting of grids, stripes, jerky lines, circles and dots, like the *Nature morte aux étoiles* of February, 1925, or the *Nature morte aux clous* of March. These compositions reveal a thirst for austerity as a reaction to the sensuality of colouring and the attraction of movement which were then affecting him. Picasso was also fascinated by the abandonment of the figurative and the severity of compositions in which only form and colour divorced from reality played a part. In 1926 he filled a whole notebook with sketches in ink of a kind not yet seen in his work, consisting of intersecting straight lines reinforced by large black dots at the point of their junction and of parallel curves also ending in these full-stops. These drawings, of which sixteen were later engraved on wood and reproduced in the illustrated edition of Balzac's *Chef-d'oeuvre inconnu* published by Vollard in 1931, represented the most advanced point reached by Picasso in the direction of abstract art.

But this was not the first time that he had been tempted by the simplifications inherent in non-figurative drawing. Braque recalls: 'How many times did we not discuss, Picasso and I, the suppression of the subject. . . . But we quickly came to the conclusion that total indifference towards subject-matter would have led us immediately to an incomplete form of art,' and he adds: 'Abstract art has not accepted the truth that, by the mere fact of their existence, objects provoke new states of mind in the artist.'

In his reaction to the violence of movement and colouring which exploded in a canvas like *La Danse* of 1925, Picasso began to make use of the most humble and commonplace materials. One day, he noticed a floorcloth lying in the bathroom. In a spirit of defiance, perhaps, he determined to make use of this nondescript object. He fixed the cloth to a canvas with nails driven through the frame, stuck a strip of newspaper beside it and stretched two pieces of string across a hole made in

M

the middle of the rag. According to Zervos, this *Guitar* of 1926 (property of Picasso) is one of the first object-pictures known, but psychologically and almost physically it upsets the spectator—a prelude to the agonies which Picasso's future works were to provoke.

In the torment which beset Picasso at that time and to which he gave diverse and unexpected expression, there was a sexual element, an obsession which may have been previous to his distress and even its precipitating cause. On a sheet of an album dating from 1925 appears a phallic symbol accompanied by two breasts with upturned tips and a navel. The whole suggests a fabulous beast escaped from a medieval bestiary, it is as obscene as an apocalyptic vision. 'Art is never chaste,' Picasso said to me one day. 'It ought to be forbidden to the ignorant and the innocent; those who are not sufficiently prepared should never be brought in contact with it. Yes, art is dangerous. Or if it is chaste it is not art.' Picasso said this in a conversation where he seemed to be joking, enjoying the fireworks of his usual sallies, smiles puckering the corners of his eyes. But suddenly his face hardened and became very sombre. His sexual obsession has always been and still is the fertilizer of his inspiration, becoming accentuated or appeased in artistic expression, glorifying forms when desire is fulfilled and destroying them when his masculine urges revive. During those years, destructive rage was paramount. The universe which he then constructed according to his appetites was, as Cassou has said, a hypothetical universe, the *Welt als ob* of German philosophy. A return to monochrome underlined its particular character. The spectral curves of the *Atelier de la modiste* (National Museum of Modern Art, Paris) emerge from a twilight world. The forms are kept fluid as though Picasso were anxious to prevent them conveying the least impression of depth. Arms float like ribbons, ball-like faces are split up by the lighting, bodies are like festoons, lights and shadows undulate as though they were spirals of smoke. This nocturne may be difficult to decipher, but it is a reflection of something actually seen. The strange choice of subject is explained by the fact that, from his apartment in the Rue La Boétie, Picasso could gaze directly into a workshop across the way and see customers and *modistes* moving to and fro behind the windows.

In *Le Peintre et son modèle* or *L'Atelier* (Museum of Modern Art, New York) Picasso's phantoms move in a monochromatic world, but one in which violent contrasts of light and shade split up the forms within firm outlines which are independent of them. These visions also emerge between brightly-coloured planes framed by curves like lead in a stained-glass window. In this period Picasso's phantoms became monsters; some critics have spoken of figures 'totally re-invented'. It has also been called the period of 'abstractions', an inaccurate description, but one which Picasso, who is indifferent to interpretations of his art, has allowed to subsist. A more useful term for classification purposes is 'metamorphoses'. Cassou has put his finger on the main quality which projects Picasso so abruptly into the unknown when he speaks of his heroism, for 'the hero has no memory and does not sustain the image of a continuous personality'. But this suggests that there is nothing permanent in Picasso, whereas in fact anxiety is constantly with him. It may be concealed from time to time by a period of reduced vitality or allayed by a temporary re-conciliation with life, but it soon surges up again stronger than ever.

'Picasso tries to persuade me,' wrote Gertrude Stein, 'that I am as unhappy as he is.' This basic feeling of distress is the very core of his creativity. Periods when he came to terms with life, such as the Rose and the Classical periods, are only passing phases and the longer they last, the more violent the explosion of accumulated resentment which follows them. The period of metamorphoses which began about 1926 represents a return of the familiar anxieties which find expression in a new form of monster.

There is also in Picasso an obscure impulse to take revenge on faces he has loved or bodies he has desired. But this avenging instinct, a sort of disgust with the eternal betrayal of nature which offers a mirage of the beautiful to lull the vigilance of the mind, is not unique to Picasso. The caricatures of Leonardo, the monsters of Bosch and Goya or those conjured by the image-carvers of Flanders were engendered by the same disgust. Only the form of his monsters is peculiar to Picasso.

In *Le Peintre et son modèle* of 1927 (private collection) appears a deformed creature with asymmetrical eyes, scanty hair, sunken breasts and strongly defined sexual organs. Picasso's sexual obsession thrusts its way into his work in the most unexpected fashion. The *Femme endormie dans un fauteuil* of January, 1927 (property of Picasso), inaugurates a series of women whom he surprises in an abandoned attitude. Among the distinctive features of these female monsters are elongated muzzles like the nostrils of a horse, mouths in the form of a circle planted with teeth or blocked with vertical bars, pendulous breasts and hands with crossed fingers in the form of laces or nails. *L'Atelier* (Museum of Modern Art, New York), which dates from 1927-8, is an isolated application of a new formula. Picasso was striving at that time to vary his plastic expression as though to seize a truth which escaped him or could only be translated in part. 'He alone among painters,' wrote Gertrude Stein, 'did not set himself the problem of expressing truths which all the world can see, but the truth which only he can see—and this is not a world which the world recognizes as a world.'

In the experiments made according to his own particular vision of truth, *L'Atelier* was to serve as a point of departure for three-dimensional linear constructions, sculptures in wire. Representing a reaction to excess, these in turn, however, were to provoke violent reactions springing from a taste for contrast. During the summer of 1927 which Picasso spent in Cannes he covered innumerable pages of his notebook with charcoal drawings so strongly modelled that they seemed to represent sculptures or be preparatory studies for sculptures of his own—sculptures in wood whose characteristic texture the drawings reproduced. The principal theme of these isolated figures is men and women bathers caught in various positions at the moment when they are inserting a key in the door of a bathing hut. The linear deformations usual at this time persist in these monsters carved or turned in wood.

The desire to convey a three-dimensional effect in these drawings was not a mere game for Picasso, nor another change in his pictorial technique. Barely aware of any limits to what he might achieve, he was thinking at that time of translating his visions into sculptural terms. He imagined a series of monuments to be erected along the Croisette in Cannes, anthropomorphic figures symbolizing the cleavage separating man-made structures from free organic growth, and creating a link between nature and the surrounding architecture.

In August, 1928, Picasso returned to Dinard. The picture which he painted there on 5th August—he had started dating his small pictures again—still had the three-dimensional modelling. A human body is represented by stalks supporting a small convex disc. Far removed from reality though the symbols were which he invented to convey the human body, the pictures he painted did represent what he had seen: people sun-bathing, games on the shore, bathers putting keys into cabin doors—this key which plays such an important part in Picasso's' imagination. In one of two pictures painted on 9th August Picasso's sexual obsession finds new expression in a female form surmounted by a horse's head, the long neck planted on a rounded rump. Like certain others of his nudes, the *Baigneuse couchée* of 28th August gives the measure of his sexual frenzy which made one continual amorous adventure of his private life and of his art a means of freeing himself of his obsession. The picture suggests a positive fury of desire and only the deformation of the figure prevents it from featuring among the artistic products of erotic delirium.

Whereas Picasso's cubist inventions were sometimes like prisms assembled under a kaleidoscope, his Dinard visions resembled those glass balls which you shake to create an artificial snow-storm obscuring the details of a small scene imprisoned inside. His sexual obsession remained one of the main elements of this agitation, but despite the exaggerated depiction of the sexual attributes of some of the women in the Dinard pictures, others, with arms and feet like oars or paddles, seem to represent merely the *joie de vivre* felt in running or playing a game.

The so-called 'Dinard period' petered out through the very excess of its own dynamism. Picasso now suddenly returned to sculpture which he had abandoned since the *Verre d'absinthe* of 1914. The sculptures in iron wire which he made on his return from Dinard are almost abstract constructions, diagrams projected in three-dimensional space. Their rectangles, triangles and spoked wheels are motionless, but they are designed as a whole to capture movement from the changing sky and shifting light, an aim which was pursued by con-structivist sculptors. This sculptural vision of Picasso's, which was entirely geometrical, was then close to his pictorial vision and was sometimes identical with it.

Convex oval plaques placed on a tripod show the same extreme schematization of human forms as *L'Atelier* of 1928 where the body is conveyed simply by an arrow, or *L'Artiste et son modèle* (Sidney Janis Collection, New York) where two-dimensional heads have saw-toothed edges and eyes placed one above the other.

On these women-objects, like the *Baigneuse debout* of 1929 (property of Picasso), Picasso lavished all the richness of his palette. His purely pictorial abilities have often been questioned, and even his most fervent admirers have drawn attention to the clash of violent colours which characterizes his periods of transition, his recourse to monochrome in his greatest pictures and the supremacy of form over colouring in his most important works. But nothing is ever exactly right or completely wrong in what is said about Picasso, and the bathing women who appear in his painting from 1929 onwards are the best evidence of his extraordinary pictorial sensitivity.

Meanwhile, his dummies with female attributes were acquiring an increasingly robot appearance. Ducks' heads were replaced by a hammer with two holes for the eyes, and these robots are the most fearsome of all Picasso's creatures. This man of unsatisfied passions who is always seeking to make new conquests, for ever greedy and for ever disenchanted, is a misogynist who rarely and then only temporarily forgives the women who have enslaved him by desire. All that an exasperated individual can find to abuse women Picasso has expressed in his painting. The mechanisms which are labelled female are mechanisms of destruction. The hammer-head did not sufficiently convey their baneful power; he gives them a pincer-head with the two arms terminating in sharpened points, the better to crush their victim.

Even in moments of despair—and perhaps in those moments more than ever—Picasso's ambitions were inordinate. The *Baigneuses* belong to that borderland between painting and sculpture which fascinated artists of the period and induced Braque, Gris or Léger to make isolated experiments. But Picasso was not content to introduce sculptural forms into his painting. He dreamt of monuments which, like his women-crushers-of-men, would have the whole sky as background. To a man whose principal characteristic was to invade all frontiers and exceed all the norms of life and art, it seemed natural to think of women's heads set up by the Mediterranean as human habitations. One of these architectual projects minutely elaborated in 1929 represents a bare block of houses with slanting elevations and, fitted over one of them, an immense rectangular frame. In the middle of this frame a huge vertical window stands out in relief, lined with sharp-pointed teeth. High up on the building two round holes simulate the eyes and three wavy lines indicate hair blowing in the breeze. This house-in-the-form-of-a-head is catalogued in Picasso's works under the title, *Femme au sourire*.

None of Picasso's architectural projects has been realized. 'The only creative thing in a creator,' said Gertrude Stein, 'is the contemporary thing, but in daily life it is a different matter.' She relates that a friend who had had a modern house built for himself suggested that Picasso should do the same. 'No, I certainly won't,' he replied. 'I want an old house. Do you think that Michelangelo would have been pleased if someone had given him a fine piece of Renaissance furniture? Not at all. He would have been pleased if he had been given a beautiful Greek sculpture, obviously.'

At the time when he seemed to be exclusively preoccupied with his monsters, he gave proof of the acuity of his visual memories by painting his son at the age of four in the costume of a pierrot (property of Picasso) just as he had painted him in his calmer period. In fact, the child was eight when the father made this new portrait. It was a strange idea to retrace the course of time, like conjuring an apparition, and in the picture the figure has the shadowlessness and weightlessness of a ghost. He stands, white and vaporous, with a bouquet in one hand and a stick topped with flowers in the other. With this souvenir portrait or this regret for a grace that was no more, it seems that the series of portraits of the son who in his early childhood had so often served him as model came to an end.

Nostalgia for gracefulness persisted in Picasso. In his notebooks monsters jostled with the purest of classical evocations, but these were reserved for his engravings which now established a separate identity from his pictorial work. He returned to engraving by pure chance. Vollard introduced him to an expert engraver, and Picasso set to work without knowing exactly what subject he would choose. A woman's face appeared, half in shadow, half in brilliant light. Then he drew a bull-fight and once in the Spanish atmosphere encountered the shades of Goya who is never completely absent from his art. He conceived the idea of illustrating the *Tauromaquia* of Pepe Hillo, the great hero of the bull ring in Goya's time. Then he abandoned the project for a time.

But during the course of these distressful years and at this turning-point of 1927 when he was preoccupied with the problems of creation, Picasso's attention concentrated on another subject, that of the relation between the painter and his model, between inspiration and the human being who stimulates it. He engraved the plate, *Le Peintre observé par le modèle nu*, introducing a figure which henceforth was to appear only in his engravings, a bearded artist with a head like Zeus, a curious projection of himself who in the picture is painting the nude with his back turned to the model. Several of these plates were used by Vollard to illustrate Balzac's *Chef-d'oeuvre inconnu* which he published in 1931. The work has been considered by the more competent American critics, including Alfred Barr, as 'one of the most remarkable books of our time', and the illustrations represent a kind of cross-section through Picasso's work as well as a key to the artistic history of the period. Speaking of the public reaction to the book, Vollard notes in his memoirs: 'Each new work of Picasso's scandalizes until the moment comes when astonishment gives way to admiration.'

In the same year of 1930, Picasso received another commission, this time from Albert Skira, to produce illustrations for Ovid's *Metamorphoses*. Once more Picasso revived his classical vein. With very few exceptions the illustrations avoid all excess, all brutal accents, any interruption of the fluid curves and the unity of the drawing. The plates for the *Metamorphoses* seem to express complete serenity.

Picasso was fifty when he engraved them. His fierce appetites seemed to be appeased, but he was in fact only on the threshold of his great adventures. Materially the period of struggle was long since over. He had arrived and the degree of prosperity he had achieved was marked by the purchase of an estate, the Château de Boisgeloup near Gisors. One would have expected material security to react on his state of mind, but there was no trace of this. The very diversity of his work showed that the old torment was still alive and continued to ravage him. With his friend Gonzalez he continued his experiments in curious iron-wire constructions, half way between the human and the vegetal. Other experiments in sculpture or semi-sculpture were made in the summer of 1930 at Juan-les-Pins and date from the same period as the *Metamorphoses*, such as *L'Objet à la feuille de palmier* or *L'Objet au gant*, both of surrealist, or rather dadaist inspiration, the latter consisting of a long glove filled with bran against a background in bas-relief. Picasso's continuing anxiety was also revealed in the choice of new subject-matter. Hitherto, religious themes had little attracted him, at best his Virgins were apprehensive mothers, but from 1929 onwards he began making sketches for a Crucifixion, at the same time continuing to draw nudes and classical profiles.

Though he did draw inspiration from existing art, it is curious that Picasso did not turn to Spanish representations of the drama of Golgotha, perhaps because they were too familiar to him. One of the friends of his youth said of him: 'Picasso sees nothing from nature, but only through the representations of objects made by other artists.'

Though this comment was deliberately malicious like many passed on famous men by the friends of their youth, it contains a kernel of truth which Picasso himself has expressed: 'What is basically a painter? He is a collector who aims to form a collection by himself, painting the pictures of other artists which he likes. That is how I begin, then the picture becomes something different.'

In reality, the pictures of the masters released a very personal creative spring in him. One of his first attempts at copying—which also became 'something different'—was of the central panel in the altar at Isenheim, by Mathias Grünewald. After making a number of sketches, Picasso painted his *Crucifixion* on a small wooden panel in brilliant colours, accentuating still further the distortions he inflicted on the work which inspired him. The contorted figures which he reduced or enlarged inordinately in size allied to the vivid, contrasting colours make the drama of Calvary seem like a formal explosion of violence as distinct from the inward feeling of desolation which characterizes the altar at Isenheim. In the final analysis, Picasso's *Crucifixion* merely reflects the agitation and agony which were in himself and were seeking an outlet. 'Picasso's despair is total,' wrote Claude Roger-Marx, and it is to this period of his life as much as to the infinite variety of his means of expression that might best be applied this other penetrating criticism: 'Despite the endless discussion which his frenzied production has provoked, it could well be that, one day, the very fact of his existence might be doubted, like Shakespeare's, and that all that has seen the light of day in the course of half a century might be attributed to different hands.'

CHAPTER XII 1931–1935

The Minotaur

IT WAS a Sunday afternoon, 24th January, 1932. Picasso wrote the date on the frame of the picture, as though it was particularly important to him.

The picture known as *Le Rêve* (collection of Mr. and Mrs. Victor S. Ganz, New York) represents a woman in a chair overcome with sleep in such an attitude of abandon that she hardly seems even to be dreaming, any more than succulent plants have dreams. With its soft yet resistant consistency, its matt surface and its green colour touched with a silvery bloom, her large body looks, in fact, like some juicy plant. The attenuated green turns in the shadows to mauve and gives the bare flesh an appearance of close texture and transparency. The liveliness of the colouring contrasts with the harmony of the lines; the violent red of the chair clashes with the green of the window; the freshness of the silvery flesh tones is counterbalanced by the warm brown of the curtain.

Le Rêve marks a new stage in Picasso's work and on the threshold stands a tall, very fair girl with a clear skin and a fresh smile. Picasso had met her in the street and everything about her captivated him: her youth, her figure, her fairness, her lively temperament, her gay and uncomplicated character. Marie-Thérèse Walter was sufficiently carefree not to worry what future there might be in their liaison and reasonable enough to be satisfied with a marginal position in the life of a man who was married to a jealous spouse who attached great importance to her wifely prerogatives. For Olga Picasso was not only jealous in the present, which was beset by continual alarms, but also of her husband's past. Against all the evidence, she had taken the improbable decision to ignore it, apparently being endowed with a peculiar ability to disregard whatever was distasteful to her. The mere mention by Gertrude Stein of the name Fernande Olivier, of whom Olga had not yet heard, was enough to make her turn pale and leave the room in a fury, and it was a year before she would set foot again in the house of the American woman who she believed had insulted her in her dignity as the legitimate spouse. Resolved to ignore Picasso's past and his amorous present, she succeeded in building an imaginary world for herself in which she reigned as absolute sovereign.

Marie-Thérèse was content to live in the shadows remote from the susceptible Olga, but she triumphantly invaded Picasso's work in a way which left no doubt as to the nature of her association with him. A picture dated 16th December, 1931, *Le Fauteuil rouge*, marks one of the first of these intrusions. It is also a striking example of a face seen simultaneously head-on and in profile. From now on this simultaneous treatment became frequent in Picasso's pictures, as though he was particularly struck by the contrast between the girl's severe profile with the high-bridged nose falling straight in line with the forehead and the soft impression of her full face with its broad eyes, small mouth and ample chin. This double visage is painted white, the yellow hair falls in an uninterrupted cascade and the body is divided into segments of a circle which intersect to form the shape of a heart. These rolling curves and rounded segments are typical of all the pictures which reflect the blind presence of Marie-Thérèse. Amidst no matter what distortions, Picasso seems to reproduce a characteristic attitude of his model, the attitude of women who love to coil up and warm themselves with their own femininity, like leaves protecting a bud or the pulp of fruit enclosing the kernel. The white face in its double aspect stands out against violently coloured planes of opaque greens, violets and browns contrasting with strident yellow and orange. But it is not only when she is present in the canvas that we find rolling curves and the juxtaposition of pure colours. The whole of Picasso's plastic vision took on this rocking rhythm and this undulating intoxication of tones.

In the *Nature morte sur le guéridon* dated 11th March, 1931 (property of Picasso) everything is in waves, even the mouldings on the wall, as though stirred by a breeze. The impression is so strong that the forms seem to move before one's eyes: a pitcher seems like a curving hip in the act of stretching, a fruit-bowl seems to be melting in an attitude of obeisance, fruit is caught in the act of levitation off a plate, the acidulous yellow of the pitcher is climbing up towards a warm cyclamen mauve, reds are closing round green cores. Only a black stroke prevents a periwinkle blue or a jade green from flowing over like quicksilver on to the white of the canvas.

Since they must have a name, the pictures of this period are grouped under the title, 'Curved Graphism'. The expression only covers the manner of drawing, it reveals nothing of the animation which then reigned in Picasso's pictures. The repose of the blonde woman whom Picasso painted reclining and often asleep is a repose which excited him and he deliberately made exciting in the form of waves circulating round the body. In one of these recumbent nudes, consisting of inter-twining arms and enormous thighs and breasts, the wall-paper in the background is patterned with violently undulating lines which seem to emanate from the body itself like an electric discharge.

Though curves seem to appear in Picasso's painting at the same time as the fair-haired girl they are not his only means of conveying her. 'As on every occasion when he forms a lasting attachment,' notes Sabartés, 'each of his previous manners leaves some trace in his canvases.' Now he painted the young woman in the style of past distortions, seeming to lead her through the successive stages of his art, making her take part in his own story as though she had always been at his side and he wanted, as the supreme gift to the woman he loved, to endow her with a permanent presence. By this process he also aimed, as Sabartés adds, 'to evaluate the influence which a new source of inspiration might have on him'.

In this sort of artistic pilgrimage on which he took his young friend he also led her to the three-dimensional monsters which closed the Dinard period. The games on the beach which he now painted in no sense represented current reality even in their background of sea and sky. They were merely artistic reminiscences, summer-time memories revived in the middle of winter and filled with a new presence. The *Baigneuse jouant au ballon* with her enormous legs of turned wood has penguin's flippers instead of arms and the head of a golf club with a duck's eye in the middle, but this is not a return to an abandoned field either, but rather an excursion to a site revisited in good company. But the three-dimensional vision was constant with Picasso. As always, he needed a combination of favourable outward circumstances before he could completely release a creative vein. He had quickly suppressed effects of perspective in his painting by establishing a single dimension and his struggles with relief, replaced at the time of cubism by a prismatic vision, had been equally violent and destructive. But the nostalgia for three-dimensional forms, which he had fought for so long, remained in him and burst out at times in his paintings before becoming an independent means of expression.

The purchase of the Boisgeloup estate enabled him to find the best possible solution to his material problems. He transformed the huge stables of the château into a studio where he could do large-scale sculptural work. The meeting with Marie-Thérèse crystallized another aspect of his creative process. For her and through her he invented his purely linear mode of presentation in wide curves, reproducing the slow movements of her body and coloured planes which best conveyed the luminous tints of her skin and hair. But the strong lines of her head with the broad-bridged nose and her firm, slim body with its well-proportioned limbs were particularly well suited to sculpture. Thus external circumstances were at that time so favourable that his sculptural mastery which was now revealed seemed like a spontaneous development.

The *Tête de femme* in gilded bronze was interpreted in the purest classical spirit, as though it were the result of long effort and not one of his first attempts. It was a portrait of Marie-Thérèse and no doubt a very good likeness, but it was also her apotheosis. The bust was the starting point for all sorts of interpretations which placed her young face on a par with the eternal goddesses.

Picasso as an innovator, a revolutionary and a destroyer has always been much discussed, but perhaps his attachment to the past has not been sufficiently stressed; his facility in creating forms close to those which were born when man's faith or terror conjured images encouraging him in his enjoyment of life or his fear of death. Among the completely new forms which Picasso has created are some which one feels obscurely must have existed at some time and place in the distant past, and it is only one's forgetfulness which makes it impossible to say precisely when and where. Perhaps the large-nosed, bulging-eyed women whom he sculpted at this time at Boisgeloup were based on the ancient goddesses of fertility with a cornucopia growing out of their foreheads. At any rate, though Picasso had made hardly any attempts at sculpture for nearly twenty-five years, he now showed that he possessed all the techniques as though he had never ceased to perfect them.

In June, 1932, with the first great retrospective exhibition of his pictorial work in Paris and Zürich, a new chapter seemed to be opening in Picasso's life. The success of the exhibition might have persuaded him to turn his attention more exclusively to sculpture— acclaim in one sphere often has the effect of making him turn to another —but instead a passion for engraving seized hold of him. Starting in 1930, he had begun to execute the series of engravings on classical themes commissioned by Vollard. The major part of this work, about one hundred plates, was performed in 1933 and 1934. Two main themes were represented in it. The first, 'The Sculptor's Studio', comprised forty-five plates. But there was a series of four further plates where the subject was due to chance. 'I had a plate to which an accident had happened,' he told Kahnweiler. 'I said to myself, it is ruined, I will just scribble anything on top of it. I began to scratch and it turned into Rembrandt. I even did another one of him, with his turban, his furs and his eye—that elephant's eye.'

The plate began indeed with a sort of doodle, those little circles that the hand traces on a sheet of paper when the mind is wandering. Taken together, they suggest a large crumbling face. But chance alone would not have summoned this vision of Rembrandt if there had not been some connection between the principal theme of Picasso's work —the relation between the creator and his model—and this forceful, ageing man who stands with a small palette in his large hand con- fronting a handsome nude.

The atmosphere of erotic excitement increased while Picasso was doing these engravings, and in five plates of April and November, 1933, he resumed a theme familiar to his sexual obsession, 'Le Viol'. It was then that a symbol of violence and animal lust rose before his eyes, the Minotaur, the fabulous creature that seems to reconcile Spain and Antiquity. 'Picasso's Minotaur,' wrote Kahnweiler, 'which carouses, loves and fights is Picasso himself. It is a symbol of his naked soul. He identifies himself with it completely.'

The Minotaur series reached its culminating point in 1935 in one of the most important of Picasso's engravings: La Minotauromachie. This large plate, measuring 19½ by 27 inches, is engraved by a mixed process with particular care and to some extent represents the conclusion of the series after the manner of actors taking their bow before the foot- lights at the end of a tragedy. Through twilight the Minotaur advances menacingly, one formidable human arm raised, with an evil look in his small eye and his nostrils wide open. At his approach a bearded man dressed only in a loincloth quickly climbs a ladder. But a small girl with a large head topped by a beret, a bouquet of flowers in one hand and a candle in the other, faces the monster calmly. The candle lights up a terrifying spectacle: a horse has fallen, its intestines spilling from a mortal wound. Its head with bared teeth is turned towards a woman matador who has collapsed over its back. Her pure and handsome profile stands out against the horse's flank, her breasts have burst from her torn clothing, but she still holds a sword in her hand. Above this scene of violence and consciously remote from it, the very picture of human indifference, two women, with two pigeons perched on the sill, appear at an open window and contemplate the scene. On the low horizon in the background a becalmed sail appears on the sea. In this engraving all classical memories have faded before a picture of Spain, the Spain of bull-fights, or mortally wounded horses, of fair women spectators and of child-heroes. In the light of future events, the *Minotauromachie* is seen as a pathos-laden presentiment; it not only recalls the actors at the end of a tragedy or reflects the present, it contains most of the elements in Picasso's future masterpiece: *Guernica*.

The violence of this plate accentuated by the sharp contrasts of light and shadow is the more surprising in that it followed the calmest of Picasso's engravings: the six etchings illustrating *Lysistrata*, which was published in a limited edition in New York in 1934. In the summer of 1934 he took a long journey through Spain, passing through Irun and stopping at San Sebastian. From Madrid he took the woman he loved to see the treasures of Spanish art at the Escurial and Toledo. In the previous year he had introduced Marie-Thérèse Walter to the environment of his childhood in Barcelona. This pilgrimage reveals Picasso's particular conception of fidelity to himself, a feeling which so well accords in his mind with his need for change that he believes he can serve the present through memories of the past. At the very first contact with Spain the theme of the bull-fight came to the fore again and was represented in numerous pictures in 1934, as well as circus scenes which also seemed to be revived by an association of memories.

Eager for any experiment, Picasso even tried drawing in the dark, but the abandonment of consciousness involved in this form of automatic writing did not appeal to his lucid mentality. Surrealist incoherence was equally foreign to him, and though in that year of 1933 he did draw legs without feet balancing weights and arms emerging from closed windows, he did not share Lautréamont's conception of beauty as consisting in 'the fortuitous encounter on an operating table of a sewing-machine and an umbrella', and he himself attributed what was to him a painful lapse to the distressing circumstances of his private life: 'serious conjugal difficulties'. Other 'fortuitous encounters' seem to be represented in a page of drawings entitled 'Anatomy' where various objects, including chairs, a table, a ladder and a cushion seem to be walking about like human beings.

As soon as the conflicts in his private life became acute his creative activity slowed down. Nevertheless, during this period which was devoted especially to engraving, Picasso was haunted by grandiose visions, as though tiring of successes in a restricted field which seemed too facile for his creative ability. And no doubt he felt the need to reach beyond his personal problems towards a new plastic vision, the need also to make closer contact with his age and with the preoccupations of humanity. Long before he became embroiled in politics, Picasso, though seemingly absorbed in his struggle with the forms of artistic expression, paid close attention to everything that went on around him and to the clash of ideas in the world.

But for the time being private anxieties absorbed him entirely, provoking what must have been the severest crisis which he has had to undergo in his artistic career. The difficulties inherent in the double life which he believed he was able to lead now burst into the open in his own home. Picasso fled the storms, knowing how damaging they could be to his activity, and took refuge at Boisgeloup where, towards the end of 1934 and in early 1935, he drew and painted a series of pictures revealing the nostalgia he felt for a peaceful home life—girls reading, writing or drawing, their eyes lowered over their work, while other female figures recline, overcome with sleep, on a table.

In these pictures no trace is left of the sensuality of exhausted women. Nothing suggests desire or the lust for smooth flesh. The soothing rhythm of curves has also disappeared, replaced by angles and sharp points. The young ladies have crescent-shaped faces, without backs to their heads, and the noses protrude at an angle from excessively low foreheads. The bodies flow between abrupt lines, the breasts jut out like small unripe apples and the hands are in the form of palm leaves or immense ears of grain.

But despite his desire to avoid them, circumstances forced Picasso to take serious decisions. Marie-Thérèse Walter was expecting a child. He started proceedings for divorce. During that summer of 1935 he stayed in Paris for the first time for thirty years. His wife had left the conjugal domicile. 'I am alone in the house,' he wrote to Sabartés. 'You can guess what has happened and what I am in for now. . . .' Though Picasso disliked clandestine love affairs and needed a woman continually in his life, and though he challenged conventional morality by advertising his desires, he was at the same time revolted by all outside interference in his private life. The stir created by a divorce, particularly by one as stormy as his own, terrified him and he was deeply hurt when the lawyers of the opposing party started rummaging in his affairs. The proceedings naturally led to sordid quarrels over money. When the divorce was finally pronounced it brought him no relief; Picasso had kept his Spanish nationality and divorce does not exist in Spain. He could neither marry the young woman who was expecting a child by him nor give his name to the child. The proceedings had disgusted him. Despite the brusqueness which he likes to parade he is extremely vulnerable. Even when carried to excess, his rough manners, the vein of cruelty he show sometimes in breaking off friendships or conveying a refusal spring from a particularly sensitive nature.

Malicious insinuations, unhealthy curiosity and treacherous demands —his pictures were seized as guarantee that alimony would be paid— upset him to such a degree that a spring seemed to be broken in him.

'He refused to set foot in his studio,' Sabartés recalls. 'The mere sight of his pictures and drawings exasperated him, for every one of them recalled something of the recent past and every memory was an unhappy one.' This crisis in his creative activity was not only due to disgust at what had happened to him: his basic integrity as a creative artist obliged him to use all his powers and he disliked working when he felt that he was not at his best. The troubles of his private life had shaken his self-assurance. The result was that he suddenly stopped painting. 'For two years,' wrote Gertrude Stein, 'he painted and drew nothing. It is extraordinary that a man can stop doing what he has done all his life, but that can happen. It still astonishes me that Shakespeare never took up his pen again once he had stopped writing, and other cases are known where something has happened to destroy all that has forced a human being to exist. But does an identity which depends on things which have been made continue to exist or not?' On the whole, yes, she concludes. 'A genius is a genius even when he is not working.' But the urge to express themselves still torments those who are blessed or cursed with creative talent when they find it suddenly blocked. They then look for a secondary means, a side-road which can cheat their distress. Picasso found his. He began to write. For a long time he was reluctant to show what he had written. 'A kind of bashfulness restrained him,' relates Sabartés. 'A kind of fear or timidity has always been apparent in him which makes him hesitate to show anything new that he has done.'

Picasso wrote in Spanish. His pictorial language was obviously international, it bore no particular local imprint, but at moments of heightened tension his native idiom, compounded of distant memories and impressions which he himself believed he had forgotten, was expressed in his work. Spanish had remained in him like virgin soil that had never been ploughed. Suddenly, the poor primary-school scholar, the man whom his friends claimed never to have seen with a book in his hand, began to write 'in a very polished literary style'. He wrote poems, painter's poems consisting of colours aligned on the paper without any link between them. Picasso was still obsessed with colour and he wrote his poems with multicoloured pencils until the pages of his manuscript looked like 'a parrot's plumage'.

The surrealist influence which he would not admit into his pictures dominated his poetry. He could easily have painted the separate visual sensations which he traced in words on the paper, but in that case he would have subjected the isolated fragments of reality to pictorial laws which he had indeed revolutionized, but which still existed for him. But in writing he allowed his thoughts to wander, bringing diverse elements together through an association of ideas. 'His writings were never his writings,' wrote Gertrude Stein. 'After all, the egoism of a painter is not at all the egoism of a writer. There is nothing more to be said, it simply isn't.'

Writing became a passion with Picasso, one of those violent and ephemeral passions which blossom in sterile days. 'He did not mind where he wrote,' notes Sabartés, 'on the corner of a table or a piece of furniture, the arm of a chair or on his knee. . . . So long as nobody moved. . . . As soon as he was alone he brought out his notebook and started writing; if someone disturbed him he would hide it and frown: "What is it?" He shut himself up in his room or in the lavatory to be sure that there at least no one would come and look for him.'

His childhood friend and confidant, whom he often used as a sounding-board and who had just returned to Europe after spending

some years in South America, received the first-fruits of Picasso's
literary efforts while their author was still uncertain and almost ashamed
at trying to compete with his friends the poets. In September, 1935,
Picasso sent some of his work to Sabartés in Madrid, writing in his
letter: 'The hours fall into the well and remain asleep for ever, every
clock that sounds its bell knows what it is and has no illusions.'

To start with, Picasso separated the phrases in his poems by longer
and shorter dashes; later, he abandoned all punctuation and capital
letters. One day, he even conceived the idea of no longer separating
the words. The objection that intelligibility would thereby be made
even more difficult seemed not to deter him, but on reflection he
realized that there were limits to innovation which he could not
exceed.

Carried away by his enthusiasm, he then risked writing in French.
When Sabartés pointed out some spelling mistakes he replied calmly:
'So what? It's by the mistakes that you recognize personality, *mon
vieux*. If I start correcting the mistakes you mention according to rules
that have no relation to myself, my own distinctive note will be lost
in grammar which I have not assimilated.'

Whether written in Spanish or in French, Picasso's poems bear
witness to his visual acuity:

Une main au bord de l'ombre fait de l'ombre à la main. . . .

or:

Le soleil-lumière dans le blanc découpe un loup étincelant. . . .

But as Gertrude Stein said: 'For him who could write so well with
strokes and colours, writing with words was not writing at all. And
Picasso knew this well enough.'

A photograph taken of him in 1935 shows him with a broad face,
heavy chin, vertical lines between the frowning eyebrows and an
expression about the mouth, unusual for him, of resentment. He looks
like a man who is sulking his way through life. And yet in that same
year his Spanish soul was delighted by the birth of a daughter. He gave
her the name of Maria de la Conception. She was called Maïa.

To Picasso, this child was like a second miracle and, being exiled
from his other home, he was the more anxious to take personal care
of her. 'One day,' wrote Sabartés, 'being absolutely determined to do
something different, he set to washing nappies—that, at least, had
nothing whatsoever to do with his previous occupations.' The child
had fair hair, a clear skin bursting with health and her mother's blue

eyes. But one day she would come to look strangely like her father, she would have his impulsiveness, his sudden changes of mood and the vitality exuding from every pore that makes other people seem bloodless. Sabartés writes that in looking after her when the child was still small and confining himself to material matters, her father found both satisfaction in physical effort and, as he was so pleased to be close to her, 'the advantage of not seeing undesirable figures around him'.

At the beginning of 1935, Sabartés and his wife came at Picasso's request to live with him. To a man accustomed to a female presence the empty house seemed too forlorn, and to underline the fact Picasso had covered the second twin bed with newspapers. Picasso, who had just reached the age of fifty, was now to live with the same close observer of his activities as he had had in his early youth. Among the Boswells of the world Jaime Sabartés holds a place apart. With his unusual receptivity and his very personal viewpoint he is an authentic poet, and when he reports events, relates conversations or describes people real or imaginary he notes above all the atmosphere which surrounds them. More than in what they think, he is interested in the way they think, more than in what happens to them, in their reactions to events, since to his mind events are fortuitous while reactions reveal permanent characteristics. In describing the life of his friend, Sabartés, despite the accumulation of small details, has conveyed excellently the atmosphere of perpetual tension in which alone Picasso seems to be able to breathe freely.

Sabartés's outstanding characteristic is his unshakeable loyalty. One day, someone was talking of a man who intended to publish his memoirs after his own death or after Picasso's. 'In that case he has got things to say which won't be pleasant to hear,' said Sabartés with a trace of apprehension. At the same time he is not the dupe of his admiration. He hovers in the margin of Picasso's lively existence with the ease of an officiating priest, but though convinced that the soil on which he treads is sacred he does not take himself too seriously. Only a Spaniard is capable of combining so much gravity with so sharp a sense of humour. As soon as he arrived in Paris summoned by Picasso he fitted himself into the life of his friend without any ambition or illusions, quite ready to abandon his own life and his own activities and observing almost with affection the chaos in which Picasso lived.

Nothing had changed since the time when objects piled up on the small table and along the walls of Picasso's first studio in Paris, except that now there was more room the litter had increased proportionately. The bed was heaped with important letters, invitation cards, catalogues, magazines and books. The daily post Picasso deposited without sorting it on a chair, on the mantelpiece or under the telephone which served as paper-weight. Among picture-postcards stuck between a a mirror and its frame, among tubes of paint, bottles of oil and turpentine, an earthenware jar full of brushes and a tall bronze sculpture with ramifications like a Christmas tree, were heaped mementoes of the more or less recent past, things which for a brief while had some significance for Picasso and were preserved to remind him of a forgotten sensation, a moment of joy, a person long since vanished from his life. Thus, in proof of his own fidelity to the past, he could remember the occasion when he had put this champagne cork on the mantelpiece, a small flag, a doll, a feather, a harlequin's cap. His pockets mirrored the chaos of his home: crumpled letters and bills, packets of cigarettes, matches, lighters incapable of lighting or ones that would suddenly burst into flame, keys, nails, pocket-knives, bits of cardboard, shells, string and ribbons.

One day, Sabartés could not restrain the comment: 'I cannot explain your mania for keeping things, considering you are an innovator by temperament.'

'You are confusing words, *mon vieux*, which have no relation to one another. The main thing is, I am not scatter-brained. . . .' And he added magnificently: 'Why should you want me to throw away what has done me the favour of coming into my hands?' As usual he had not explained himself. The contradiction went too deep and not the least part of it is that he likes simplification and is exasperated to find his existence cluttered with people and things. He would like to strip his life of everything superfluous and live according to the law of minimum effort. One day during his communal life with Sabartés he decided, for instance, to take his meals in the kitchen. 'You've got everything to hand there,' he said. What annoyed him was to have to leave the dining-room where he had settled down with a book, a newspaper, cigarettes, matches and a pile of other things and see them all removed so that the table could be laid.

In reducing his life to the minimum of effort Picasso was succumbing to the lassitude which had invaded him. Months passed in a kind of paralysis, the greater by contrast with his former active life. Other creative artists have known what it is to wait for a jolt that will release them from themselves. One can imagine that Picasso, who is such a slave to his work, found inactivity a greater trial than anyone. Those who knew him well found him sunk in a coma from which he seemed to have little desire to awake. 'To some extent it suited him,' wrote Gertrude Stein. 'It meant one responsibility the less for him and it is pleasant not to have responsibilities. It is like soldiers in war. War is terrible, they say, but during a war you have no responsibility, neither for life nor for death.'

CHAPTER XIII 1935-1939

Guernica

'THE time has come,' said Paul Éluard in 1936, 'when all poets have the right and the duty to declare that they are profoundly involved in the lives of other men and in communal life.' He had just come back from Spain where he had gone to talk about Picasso in connection with a retrospective exhibition of his works, which was the first to be held in Barcelona since 1902 and was now shown in several other large towns. At his lectures, at which Ramon Gomez de La Serna had read some of Picasso's poems, Éluard had met some of his writer and poet friends, such as Lorca, Alberti and Bergamin. As though they had a presentiment of the coming world drama, Spanish intellectuals were particularly sensitive to contemporary political currents and they succeeded in instilling into their French guest a sense of urgency in the face of a common danger.

On his return from Spain, Paul Éluard published a collection of poems with the characteristic title, *Les Yeux fertiles*. He had known Picasso for a long time and though fifteen years younger had become increasingly friendly with him. In 1935 Picasso had done four etchings for a previous collection of Éluard's poems, including a portrait of his wife, Nush. Now Picasso drew another portrait of Nush, moving in its delicacy, for *Les Yeux fertiles*. In early 1935 Picasso was feeling more distraught than ever. In February and March two exhibitions had taken place in Paris and their enormous success had again attracted the curiosity of the general public to him and plunged him in a whirl of distracting commitments. He took flight, aiming at complete anonymity and suggesting to Sabartés that he post on his mail to him under the name of Pablo Ruiz: 'Yes, Pablo Ruiz, as in the days when we were small.'

But his wanderings along the coast did not lead him to discover a village off the beaten track where he had never been before, but to a place which he knew and where many memories awaited him: Juan-les-Pins. After some temporary relief, distress returned to him, finding its way into the sprightly tone of his letters to Sabartés whom he informed one day that he had dropped everything, even poetry, 'to devote himself entirely to singing'.

Despite his desire to bury himself, troubles pursued him in the form of promises to collaborate which he had allowed to be extracted from him and he was now reminded of, as though they were a kind of debt which he had contracted. 'I cannot stay quiet while busying myself with so many things which are neither mine nor yours, but which we attend to, you out of kindness to me, and I for I don't know what reason.' Some days later, he wrote to Sabartés in exasperation: 'All this puts me in such a bad humour that it would be better for me to start working again than to write so much nonsense.'

Picasso had, in fact, resumed work. Towards the end of May he returned to Paris, but hesitated to show his recent drawings. They contained, in fact, several elements which would one day be used by Picasso in his great picture, *Guernica*. Meanwhile, they seemed to Sabartés to reflect his distress, the insistent shadows which the southern sun had not succeeded in dispersing.

On his return to Paris, Picasso decided to resume work on the engravings which he had promised to Vollard, 'no one knew how long ago'. These were the illustrations for Buffon's *Histoire Naturelle*, a strange undertaking for him, but one which reveals his abilities as an acute observer of reality and also the degree to which a complete contrast in style and technique can release his inspiration. Picasso, who had so much affection for animals and always liked to be surrounded by them, was particularly well qualified to depict them, not only in their external aspect, but also in their attitudes. He drew as though he had the model in front of him, trusting to his prodigious visual memory to seize every detail down to the texture of hair or plumage. The patient detail of his drawings reveals also perhaps a need to resume contact with the springs of reality and to borrow a little inward calm from the calm which such delicate work demands. Apart from precise and elaborate drawing, the aquatints reveal a rare delicacy of tone. Picasso enjoyed this work and seemed to be soothed by it. The plates were finished regularly, at the rate of at least one a day. They were prepared by the sugar process and immediately printed in Lacourrière's work-shop, but were not published until 1942, according to Robert Maillard eventually becoming, with Ovid's *Metamorphoses*, one of the works most sought after by collectors.

Slowly Picasso ceased to be a recluse. In the warm evenings of early summer he would go out with Sabartés to exercise his dog Elf. Reaching the Champs-Élysées he would ask: 'Shall we go back or go to a café?' The empty flat with the twin bed covered with newspaper held no attractions for him. Uusally they would finish the evening in one of the cafés in Saint-Germain-des-Prés with Picasso sitting over an Évian water and Elf begging sugar from the neighbouring tables. Often they would meet Éluard there or Breton and sometimes Braque.

One day at the 'Deux Magots', Picasso noticed a girl at a nearby table. His glance lingered on her black gloves embroidered with large flowers. He made a remark in Spanish. The girl recognized Picasso and smiled. She had lived for a long time in Argentina. Her smile lit up unexpectedly a serious face with regular features caught in a remote yet attentive expression. The pure oval of her cheeks broadened slightly towards high cheek-bones, denoting Slav origin. The face was dominated by clear unwavering eyes set between long, dark lashes beneath haughty eyebrows. The Croat blood of her architect father and the French blood of her mother's family, which came from Touraine and le Poitou, fought for expression in the youthful face which varied between the liveliest attention and paralysing timidity. As it happened, Paul Éluard knew the girl. Her name was Dora Maar. He introduced her to Picasso and thus chance sealed her destiny as a woman and marked the beginning of one of the decisive periods in Picasso's art.

Of all the women who up till then had shared Picasso's life for varying lengths of time, none seems to have been so conscious of what was happening to her as Dora Maar. She was young enough to be influenced by his powerful personality, at the same time she had lived her own life long enough to have established an independent identity. Moreover, she had a job which enabled her to enter Picasso's life as it were on an equal footing. She had been a painter, but, doubting her talents, had abandoned painting and taken up photography. Later, she was to make wide use of the facilities offered by this second employ-ment to record the stages in Picasso's creative process.

At the same time as Dora Maar entered his life Picasso received alarming news. On 18th July it was learnt in Paris that civil war had broken out in Spain. Several compatriots knocked at his door coming from both the opposing camps. But from the start Picasso had decided his allegiance. The Republican Government immediately made use of his fame by appointing him a director of the Prado. Soon after, Picasso learnt that the masterpieces had been removed from Madrid to a place of safety. 'So I am a director of an empty museum,' he said. He paid close attention to reports on the security measures decided by the Government. When Bergamin told him that he had supervised the arrival of the Madrid pictures in Valencia and that on unrolling a canvas he had discovered Velasquez's *Las Meninas* in his hands, Picasso sighed: 'How I should have enjoyed that!'

The civil war in Spain touched him more deeply than any other world event has ever done. Perhaps he was waiting more or less consciously to identify himself with something greater than the torments of his own creativity or perhaps he was trying to rediscover a link with men or things that he had long since lost.

In the course of the years lived with Dora Maar and in the frankness of their intimacy, a groan often escaped him at his ultimate solitude, the curse of all creative individuals. In an ironic tone ill-concealing the tragedy in him, he borrowed de Vigny's line to express his irremediable anguish:

Hélas! je suis, Seigneur, puissant et solitaire.

The reactions of the Spanish people in their fierce struggle for liberty awoke a feeling of solidarity in him and broke the circle of his isolation. In his passionate commitment there was also an element which Gertrude Stein has detected. His renunciation of painting had been voluntary, but it reflected all the same that agony of sterility which at some time or other assails every creator with greater or less severity. The civil war coincided with this agony in himself. 'It was not the events themselves that were occurring in Spain that awoke Picasso,' wrote Gertrude Stein, 'but the fact that they were happening in Spain; he had lost Spain and now Spain was not lost, it existed: the existence of Spain awoke Picasso, he, too, existed. . . . Picasso began to work, he began to speak as he has spoken all his life, in drawing and colour.'

When the civil war broke out, however, no one seemed to understand the trial of strength it represented or what this trial meant for the whole world. Picasso was still absorbed in his new love affair. Placed as he was between the demands of his wife and his attachment to the mother of his daughter, the appearance of Dora Maar in his life seemed to complicate it inextricably. But in fact she offered a way out of his difficulties. Dora Maar was not one of those who haggle over their surrender. At the same time, as she was living with her parents she was obliged to observe certain proprieties and had to return home at an early hour. When she left the flat in the Rue La Boetié, Picasso would lean over the balcony with a lamp in his hand to light her path. This beacon, the symbol of his awakened passion, would one day leave its trace in the light that cleaves the darkness of *Guernica*.

Towards mid-August Picasso left Paris in search of the sun in the South of France. He settled in the mountain village of Mougins, half an hour from Cannes. Dora Maar was with friends at Saint-Tropez. With a lover's impatience Picasso went and fetched her. The whole of Mougins even to the dining-room of the 'Hotel Vaste Horizon' was full of revolting pictures by a rural policeman, which amused Picasso greatly. In the hotel Dora Maar discovered two girls employed as chamber-maid and cook whom they took back with them to Paris, and of whom one, Inès, was to stay with Picasso through all the vicissitudes of his existence. Every year thereafter on her birthday Inès would receive a portrait of herself drawn in realistic style by Picasso with her pure features standing out against a shadowy cloud of hair.

With his eternal youthful sentimentality Picasso disliked keeping his passion a secret. 'I do not travel incognito,' he wrote to Sabartés. Soon Dora Maar's handsome face was dominating his art, and would do so for years. One of her earliest portraits (collection of Mme Cuttoli, Paris) shows her with hair still very short as it was on their first meeting, but with a false plait round her head while, at Picasso's request, she let her hair grow. In her face which is leaning against a very small hand—Dora Maar's beautiful hands attracted him greatly— the eyes are unnaturally large and have an intense look both withdrawn and challenging.

Sabartés writes that Picasso at this time liked to parade his conquest, but he also wanted to integrate Dora Maar in his life and this involved taking her on a pilgrimage through all the stages of his art, a task in which Picasso acted as a very conscientious guide. Dora Maar was now associated with all the monsters that his imagination had engendered.

New figure-heads rose beside the Mediterranean shore. The *Jeunes Filles avec le petit bateau* (collection of Mme Meric Callery) of February, 1937, presents a pair of robots playing with a toy boat. The figures are constructed of wooden slats and spheres with golf-club heads reminiscent of vipers. *La Baigneuse nue* is in the same mosaic style with a small spherical head in which the features are barely indicated. It is painted in a faded ochre colour resembling wood with highlights scratched on the canvas contrasting with a strip of deep blue sea and a pale summer sky. *La Femme assise avec un livre* is another similar work which, thanks to the severity of the composition, assumes an almost monumental aspect.

But after this journey into the past Picasso began to adopt a different visual approach in the depiction of Dora Maar's features. Hitherto he had achieved the double presentation of the profile and the full-face view by linear drawing which made it less convincing. (Incidentally, it was a curious fact that the fair-haired girl, whose big firm body and powerful profile had awakened Picasso's sculptural vein, appeared in his pictures divided into planes outlined by curves or circled with dark strokes after the manner of a stained-glass window or ceramic painting.)

It was thus that he painted the portrait of Marie-Thérèse Walter in January, 1937, in an attitude of imperturbable calm, sitting in a chair with a hat on her head but with her two breasts protruding from her low-cut dress and the lights in her skin and hair rendered in pale green. But in a portrait of Dora Maar probably painted about the same time, or slightly later, the modelling has suddenly changed. The face which is treated not in planes but in strong relief emerges between flowing, blue-black hair and a nose seen in profile placed side by side with a nose seen full-face, while an eye placed in profile but turned inward, in green, confronts a calm, full-face eye in red. Picasso achieved the same *tour de force* as in his cubist portraits; despite the distortions he inflicted on the regular features, the resemblance remained a striking one, even down to the delicate hands represented as ears of corn and the red, pointed nails reproducing the characteristic gestures of the model. The space behind the seated woman is reduced to walls covered with white slats, and this restricted setting, reminiscent of a monk's cell or the walls and bars of a prison, continued to feature in further portraits of Dora Maar as though representing the desire of a jealous man to keep the young woman prisoner.

While his amorous ardour and the anger and distress with which he followed the uncertain course of the war in Spain persisted, the taste for work suddenly returned to Picasso. Only the intellectual *élite* of the world seemed able to gauge the importance of the war that was raging in the peninsula. In the Anglo-Saxon world where official policy prevented all aid to the Republicans, people were stirred in their imagination as they had not been stirred since Byron had espoused the lost cause of Greek independence. Beyond ideologies and beyond even the atrocities committed by the opposing forces, there was some particular characteristic in this Spanish revolt against misery and the oppression of a still almost feudal régime that awakened the loyalty of man to man.

The two Fascist dictators knew well enough what was at stake in the struggle, and while they were supplying Franco with heavy weapons and aircraft it was paradoxically under the aegis of Léon Blum that France proclaimed a policy of non-intervention, as though anxious to ignore the fact that the explosion of shells on the Guadarrama was the signal for a general conflagration.

With his passion for ideological struggles, yet withdrawn in his creative solitude, Picasso became alarmed at the turn which events in Spain were taking. He knew of the ravages of Fascism in Italy and knew what horrors were taking place in Germany, but these crimes did not summon such familiar images in him as the atrocities perpetrated on Spanish soil. The blood which was flowing, and flowing in vain, was the blood of his friends. The monster Franco was also well known to Picasso. He was a continuation of the scourges which have assailed the history of Spain, he was the incarnation of all the nightmares which have descended on his country, all the demons which have held it prisoner in the darkness. It was in the features of Franco that Picasso, assuming the heritage of the Spanish revolt, reproduced the formidable and grotesque face of dictatorship. In doing so he revealed his basic character which is typical of his country: when a Spaniard speaks his own language, when he strikes a truly indigenous note, he believes he is speaking in the name of humanity; when he expresses emotions which are peculiar to himself in words which are his very own and in images which he invents for his personal use, he is convinced that he is using that *idioma universal* which Goya quoted as his authority.

It was as a direct heir of Goya that Picasso drew up the indictment in words and pictures known as *Sueño y Mentíra de Franco*, 'Dream and

Lie of Franco'. The Spanish words which came to his lips had all the violence and extravagance of a Spain in anger, the force of anathemas pronounced by popular preachers, the vulgarity of impotent popular laughter and the lively imagery of its invective.

The text of the pamphlet was written straight off on 8th and 9th January, 1937; it was originally illustrated with fourteen etchings. The only link between these and the text was a violence common to both and their common origin in popular imagery and Picasso's own furious contempt. In choosing this form of illustrated strip Picasso seems to have revived a very distant memory. In the days of the Bateau-Lavoir he had enjoyed looking at a feature in American newspapers which Gertrude Stein passed to him. This was the adventures of the 'Katzenjammer Kids', a predecessor of the modern comic strip. He made a point of asking for these newspapers when Gertrude Stein forgot to bring them to him. The 'Katzenjammer Kids' had been based on the famous German series full of stark and often cruel humour, featuring the exploits of Max and Moritz. But the figure of Franco is given features for which no model is known, any more than it is known what inspired Goya's ghosts and phantoms. Franco is given a flabby shape similar to the figure in Michelin advertisements and a slug's head crowned with a head-dress.

In these etchings the significance of the battle raging in Spain is defined unequivocally. The loathsome, flabby monster, his slug's head topped by the hat of a religious pilgrim, is shown kneeling at a *prie-dieu* in front of an altar surrounded by barbed wire on which a Duro stands as the object of worship. In another picture the horrid figure has pierced a winged horse with his lance and the animal falls at his feet. A woman with a pure profile lies stretched out dead in a field (in the struggle for freedom in Spain women fought with their menfolk). Further strips show a foul, hairy beast with a sneering mouth in the middle of its stomach confronting the calm head of a ram. Finally, eternal Spain ends by putting the creature to flight: a monster with an obscene head terminating in a zebra's body is disembowelled by a bull and writhes while its entrails spill on the ground.

The fourteen plates composing the *Dream and Lie of Franco* were completed later by four others depicting fresh atrocities committed in Spain: slaughtered women, women sobbing with their cheeks streaked with tears and mothers with the corpses of their children clutched to their breasts. This series of eighteen plates touched up with aquatint were also to be published later in the form of postcards and sold for the benefit of Republican funds.

In the same month that Picasso produced his virulent pamphlet, the Republican Government asked him to decorate a wall for the Spanish pavilion in the international exhibition that was due to be held in Paris. Picasso promised his help, but was slow in setting to work. For a large mural he needed more space around him. He had left the estate at Boisgeloup to his wife. He also felt the urge to get out of Paris. Vollard rented him an old house in a large garden which he had bought at Tremblay-sur-Mauldre with a barn which had been converted into a studio. Here Picasso set to work, dividing his time between the country and Paris.

The still-lifes which he painted at this time were mostly set against the bright background of a window with a very salient and often disproportionately large window-catch. Sometimes the background is a wall-paper of stripes and flowers with a mirror that catches the light. Among the objects a flower-vase appeared again, a pitcher, a candlestick with a lighted candle whose flame is depicted as an open eye, a negro sculpture and a woman's bust whose features are those of Dora Maar. These very brightly-coloured still-lifes are among the most intense that he ever painted and reflect his joy in having a home again and a full daily life.

The urge to create now returned to him after the sterile years, and the feeling of being able to work continuously demanded an end to the journeys in and out of Paris. He rented two floors of an old seventeenth-century house in the Rue des Grands-Augustins. The studio there was well suited to a large-scale work. Picasso's countrymen were becoming uneasy about the composition which he had promised them for the international exhibition. It was already April and he had not yet started work or even sketched a project. He was surrounded by an atmosphere of expectations, of tautly stretched hopes which almost made the air vibrate. José Bergamin writes: 'I consider Picasso's painting up to this time as an introduction to his future work,' and he adds: 'The recent war of independence in Spain gave Picasso, as the former war gave Goya, a full awareness of his pictorial, poetic and creative genius.'

In these delays and this hesitation to start work there was perhaps something of the anxiety which all, even the most self-assured creative artists, feel at the thought that they may not be able completely to

197

satisfy the hopes which have been placed in them. At any rate, the delay did not escape the opponents of the Republican Government. Had its reverses, they wondered, convinced Picasso that it would be hopeless to continue the struggle? Was he, too, accepting passively the *fait accompli*? Rumours were current that Picasso had transferred his allegiance to Franco. Later he reacted violently to them in a declaration published to coincide with an exhibition of Spanish Republican art in New York: 'The war in Spain is the struggle of reaction against the people and against freedom. My whole life as an artist has been one continual struggle against reaction and against the death of art. How could it be thought even for a moment that I was in agreement with reaction and evil?'

Later still he also said: 'I have always believed and still do believe that artists who live and work with spiritual values cannot and should not remain indifferent in the face of a conflict where the highest values of humanity and civilization are at stake.'

But strong as were his convictions and constant his desire for absolute freedom, he needed another jolt, a powerful shock before his creative springs were completely released. On 28th April, the town of Guernica was destroyed by German bombers; women and children were overcome by a terrible death in this first latter-day massacre of the innocents. Here the new face of war was revealed, the collusion of all the forces of evil. It was a check to the democracies and indeed the beginning of their final downfall.

The shattering impression of this news on Picasso was shown in the fury with which he set to work. He was to call the great composition which he undertook for the Spanish pavilion, *Guernica* (Museum of Modern Art, New York). Zervos states: 'In its first state the picture was conceived in a mood of exaltation.' By 1st May, Picasso was already showing pencil drawings on blue paper to Sert. These revealed a rapid sketch of the central theme besides more elaborate details, such as the magnificent sketch of the stricken horse. From now on, Picasso's creative fury worked at full pressure.

The main lines of the composition had been fixed in a single burst; thereafter, during the course of work, they were slowly to be modified in the sense of increasing simplification and a more rigorous presentation of the emotive element. Picasso was determined to marshal all his forces and leave nothing to chance. About a hundred studies have been counted for and around the theme of *Guernica*. Most of them have been published and they provide the surest and most revealing guide to his creative process. If we knew nothing else about him, these preparatory studies for the great composition would still provide us with complete insight into his manner of conceiving and executing a work, into his joy and anguish, his often despairing efforts and into the felicity of his sudden brainwaves.

Dora Maar was with him while he was painting *Guernica* in his studio in the Rue des Grands-Augustins. She realized at once the importance of the event she was privileged to witness. A week after Picasso had started work, she conceived the idea of photographing its successive stages to show the choice he made between different pictorial elements and his agonized search for the best and briefest way of expressing the vision which had appeared to him in the upsurge of his fury and compassion. Thanks to these photographs and to the numerous published studies, one has the feeling of having broken into his studio like a cat-burglar.

The stricken horse which he placed in the centre of the composition was his first concern. Among the studies made on the day following the initial sketch, there is a monochrome painting of the animal's head crying out with such an expression of terror that Barr has considered it the most unforgettable vision in the whole of Picasso's work.

One of the main accents in the terrible drama is supplied by the grieving woman clasping her dead child. Picasso had at first imagined her staggering down a ladder from a collapsing house from which she has rescued the child's corpse. Two days later, the definitive image imposed itself of an enormous head thrown back with a mouth wide open in a howl of grief and a pointed tongue projecting. The child's body has collapsed like a dislocated toy. According to the photograph taken by Dora Maar, the whole of the vast canvas ($11'5''$ by $25'5\frac{3}{4}''$) was sketched by 11th May. Picasso had modified the position of the horse: its head now fell near the warrior's who had collapsed, as though in terror at the violence of the animal cry echoing the cries of men. While painting the canvas he continued the detailed studies, for instance of the bull's head with its human lips and tranquil Napoleonic features. Several sketches were made in coloured pencil. Picasso had sketched the canvas in monochrome; he now thought of finishing it in colours. But the effect of the picture was already so powerful that his friends tried to dissuade him. To judge the effect that colours would have he tried introducing papier collé. In one of Dora Maar's photographs, strips of striped or flowered paper can be seen, employed to render clothing, and on the head of the woman on the right a paper napkin representing a tartan handkerchief.

Picasso realized that the evocative power of the canvas was weakened by these effects, but he was reluctant to abandon any introduction of colour. He cut out a red tear which he tried in various positions on the canvas under the eyes of the victims. Finally he stuck it to the eye of the bull. But the red blob was out of place and regretfully he removed it, joking as always at his own brainwaves and calling it 'the furtive tear'. When the picture was exhibited he said to Bergamin: 'We'll put it in a jewel-case and go and stick it on the bull at least on Fridays.'

As he developed the canvas he continued his rigorous simplification, sacrificing all facile symbolism or decorative effects. In the final stage of the work he drew weeping women, their cheeks streaked with tears, but excluded the contortions of sobbing mouths. But in the ultimate canvas even the tears have gone, to be replaced by tear-shaped eyes.

After the sacrifice of innumerable details, *Guernica* emerged almost in monochrome from a bluish grey half-light. The canvas is painted in large planes almost without relief, but these planes are arranged so judiciously that, without any recourse to perspective, they create a fictitious depth as though they culminate in the very heart of night, and they are so finely graduated that they do not seem to have been deprived of colour, but rather to have lost it, swallowed by the shadows, the twilight of catastrophe. It was in the shades of the Apocalypse that Picasso placed his interpretation of the drama. Of a world ravaged by crime only a schematic bird fallen on a table and the vague contours of a flower remain, visible near the hand of the warrior and his broken sword.

Exhibited in June, 1937, in the Spanish pavilion, *Guernica* was immediately considered to be the most striking work of the twentieth century. It has undergone the most varied and contradictory interpretations. Picasso's silence on the meaning of his work which seems to him to require no explanation has given free rein to every kind of speculation. To some people the picture has seemed too clear, to others too obscure. According to Barr, the Director of the Metropolitan Museum, Taylor, accused it of the banality of overstatement and compared it to Tennyson's poem, 'The Charge of the Light Brigade'. Other critics have found that Picasso expressed himself in an over-intellectualized, sophisticated idiom incomprehensible to the average man and complained that he stripped the subject of all emotion, employing an involved hermetic symbolism instead of representing the event itself. But in fact Picasso had no intention of depicting the atrocities of Guernica, and it is the very absence of the narrative element which makes his great picture a contemporary work. 'The first characteristic of modern art is not to tell a story,' says Malraux.

Even those who accepted the symbols of the dying horse and the impassive bull as the protagonists in the drama have attacked Picasso for having made a ridiculous monster out of the wounded horse, and scarecrows of the victims of the air attack.

But the form which Picasso gave the work was as deliberate and as clearly sought after in his innumerable studies as the distance which he put between himself and his subject. Though he was profoundly upset by the news of the terrible attack and the interval between his initial emotion and the sketching of the work was short, he knew that it was not the horror of a single night which he intended to paint or the destruction of one small town in his country, but all the 'Guernicas' that were yet to come throughout the world. It was this more or less conscious foreboding which made him choose animal forces to represent the horrors to come. The bull with human eyes which rears motionless, close, too close to the woman with the dead child, seems like the incarnation of an indestructible power emerging from primeval night to triumph in future times.

Even those who refuse to admit that Picasso has his own personal vision and that his distortions are systematic rather than arbitrary might ask themselves whether the horror of Guernica could be rendered by any other means. About a century and a quarter have passed since the *Dos de Mayo*, which was also painted in a mood of compassionate fury. Like Goya's masterpiece, *Guernica* is also an anticipation of horrors to come, and the distorting mirror of the picture has captured the true face of our distracted world. Critics who reproach him for having painted a picture 'incomprehensible to the average man' talk on the assumption that only the lowest level is intelligible to popular taste. But the relationship of the masses to art is much more subtle. When *Guernica* was exhibited in Paris in 1955, silent spectators could be seen on the benches facing the picture with the same rapt expression as visitors confronting the *Sistine Madonna* in the old Dresden Museum or the *Night Watch* in the Rijksmuseum in Amsterdam.

Complaints have also been raised that Picasso did not define clearly enough his attitude to Franco. While he was working on the picture, rumours of his adherence to the Franco Government continued to circulate until he felt obliged to declare that in his work he was clearly expressing his detestation 'of the military clique which has plunged Spain into an ocean of suffering and death'. In the same declaration he protested vehemently against allegations raised by Spanish Fascists concerning the destruction of works of art. All foreign visitors to Spain were unanimous in stressing 'the great respect of the Spanish people in arms for their immense artistic heritage'. They were Franco's planes which bombed the Prado and it was the men of the Militia who saved the artistic treasures at the peril of their lives. 'There is no possible doubt on this subject,' asserted Picasso angrily.

Reluctant as he was to take up his position publicly, Picasso addressed numerous appeals to the conscience of the world. Even the defeat which he knew to be inevitable did not halt his efforts. They took the form of material aid for the sorely tried population. To supply it he was obliged to sell pictures which he had intended to keep. One of the Spaniards engaged in the distribution of food, Juan Larrea, claims that Picasso gave 400,000 francs towards supplying children with milk, and that later he continued his gifts for the support of intellectuals apart from what he distributed privately.

He also helped the refugees whom defeat brought flooding into France. Sometimes his help took unusual forms. When an exhibition of the works of exiled Spanish artists was organized in Paris in the spring of 1939, Picasso, relates Larrea in a letter to Barr, stopped in front of a dreadful picture, a sort of enlargement of a picture-postcard, and bought it for a good price. To a friend expressing astonishment, Picasso explained that nobody else would have bought it if he had not. 'The artist's pride is impossible to describe,' concluded Larrea.

The completion of *Guernica* did not release Picasso from the agonies experienced during the long weeks of work. Though the fever of execution subsided, the shock which had plunged him into a creative whirlwind and the tension which never ceased to stretch his nerves persisted. He continued to dream of the horrors of Guernica and to paint the nightmare visions which he had not incorporated in his picture, for example weeping women. The motif of tears coursing down cheeks seemed to obsess him, he followed their path with an apparently detached curiosity, and under his pen or his brush these strange tracks assumed an almost ornamental appearance.

It was the face of Dora Maar which these tears distorted with increasing ferocity. In their intimacy she and Picasso, who were endowed with the same volcanic temperament, knew moments when they faced one another as enemies. Sometimes Picasso felt a kind of dull anger at his enslavement. But Dora Maar knew that she had no real hold over him and that despite her sorcery those terrible eyes fixed on her remained very lucid. She, too, was liable to sudden anger and passed through crises of absolute despair prompted by her Slav temperament. Ravaged by anger and made ugly by tears, the handsome face of the woman he loved seemed to Picasso even more attractive and he studied her closely: the open mouth baring the gums, the strongly rooted teeth, the pointed tongue, the palate, the contracted eyebrows, the eyes screwed up in anger, the tears flowing down cheeks already swollen with weeping.

Picasso's weeping women reached a climax in a picture painted in October, 1937 (Roland Penrose Collection, London). The violence of the colouring is in tune with the violence of the young woman's emotion. Sitting in a bright red chair in total surrender to despair, she is dressed as though she had come on a visit, wearing a little red hat with a cornflower pinned to the top. The eyebrows painted like ears of corn rise in a circumflex accent towards a deep furrow creasing the forehead. From orbits assuming the form of small oblong slits the eyes literally pop out of her head. Fat tears are coursing down the cheeks and along a nose planted in profile on a three-quarter face. The mouth is drawn back in a rectangle. The teeth bite furiously on a handkerchief to stifle the cries surging up from the throat. Rarely has such violence been done to a human face.

And yet Picasso's weeping women are more than an episode in his emotional battles. They arose at the beginning of those years when despair, violence and cowardice were preparing the future cataclysm. All the tears shed anywhere in the world by the victims of barbarous oppression, all the strangled sobs, the anger and the impotent revulsion were reflected in their distorted features. If those years when an uprising of the free world might still have averted disaster and every opportunity was irretrievably lost could be represented in a single symbol, one would choose the tormented face of Dora Maar.

In the summer of 1937 Picasso sought relaxation at Mougins, after the efforts and distress imposed on him by *Guernica*. He was accompanied by Dora Maar and his great Afghan hound, a lean, raw-boned animal with a pointed head and ears like drooping wings covered with long hair. Animals continued to play a large part in his life, and he was particularly fond of this huge dog which was called Kazbek after a mountain in Spain. But the relief and relaxation he sought eluded him. He continued to be haunted by weeping women and at Mougins he was assailed by new nightmares. While there he painted the extraordinary *Femme allaitant un chat* (collection of Mme Cuttoli, Paris), as unexpected in its choice of subject as in its colouring: the wide-eyed, grinning monster is plunged in a green phosphorescence.

These fresh nightmares were accompanied by a new method of treatment. The sharp relief which had characterized the portraits of Dora Maar was succeeded by a taste for a broken-up surface, horror rationed out, as it were, in ornamental fragments of the most intensely strident colouring. In his drawings this increased fragmentation is achieved by straight intersecting lines which cover the faces like a multicoloured spider's web and then turn into curves and spirals, a kind of ornamentation based on some unknown folklore or popular primitive art. The portraits which he produced at that time are like the painted faces of barbarian warriors or Mexican masks.

This destructive process took place in a mood of ferocious gaiety. For the time being anything striped and multicoloured attracted Picasso; even his letters were written with coloured pencils, each phrase in a different shade. He painted *Les Coqs* (collection of Mr. and Mrs. Ralph J. Collin, New York) standing arrogantly on their strong feet with their bright plumage, combs erect, beaks open and pointed tongues protruding. 'There have always been cocks,' said Picasso at that time to a young American painter, 'but like everything else in life we have got to discover them, as Corot discovered morning and Renoir young girls.'

In February, 1938, Picasso painted the *Jeune Fille avec un coq* where the bird with tied feet is struggling on the girl's knees with squawking beak and beady eyes. The huge-faced monster holding the cock is barely less ferocious: the eyes are raised almost level with the top of the head, one in profile appearing immediately beside another seen full-face, and the mouth in a gigantic profile is open as though about to emit a piercing cry. This tendency to break up the face with interior lines characterizes a portrait of Picasso's daughter Maïa (property of Picasso) in which a moon-like visage reveals highlights in the form of suns, an ornamental effect underlined by the drawing of the tartan dress and a beret with a striped ribbon.

This pictorial disintegration produced yet further monsters. Composed of tight spirals of woven rushes, a profile emerges with the nostrils of a horse and surmounted by a ridiculous hat. Some monsters have two enormous rhomboids instead of nostrils, breasts made of rustic embroidery and a crescent-shaped face like a piece of twisted cloth with a lock of hair like a horse's tail. As though under the impulse of repressed rage Picasso was committing every kind of violence. From time to time, almost in spite of himself, the model triumphed over the martyrdom inflicted on her. There is a portrait of Dora Maar, for instance, wearing a hat with one gloved hand against her cheek and the upper part of the face plunged in shadow from which the whites of her eyes emerge, seeming to reflect the combined intensity of model and painter.

Curiously enough, the fragmentation of the portraits was absent from the still-lifes which Picasso painted in the same period. But two of them reveal the whole range of his invention in treating an almost identical subject, a bull's head beside a lighted candle and a palette with brushes placed on an open book. One of them is painted in great luminous planes contrasting with the black head of the bull which is drawn in classic linear style. In the other picture the bull's head rears three-dimensionally on a pedestal. The plasticity of the objects is matched by the violence of the colouring, as though the lighted candle with its small triangle of jade-green light was really plunging the picture into an artificial illumination. The bull's head in vivid red and bright orange stands out against a cold background of blues, greens and acidulous violet.

This period of pictorial fragmentation and strident colours reached its peak in the works painted in the summer of 1938 and ended with them. It was a summer troubled by rumours of war when the conflict seemed very close. Picasso suddenly left the South of France and returned in the middle of the night to Paris. 'As though peace were essential to a man who could not live without battles,' wrote Sabartés, 'he feared war because it might affect his work.' Munich brought a deceptive pacification and a reprieve which merely aggravated the violence of the conflict when it finally broke out. From these days of agony Picasso emerged breathless with relief.

In December he contracted a bad bout of sciatica, and when Christmas came he was still moving with difficulty. But on Christmas Night he drew Sabartés on an odd scrap of paper which came to hand. One day Sabartés had said to him: 'I would like to have my portrait done in a ruff like a sixteenth-century gentleman and a feathered hat on my head.' 'Some day I will draw you like that,' Picasso had promised him. Now the promise was kept: Sabartés emerged, drawn in masterly style as though Picasso had no difficulty in his movements, with a broad ruff and a plumed beret. But Picasso was not satisfied. Next day he surprised his friend with two more portraits drawn on the previous evening from memory, one of them showing him in a tall ruff, the other, a striking likeness, in monastic homespun with folded arms.

Picasso recovered quickly. As though impatient at the interruption of his work, he launched immediately into new experiments, attempts at engraving in colour, combining, as in every new undertaking, infinite patience with passionate enthusiasm. Each day he went up Montmartre to Lacourrière, showing enormous interest in the manual side of the work, striving to obtain colours as fresh as if he were using paint and brushes and experimenting to find the best paper for the desired effect.

Six women's heads varied the features of Dora Maar. He engraved her full-face with clear impressive eyes in a calm, dark-skinned face and in profile with a nose with double nostrils, accentuating the hugeness of her eyes and her fine, sad mouth. He constructed her face in rectangular planes with slashes on the surface giving it the appearance of some diabolical creature, and on 29th March, 1939, he painted the *Femme aux cheveux bruns* where she appears, still extraordinarily distorted, with a white face bathed in blue shadow and planted on a red neck. The portrait stands out against a yellow background and the reds and blues of the dress combine to give the model the appearance of an Aztec goddess.

Dora Maar was also one of the numerous women he painted lying down with a book. Never perhaps has the most peaceful of occupations given rise to so disturbing a picture. The young woman is curled up on the sofa like a seal, spherical breasts protrude from the curve of her arm and two small dancing shoes from her thighs. The small coiled body is dominated by an enormous head. The nose is in profile like the chin. One eye is full-face; the other in profile is looking at the book, and in this restricted space appears a pale half-open mouth drawn with soft and innocent contours. Above the sofa is a window with casements giving the effect of bars set up by the jealous lover for his diabolical prisoner.

They were anxious times, but as though to convince himself of universal stability, Picasso now finally set up house in the Rue des Grands-Augustins, installing central heating at considerable expense to make the two floors habitable. He also decided to make an engraver's workshop and had his old press and all his material brought from Boisgeloup. This project necessitated special electrical fixtures. Lacourrière supervised the fitting out of the workshop so that nothing should be missing. Vollard also called frequently, enthusing over the publishing plans which Picasso was cherishing. Towards the end of June the alterations were complete. The world seemed cradled in peace. But Picasso's monsters seemed to sniff sulphur in the air. The *Chat qui a pris un oiseau* (painted on 22nd April, 1939) stood menacingly on the threshold of things to come. 'Yes,' says Picasso, 'the subject obsessed me, I don't know why.' The pointed head of the animal with unequal phosphorescent eyes is still a cat's, but the body, crouched, ready to spring was also the incarnation of some evil force that was about to spring from the bowels of the earth.

CHAPTER XIV 1939-1944

A World Distraught

ON 15th November, 1939, a retrospective Picasso exhibition was planned to open at the Museum of Modern Art in New York, entitled 'Forty Years of his Art' and intended to establish his reputation definitely in the United States. The Art Institute of Chicago was collaborating with New York. All the American museums, all the galleries, all the collectors had sent in works. Many pictures from private European collections had already arrived in New York and in that autumn of 1939 others were on the way to the United States. Preparations for the exhibition had long been in train. In Alfred H. Barr, the Director of the Museum of Modern Art, who was preparing the catalogue, Picasso had found a most conscientious and understanding interpreter. The artist had sent many works from his own collection, even some which he was reluctant to part with. Some sculptures had been cast in bronze specially for the occasion. But certain pictures failed to arrive by the time the exhibition opened, for by then Europe was plunged in war.

In that same year Picasso's mother died at the age of eighty-three in distant Barcelona, where the political attitude he had adopted prevented him from visiting her. It was more than fifteen years since he had last painted her portrait and she had been an old lady then, but with very lively and piercing eyes. He had remained in correspondence with her, writing less frequently than she would have liked, but she had retained the same faith in him and considered his dazzling success merely as his due. Despite their separation a profound link had remained between the old woman and himself, and his Spanish filial loyalty had been accompanied by gratitude for her continual support. Like all his deeper feelings, his grief was unexpressed.

In the summer of 1939, Picasso, as always, was drawn to the South of France. Travelling was now easy for him; he had a car and a chauffeur, Marcel, who became, incidentally, an important personage in his life and indispensable like all those who served him for any length of time. Thanks to Man Ray who gave him the keys of a small flat in the Palais Albert Ier., he chose to stay this year at Antibes, removing the furniture from the largest room to make a studio. Once installed, he felt the urge to start a major work, explaining to Sabartés that his zeal sprang from the desire not to throw himself out of the window. But the sense of urgency underlying his creative efforts was always that of a hunted man.

He had not yet decided on a subject when he covered three walls of the studio with a large canvas that could be cut into sections. 'Picasso wanted to paint whatever came into his head without being confined to the limits of a frame,' Sabartés explains. Before starting work he had already soaked himself in the atmosphere of the countryside. He showed Sabartés the points on the coast which particularly delighted him, the ramparts plunging steeply into the sea like the sides of a gigantic stone ship dominated by the imposing mass of the Château Grimaldi with its stark walls gilded by the sun. But though he was a fanatical sun-worshipper it was not bright daylight which arrested his attention, but a nocturnal scene, as though the colours half hidden in summer nights seemed to him more precious than those revealed by the light of day.

A genre scene served as point of departure. In Antibes harbour fishing is done at night with harpoons by the light of torches. On the jetty in Picasso's picture two young women are watching the fishermen at work. One of them, holding a bicycle, reveals a deformation of Dora Maar's features, the other is reminiscent of Jacqueline Breton-Lamba. 'It was warm that evening when we walked round the harbour,' recalls Dora Maar, 'and we bought some ice-cream cornets'; in the picture the girl with the bicycle is licking a double cornet with her pointed tongue.

But for Picasso the genre scene and anecdote were merely a pretext to transpose a nocturnal fairyland into his own particular world. In a velvet blue sky swims an enormous russet moon fringed with eyelashes and emitting light like an eye drops tears. The façades and roofs of the houses stand out violet against the warm summer sky; the sea casts a greenish-blue sheen on the blue jetty, one of whose walls shines green under the artificial light; from the bottom of a small violet-blue boat some fishermen emerge like pale phantoms. Human beings and objects appear like vague whirling forms in the depths of a moon-lit night. Even the commonplace bicycle is distorted into dancing curves which, with flying arms, hair and clothing give the whole picture a feeling of transitory reality on the point of dissolution. Those who experienced those August nights in 1939 in the South of France will remember their soft and poignant beauty. The *Pêche de nuit à Antibes* (Museum of Modern Art, New York, Mr. Simon Guggenheim Fund) recalls them with crystal clarity.

From now on, Picasso worked frenziedly and against time. Customers of the café in the Place Victor-Massé discussed the serious international news with growing alarm. They clung to hope as though those summer nights could never come to an end, and Picasso painted his peaceful harbour scene, almost in spite of himself, while the world hovered on the brink of disaster. When the news became yet more serious he clung to his routine from an instinct of self-preservation, and when the first mobilization notices appeared at the town-hall he groaned aloud: 'Now, of all times, when I have just started work!' The café in the square and the square itself became deserted. Lorry-loads of troops started passing through the town. The black-out was imposed and suddenly dense night descended on Antibes. The fishermen's lanterns no longer bobbed over the green water. All had been swallowed by the shadows. The great canvas was hastily taken down.

In Paris contradictory rumours and news true or false were exchanged in furtive, confidential tones. Unreasoning panic began to spread, and hopes even more absurd. Picasso, who had now returned, found himself inundated with callers who believed that because he was famous he would be better informed than themselves. They sensed, too, that he possessed an inner strength which they lacked and hoped to draw on it. But distraught and undecided, he himself was wandering like a blind man in the vacuum that now arose on the eve of an unpredictable war. In the Rue La Boétie and in his studio he started packing up his pictures and then stopped, began sorting his possessions and then abandoned them. Knowing the war to be inevitable, he, like everyone else, was responding to some vital instinct and refusing to admit his own certainty. Paris was emptying, a general stampede had begun. 'Every parting seemed like an eternal farewell,' Sabartés recalls.

Picasso, too, joined the exodus accompanied by Sabartés and his wife, by Dora Maar and his dog Kazbek. On that night of 1st September German aircraft were expected to appear over the city.

Basing his choice on the experience of the First World War when the enemy advance had failed to reach the coast, Picasso made for the sea. On the road to Royan his car met some groups of horses which had been requisitioned by the army. They were going in twos and threes, led by a man on foot. Picasso was impressed by their mournful and submissive bearing. Animal distress has always touched him deeply, more deeply perhaps than human sorrow. 'They seem to understand,' he said, 'that they are not going to their usual work.' The first drawings which he made at Royan, as soon as he had a pad of paper in his hands, represented these requisitioned horses.

He put up at the Hotel du Tigre and rented a room in the villa 'Gerbier de Joncs'. Though there was barely space for his canvases, paints and brushes he wanted to start work at once. 'He is always inclined to solve every problem, however grave, by subjecting himself to a work cure,' reports Sabartés, and when Picasso saw his friend with nothing to do and aggravated by his enforced idleness he recommended the same discipline: 'Write, *mon vieux*, write—no matter what. Write for youself if you like, but even if it is only for yourself you'll see how your bad temper will vanish.'

From this wise advice was born the book which Sabartés has entitled *Portraits et Souvenirs* and which provides a key to knowledge of his friend. But the same recipe could not protect Picasso from the distractions of the times. Royan and its neighbourhood had been declared a frontier zone, and he learnt that foreigners who had arrived after 25th August were not entitled to remain in the town. His fame would have sufficed to protect him against any trouble with the police, but Picasso the eternal rebel had a strange respect for authority. 'The mere knowledge that he was not completely square with the law upset him to such an extent that he was incapable of work.' So he made the journey back to Paris to obtain the necessary permit and returned the following day.

Picasso resumed work in conditions which would have repelled anyone else. He did not even possess an easel. Then one day he discovered a miserable, flea-infested hotel crammed with useless objects. The place enchanted him like his former visits to the junk-shops in Montmartre, and instead of a normal easel he brought home a

211

diminutive one that had been supporting a photograph. It was only with difficulty that he managed to refrain from collecting an assortment of other weird objects as well. Another of his rare distractions consisted in visiting the market where fruit and vegetables were piled up in splashes of colour under a permanently blue sky. Among the first pictures painted in Royan is the *Nature morte au crâne de mouton* of 6th October (Galerie Leiris, Paris), a strikingly realistic work with a yellowing skull of polished bone placed beside a quarter of red meat.

But working conditions were discouraging. He was obliged to set up his canvases on chairs and painted them bending double. He was using wooden chair-seats which he had bought in the town as a palette. Green light filtering through the trees in the avenue was bad for working by. The room became dark as soon as the sun started to go down. But with Picasso no material difficulty has ever got the better of his passion for work.

First news of the war was alarming. Poland collapsed under the unforeseen onslaught of the new strategy. The unpreparedness of the democracies opened like a bottomless pit. Picasso worked on apparently detached from surrounding events. He painted the portraits of his friends, of Dora Maar as the *Femme au chapeau fleuri* with scattered features, immense sad eyes dominating the face, a puckered mouth and a small hat incongruously perched on this mask of distress. As a surprise for him he also painted Sabartés in his absence wearing the high ruff and a black hat with a blue feather. Only the high bulging forehead has remained in its place, the rest of the face is violently twisted like a piece of material. The pointed nose painted in profile reveals the two nostrils, the mouth very characteristically drawn follows it to the left while the eyes and a small chin move sharply towards the right. Everything in the face is so displaced that even the spectacles which the model is wearing are painted upside-down with the curve of the bridge facing the bottom of the picture.

The two friends had got into the habit of taking a morning walk ending up at a café. There with a bottle of Évian water in front of him Picasso would listen to the latest communiqué. This was the time of the 'phoney war'. Closeted in his makeshift studio Picasso began to worry about the scarcity of canvases. He was so afraid of running short of material that he bought a mountain of notebooks, sketching in them the general lines of current pictures or ideas for future ones.

Brushes were also becoming scarce and he began to fear that his stock might become exhausted. So he tried his hand at making them himself, relaxing only when success showed that he could make enough to last through the war.

Towards mid-November he left with Sabartés and Dora Maar for Paris. He also visited Le Tremblay and Boisgeloup to put his canvases and drawings in a safe place and bring back tubes of paint and a proper easel.

The dining-room which he was using as a studio seemed to get smaller and darker as the days grew shorter. Finally, Picasso decided to rent a studio and a small room on the top floor of a narrow house—the villa 'Les Voiliers'—standing between the two large hotels in Royan. There was a magnificent view from the windows. 'I don't need such a panorama just for myself,' he said, 'but it is worth a lot to have nothing blocking the view.' When he moved in towards the end of January, 1940, he stood for a long time by the window watching the sea and the sky aflame with the setting sun. 'That would be very nice for someone who was a painter,' he said with a touch of envy for those who have no sense of mission to disintegrate the universe. He seemed sorry now to have left the discomfort of the cluttered room where he had to bend double to paint and bit by bit he brought over an assortment of furniture, including an armchair covered with olive green velvet and another made of twisted cane.

This chair became part of the accessories which established themselves as the sole element of continuity in Picasso's work. He painted, mostly from Dora Maar, a series of increasingly mask-like portraits which became more and more detached from the model. These seated women with decomposed features were painted as phantoms with beige flesh against a grey background or in strident, multicoloured dresses and were mostly reduced to linear planes and geometric forms. Sydney Janis stresses that this disjunction of the features originated with *Guernica* and adds: 'Just as the war itself spread from a localized Spanish conflict to a world struggle, so these deformations became amplified and inundated his art, inaugurating a new phase in his creative work.'

Picasso was feeling at this time a kind of dull rage against the madness of humanity. 'We believe we are superior to the animals,' he grumbled, 'but we are not.' Human inventions aroused his ire, like that of the clock which he denounced as a scourge. 'In spite of our scientific achievements we have lost a sense of direction,' he said, 'and now we have only sufficient instinct left to put a hand on that part of the body which we want to scratch when it itches.'

But he was still working. Apart from pictures, he was painting in oil on paper and making innumerable sketches, mostly in charcoal. Sometimes, leaving the canvas on its easel, he devoted a whole day to sketches, often taking them to a very advanced stage. 'This accumulation of pictorial ideas on paper,' he explained later, 'might eventually amount to something that I could use in my canvases, although never quite in the same form.'

In the middle of March, Picasso again left with Dora Maar for Paris. '*Je travaille, je peins et je m'emmerde,*' he wrote to Sabartés on a postcard. An exhibition of his watercolours, gouaches and drawings was to open at the Galerie M.A.I. on 19th August. In a Paris bristling with alarming rumours he became nostalgic for the calm of Royan. On 27th, 28th and 29th March he painted still-lifes and it was the Royan market that he had before his eyes when he wrote to Sabartés from his studio in the Rue des Grands-Augustins: 'I have been working. I have done three still-lifes, some fishes with a pair of scales, a large crab and some eels.'

Then the big German offensive began. Disaster on an inconceivable scale was imminent. Paris was seized with panic. Picasso returned to Royan on 17th May and, as though to erect a wall between himself and events, at once began work. But the war could no longer be shut out. Futile effort was expended on digging trenches in the town, then the first refugees began to arrive, among them friends and acquaintances of Picasso, men who were politically compromised and Jewish artists who hoped to find a ship at Bordeaux or take refuge in the South of France.

The French troops were falling back without having yet understood what had happened to them. In Royan, buildings were requisitioned and the restaurants were full to bursting. The first queues were forming at the bakers. The Germans entered Paris. 'They think themselves very intelligent,' said Picasso, 'and they are—sometimes. But we certainly paint better than they do. So many troops and machines, so much force and terror to get this far. . . . They imagine they have taken Paris. . . . On the other hand, we, without moving from here, have been holding Berlin for a very long time and I don't think they will be capable of dislodging us.'

20　Picasso with his owl

21 Picasso speaking at Wroclaw, Poland, 1948

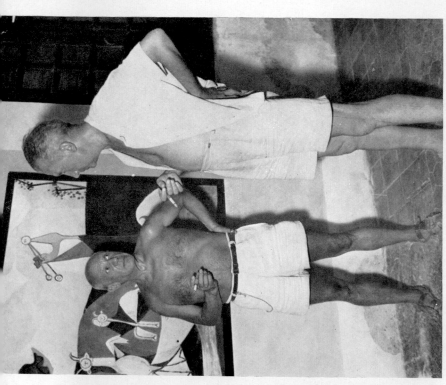

22 Picasso and Éluard at Antibes

This sounded like whistling in the dark. One evening the German troops arrived in Royan. Picasso watched them marching in from the window of his studio. The Kommandantur was set up in his immediate neighbourhood, at the Hotel de Paris.

On 15th August, Picasso painted the café at Royan, lavishing all the brilliance of his palette on a canvas where the freshness of the colouring is enhanced by the sheen of the ripolin. Above the greens, mauves and violets of the square rises a yellow building with blue windows in red frames. A small wooden balcony on which he had often leant with an awning gaily striped in green and yellow looks like some graceful stage set. The sky of crystalline blue tinged with green reflections from the sea seems swept by a fresh breeze. The picture is an explosion of gaiety and of faith in life. It was Picasso's farewell to Royan.

Soon little would remain of the town he had known. The Hotel de Paris where the Germans had so arrogantly installed themselves was to disappear in the Allied raids, and the villa 'Les Voiliers' from where he had painted the joyous face of Royan was also to become a heap of rubble. Friends now advised Picasso to leave occupied France. He was the representative *par excellence* of that 'Kunstbolschevismus' which an incompetent painter who was also the all-powerful conqueror of the hour was persecuting with venomous private rancour. It was known that the author of *Guernica* had lavished help on the Spanish Republicans and the Germans were experts in sorting out sheep from goats. Picasso received invitations from all over the world, from Mexico, the Argentine and the United States. But he decided to return to occupied Paris. Just as he was leaving and about to climb into the car with Kazbek at his heels a German officer standing stiffly in front of the Kommandantur walked over: '*Bitte,*'—and summoning all his knowledge of French—'*auriez-vous la bonté de me dire de quelle race est votre chien?*'

Picasso returned to a deserted and mournful Paris. To start with he lived in the Rue La Boétie. But travel between the flat and his studio became difficult and he decided to move to the Rue des Grands-Augustins. In the general climate of cold and hunger he started work.

In the last days at Royan, having packed up all his canvases, he painted another two portraits on the lids of the packing cases. At Royan, too, he had met a very agitated friend who had asked him: 'What shall we do with the Germans on our heels?' 'Hold exhibitions,' Picasso had replied. But in fact, compromised as he was in the eyes of the Germans, he was forbidden to exhibit in Paris. He put most of his pictures in safety in the armoured vaults of a bank, but kept more than a hundred. And he worked. 'This was not the moment for a creative individual to throw up the sponge, accept defeat and stop work,' he said later. 'There was nothing to do but go on working seriously and enthusiastically, struggle to find food, calmly continue to see one's friends and await freedom.'

But the struggle for mere survival was hard enough. It was cold in the huge house in the Rue des Grands-Augustins, for the recently installed central heating could not be used. Picasso's numbed fingers could barely hold a brush. One day he unearthed a large coal-burning stove and this was hoisted with great difficulty up the steep and winding staircase. It was impossible to find enough coal to feed it, but Picasso thought that the stove resembled a negro sculpture and was reluctant to move it again. As a makeshift he was lent a cooking stove which filled the room with smoke.

At the beginning of January, 1941—'solely as a pastime', says Sabartés—Picasso began to write, playing with words as he had toyed with pleated paper, twisted wire, metal leaves, matches, bits of horse-hair or string and made objects of them. But while his impatient fingers seemed automatically to construct coherent shapes, words with him often assumed a life of their own. His literary efforts did not reveal the discipline or the instinctive sureness of touch of his plastic vision. Surrealism had not influenced his painting—with the exception of the drawings done in 1933—but it left lively traces in his style. He jotted down notes and soon these began to take the form of a play which he wrote guided by the association of ideas and by fragments of things seen and heard. Picasso greatly enjoyed writing this play which he called *Desire caught by the Tail*.

The play reflected the privations of the times interpreted according to his own particular sense of humour. The opening of the second act represents a corridor in 'Sordid's Hotel' with two feet in front of each door writhing in agony and howling in chorus: 'My chilblains! My chilblains!' There is a memory of the smoking stove: 'My slave-Slav-Hispano-Moorish cooking stove and albumenuric servant and mistress. . . .' The isolation of people living in an egotistic world is reflected in this retort by one of the characters: 'I strike my portrait against my forehead and cry the wares of my grief to windows closed to all pity.' *Desire caught by the Tail* is a slightly forced laugh which suddenly exploded in the gloom of Paris—the Paris of the curfew, where houses were searched at any moment of the day or night and in the early mornings the Gestapo roused citizens from their beds with heavy knocks on the door.

In March, 1943, the Leiris invited some friends to their home to read through the play under the direction of Albert Camus. These were people who, like Picasso, were awaiting the hour of freedom and came together for the sake of companionship: Jean-Paul Sartre, Simone de Beauvoir, Raymond Queneau, Dora Maar and others. The sense of cohesion which friendship afforded was one of the keys to surviving those dark years which dragged by so inordinately slowly. To all those who lived in Paris or elsewhere and were uprooted from their normal lives the years of the German occupation seemed to pass at a different speed from the usual, as though time itself had been altered and clocks were ticking to a slower rhythm. Hopes too long deferred became weary and finally wore out. This tiredness often impelled even the most timorous people to action or incited others to come to terms with the enemy.

Picasso was both protected by his fame and, because of it, particularly exposed. The rumour ran through occupied France that Otto Abetz himself, Hitler's ambassador in Paris and a former professor of drawing, had gone to see him and, shocked by the coldness of his studio, had offered to supply him with coal, an offer which Picasso had refused. It was also said that Abetz had been struck by a photograph of the picture *Guernica* and asked: 'Oh, it was you, Monsieur Picasso, who did that?' to which Picasso had replied: 'No, it was you.'

Occupied France took comfort from stories of this kind which spread far and wide on the grapevine. When Picasso was asked after the Liberation if this particular tale was true he replied laughing: 'Yes, it's true, more or less. Sometimes the Boches used to visit me on the pretext of admiring my pictures. I used to give them postcards of my canvas *Guernica* and told them: "Take them away! Souvenir! Souvenir!" ' Suspect from the first, Picasso was also the target of envy. A persistent rumour had it that he was a Jew, or at least half Jewish. When asked about his origins he replied that as far as he knew he had no Jewish blood in his veins, but added immediately: 'I wish I had.'

In an article published in *Comoedia* Vlaminck fulminated against him. Camille Mauclair held him responsible for the crisis in modern art, an American Fascist tract imputed the decadence of painting to him and he featured prominently in a book by Vanderpyl with the suggestive title: *L'Art sans patrie est un mensonge; le pinceau d'Israël*.

It was at this time that Picasso's power of abstraction, his ability to shut himself off from everything that might deflect him from his path, was fully revealed. As though anxious to cling to some stability in a disintegrating world he continued to paint innumerable variations on the same motif of the seated woman. But the destructive atmosphere of his environment found a way into his pictures and distorted still further the features of Dora Maar, as for instance in the *Femme au corsage bleu* (Galerie Leiris, Paris). The bodice with blobs of white was to reappear in many of his pictures, but in fact it was never worn by Dora Maar.

But it was not only on faces that Picasso inflicted his obsessions. The numerous nudes which he drew or painted at this time reveal different aspects of their bodies growing out of one another without transition. They seem to recall the nightmares of Goya when he drew women with multiple limbs in the *Disparates*. But Picasso did not aim as Goya did to present the contradictions in a human being, but rather the simultaneous aspects of his existence. A series of sketches done in May, 1941, vary a circular view of a reclining body. A nude with almost realistic contours presents a face with two profiles joined together, one seen from the back attached to one seen from the front.

The theme of two amorous women now also appeared in his pictures culminating in the *Aubade* (Museum of Modern Art, Paris), where in the presence of a mirror one nude woman, contorted to present her in all her aspects, is stretched out on a striped divan, while another, of curiously masculine appearance, is sitting clothed on a chair with a mandolin on her knees. The different simultaneous aspects of the nude are depicted in linear planes or in facets with sharp points and deep scattered shadows. At the moment, a division into rectilinear planes was dominating his pictures with violent contrasts of colour. This treatment was continued in the series of seated women which became an exercise in interpretation carried out on a very large scale.

'I did not paint the war,' said Picasso after the Liberation, 'because I am not one of those artists who go looking for a subject like a photographer. But there is no doubt that the war is there in the pictures which I painted then. Someday, perhaps, a historian will demonstrate how my painting changed under the influence of the war. I myself, I don't know.'

The war did indeed exist in Picasso's paintings, even in the still-lifes which he painted during its course. Daily life in those years was full of sordid privations. Picasso with his Spanish sobriety found it easy to adjust himself to austerity, but even his indifference in matters of food yielded to growing hunger. One day, he painted the *Buffet du 'Savoyard'*, the restaurant where he frequently ate, with the showpiece of contemporary meals: a roll of black sausage with artichokes, a large butcher's knife and a bottle. This picture is painted in dull tones and it reveals, in Picasso's own words, 'a mournful and sombre atmosphere like Philip II'; forks and knives emerge from an open drawer 'like tormented souls in Purgatory'.

Monsters continued to appear in Picasso's work, assuming in turn the aspect of all the terrors which haunted primitive man when he was cold and hungry, when he struggled to survive. Thus the *Femme tenant un artichaut* of 1942 shows a barbarous idol with a nostril-eye, a crescent-shaped mouth and one ear climbing over an eyebrow, holding a club studded with sharp points.

Even when Picasso lavished the gayest of colours on his canvas, his still-lifes remained stamped with a sense of drama. At first sight the *Nature morte avec la guitare et l'épée de matador* seems composed of gay touches and of an assembly of peaceful objects, such as a cigar which is burning in a crystal cup. But these objects throw very blue shadows on the wall, the mirror in its brilliant gilded frame reflects a stormy background, and risen unexpectedly from nowhere a white sword with a violent red handle rests against the edge of a table.

Picasso seldom varied his subjects, but now he felt a taste for change, placing objects in his still-lifes which he had not yet employed. He also turned to an unexpected theme: childhood. In the *Child with Pigeons*, theme and composition are equally unusual. A fat, chubby-faced baby is sitting on the ground beside a chair on which two pigeons are perching, one on the seat and the other on the back. In the round head of the baby unequal eyes gaze out insistently. No child served him as model, but the features are vaguely familiar. 'We called the baby Churchill,' says Picasso laughing, 'because we thought it was like him.'

The summer of 1943 was bright with hope. The nightmare was still installed in the heart of Paris, the boots of German soldiers still hammered the streets and an increasingly inventive terror was even becoming more burdensome, but the German reverses in Russia showed that the turning-point in the war had come. Victory was changing sides. Picasso had hardly ever spent the summer in Paris, but since his return from Royan he had ceased travelling which had become difficult for foreigners. Yet when he left the house he saw close by, as though for the first time, the small garden of the Vert-Galant at the foot of the Pont-Neuf, with trees that seemed to form part of the architecture and at the back the equestrian statue of Henry IV. The garden was a rendezvous of lovers, and Picasso painted them as grotesque figures with round eyes, a moustache pressed against a mouth in the upturned crescent of a woman's face. The *Vert-Galant* and a series of embracing lovers showed that Picasso's taste for change was becoming more marked. At the same time, linear forms and planes outlined with a dark stroke were giving way to increasingly accentuated relief.

In 1941 Picasso had returned to sculpture: heavy-bodied cats, birds, vaguely human heads and small objects that could be held in the hollow of the hand. He had plaster casts dating from 1931 to 1933 brought from Boisgeloup, for he had almost completely abandoned sculpture for over ten years. But at a moment when the Germans were removing statues from Paris to be made into guns, he had great difficulty in having them cast in bronze. For his sculptures he used the most humble objects, anything which came to hand, like a cake-tin, a tailor's dummy or corrugated paper.

One day his inventive eye fell on an old bicycle saddle and handlebars. Placing the handlebars at the back of the saddle in an upright position he created a bull's head with horns. The illusion was striking and the virtuosity of the transformation conferred a kind of noisy notoriety on this *Tête de taureau*. When it was exhibited after the Liberation Picasso looked at it with an amused air. 'A metamorphosis has taken place,' he said to André Warnod, 'but now I would like another metamorphosis to occur in the opposite direction. Suppose my bull's head was thrown on the rubbish heap and one day a man came along and said to himself: "There's something I could use as handlebars for my bicycle." Then a double metamorphosis would have been achieved. . . .'

Everything that Picasso created in those last years of the war expressed his refusal to capitulate, his determination to endure. Friends in the Resistance undertook to take his plaster casts to a secret foundry at night. This was the time of fantastic feats when people distributed some tract or other without worrying too much whether it was worth risking death under torture for the effect it was likely to produce. Buried under refuse, Picasso's casts were taken in wheelbarrows to the foundry under the nose of German patrols, and the bronzes were returned in the same way. What really mattered in all this was the act of defiance in itself, the question of principle.

Picasso now embarked on a large sculptural work. He prepared numerous sketches and drawings for it which an American critic has assessed at about a hundred. These preparations were so thorough and the conception of the work down to the smallest details so complete in his mind that the seven foot high statue was executed in a single day in February, 1943. The work appears as an isolated theme in his art without any connection with the times or roots in Picasso's own past. Its main characteristic is extreme simplicity. 'Primitive sculpture has never been improved on,' Picasso had said to Sabartés during their stay in Royan, and he seemed indeed to have rediscovered the secret of primitive instincts when he sculpted *L'Homme au mouton*. It is curious that this simple vision rose in the mind of a townsman living in beleaguered Paris. The artistic antecedents of *L'Homme au mouton*, in so far as they exist, might go back to the Good Shepherd of early Christianity, but Picasso's presentation of the man and the way he holds the animal give the lie to any symbolical intention.

The war was in its final convulsions, deliverance was approaching and it was now that the German terror was redoubled. Every day brought news of the disappearance of some friend, of a Jew who had hitherto been in hiding, or a member of the militant Resistance. Max Jacob, who for some years had been living as a lay brother at the abbey of Saint-Benoît-sur-Loire, had not escaped racial persecution and had been forced to wear the yellow star. The arrest of his sister had been a cruel blow, but he did nothing to escape the same fate and even stayed on in the village where he was only too well known. He himself was arrested in February, 1944, and taken to a concentration camp at

Drancy where he died. When his body was brought back to Paris for burial in the cemetery at Ivry, Picasso was among the few friends who dared to join the funeral procession. There was something particularly terrible in the deaths of needless victims in the last stages of the war, and those that were left felt an increasing isolation.

Allied air attacks on targets in Paris were now redoubled and the nights shook with explosions. As though to lend permanence to the threatened scene, Picasso painted the Seine embankment including in the picture some of his favourite motifs. According to Sydney Janis he seemed to be thinking of some great work, a twentieth-century version of *La Grande Jatte*. Like many foreigners who had suffered terribly at the defeat of France, he was now filled with enthusiasm by the rebirth of hope and by the many deeds of anonymous heroism. On 14th July, Bastille Day, he painted two pictures with a view of Notre-Dame. During his first year in Paris he had painted the national festival with the explosive colouring he was using at that time. Now the Germans had forbidden all national celebrations, but France was showing the old spirit in fighting tyranny. Picasso has perhaps never been so French as on that 14th July when he painted the eternal Paris.

At the beginning of August, 1944, the Allied armies began their swift advance. Picasso lingered by the window of his studio where a tomato plant was growing in a pot, branching vigorously towards a clear sky against a background of grey wall. Most of the tomatoes were still green; day by day Picasso watched them grow till they became tinged with red and then, between 3rd and 10th August, painted four pictures of them.

The war drew closer, shooting broke out in the streets. There was a rumour that before leaving Paris the Germans were going to blow up the city. No one could be sure of survival. On 21st and 22nd August Picasso painted two realistic watercolour portraits of his daughter Maïa, taking particular pains as though to bequeath them to posterity.

On 24th August a full-scale battle was raging in the streets. The Germans barricaded themselves in the Luxembourg. The Prefecture, close to the embankment, became a citadel of the Resistance. Young, mostly very young men with armband and rifle mounted guard at crossroads. Soon, poignant inscriptions would appear on the walls of Paris saying simply: 'Ici, est tombé pour la France. . . .' Most of the young people who died in those last hours had not yet reached the age of manhood. Tanks now came into action. Heavy fighting had broken out in the Boulevard Saint-Michel. The windows shook in Picasso's studio. Somehow he had to break the tension, fill the period of waiting with activity and do something so different that it would have no connection of any kind with the surrounding frenzy.

Between 24th and 29th August Picasso interpreted the *Bacchanale* of Poussin according to the laws of his own vision. He had a great admiration for Poussin. He said one day to Kahnweiler: 'Look at Poussin when he painted *Orpheus*, well, that's narrative. The whole thing, even the smallest leaf, tells a story.' Some secret affinity now induced Picasso to study the *Bacchanale* and capture its secret. 'Masterpieces are the pictures which other people paint,' he said one day to Malraux.

In Poussin's great picture it seems to have been the frenzied movement which attracted him, and that obsession with sensuality common to those who skirt death by inches. 'Omitting practically nothing in Poussin, he changed almost everything,' wrote John Lucas. The *Bacchanale*, reduced to a quarter of its size and painted in watercolour, not in oil, became a characteristic chapter in Picasso's eroticism, his dreams and his nightmares. The central couple comprises one of his familiar figures, the bearded faun, and a nymph who is closer to Goya than antiquity, with a sharp profile, wrinkled neck, immense buttocks and two conjoined breasts. The goat standing by her has eyes filled with profound human sadness. The picture reveals traces of almost every one of Picasso's styles: there is a woman carrying fruit with a classic profile, Bacchantes with diminutive spherical heads, a nude with cubist facets and even monsters with Janus heads. Huge feet, enormous swollen breasts and hands like flails emerge from the intertwining bodies. A curious anthropomorphic whirlwind seems to run through the picture, where trees writhe like bodies arched with erotic desire and human limbs become trees or leaves.

Picasso painted feverishly during the battle for Paris amidst a rattle of window-panes, thundering tanks and the nearby crackle and roar of rifles and guns. Shots whined and ricocheted off a neighbouring house. To those who later expressed amazement that he could concentrate on work in such conditions he replied: 'It was an exercise in discipline.'

The Allied troops entered liberated Paris. There were rumours that

Picasso had been arrested, had died in prison or in a concentration camp. But American correspondents investigating the truth were able to inform their newspapers: 'Picasso is safe!' And somehow this news seemed very important, even to those who had only a vague idea of his work.

CHAPTER XV 1945–1949

Joie de Vivre

'WHAT do you think an artist is?' said Picasso at the beginning of 1945. 'A half-wit who only has eyes if he is a painter, ears if he is a musician, a lyre attuned to every human emotion if he is a poet, or only muscles if he is a boxer? On the contrary he is at the same time a political being constantly awake to events in the world and reacting to them with all of himself.' Picasso has always been in close contact with his time, reacting to all the currents in human thought and greatly interested in every new contribution to the intellectual life of the world. The variety of subjects which interest him brings him close to the type of creator of which Leonardo dreamed: the painter-philosopher.

Yet Picasso for whom art is life itself might have subscribed to the doctrine of art for art's sake. His opponents have frequently stressed his artist's egoism. Yet his constant state of awareness of which he himself speaks and the acuity of his social conscience complement rather than contradict his creative exclusivism. 'How would it be possible,' he said in the same interview granted to the *Lettres françaises*, 'not to be interested in other people and to detach oneself from the life which they bring us so abundantly?'

Long before the word came into use, Picasso was a 'committed' artist. He was when he painted the poor people of Barcelona and engraved the *Repas frugal*. He was when he answered Fascism with *Guernica*. Yet he only fully saw himself as a 'political' being during those days following the Liberation when a flood-tide of visitors inundated his studio in contrast to the sepulchral silence of the occupation years.

He had taken no part in the stirring deeds of the Resistance and had not endured the dangers of a double life, yet at a time when people knew little even about their closest neighbours' activities it was known throughout France that Picasso had refused to compromise with or make any concession to the enemy, in striking contrast to the attitude of many well-known artists during those dark years. Even the Resistance had contained more anonymous heroes than former celebrities. Thus Picasso was one of the few men of international reputation who could be taken as a symbol of French endurance, and in the joy of Liberation the gratitude and enthusiasm which centred round him were particularly great.

As soon as Paris was free Éluard arrived at the studio with a large album under his arm which the poets and painters of the Resistance intended to present as a tribute to General de Gaulle, the legendary figure who had kept bright the flame of hope during the occupation. The first page of the album had been reserved for a drawing by Picasso.

A photograph taken a few days after the Liberation shows him as he was after the long ordeal: thinner, with white hair growing down his neck and sunken, deeply-lined cheeks. Picasso's studio now became a centre of intellectual life that had been scattered up and down the country and was now flowing back to Paris. Gertrude Stein returned from a long retreat in the Ain where she had shared the life of simple loyal French people. Besides friends, total strangers now called on Picasso out of curiosity claiming that they were former acquaintances, and for the time being it was easy to gain entrance. Above the doorbell a card was pinned which said simply: 'Ici'. The long room began to look like a railway platform.

But it was not only friends, picture dealers and celebrity-hunters who climbed the steep staircase. Thanks to the exhibition held at the beginning of the war in New York, Picasso was one of the few names known in America. Art-critics enrolled in the Allied armies asked him questions to which he replied with an unusually good grace. Enthusiasts had persuaded the American authorities to familiarize even the ordinary soldiers with Picasso's art. From now on he was perpetually in the limelight. He was already becoming a legend.

Intellectual life so long repressed now revived with extraordinary vigour. Though the war was not yet over and the blackout continued, though everyone was poor, cold and hungry, the Autumn Salon opened its doors barely six weeks after the Liberation. It was called the Salon de la Libération. One huge gallery was devoted to Picasso's work, an honour rarely granted to a French painter and never to a foreigner. He exhibited seventy-four canvases painted in recent years and five bronzes cast during the occupation. Visitors were confronted by visions from the nether pit.

When Picasso assumes a new manner the public always needs time to adapt itself even with the best will in the world, and it is necessary to tread a long and arduous path before his intentions can be understood. In liberated Paris some people were reluctant to make this effort, and two days after the exhibition opened what seems to have been a carefully organized demonstration took place. Headed by gentlemen of solemn appearance, some young people, mostly students from the École des Beaux-Arts, burst in and started shouting: '*Décrochez! Remboursez!*'—'Take them down! Money back!' Willing arms removed the pictures from the walls and attempts were made to slash the canvases. Picasso took up the challenge. 'Painting,' he said, 'is not intended for interior decoration. It is an instrument of offensive and defensive war against the enemy!'

Just before the exhibition opened the newspapers had announced that Picasso had joined the Communist Party. People at this time were joining the Communists *en masse*—many of them were surprising conversions—usually in the belief that this was the Party to which future power belonged. Communism had emerged from the years of occupation with enhanced prestige. In every cell of the Resistance it had been found that their long experience of Party discipline and underground activity had fitted the Communists better than any other political group to carry out their perilous, furtive and exacting work. 'Isn't it the Communists who have been the most courageous in France, in Russia and in my own Spain?' asked Picasso at this time.

But it was not opportunism or even respect which impelled Picasso to join the Communist Party. In an interview given about 20th October to the American publication *New Masses*, he explained at length the reasons for his action. He stressed the principles which had governed him in the past: 'I am proud to say that I have never considered painting simply as a pleasure-giving art, a distraction; I have wanted, by drawing and colour since those were my weapons, to advance ever further in knowledge of the world and of men.' He found it easy to identify his work with action. 'Yes, I am conscious of always having struggled, through my painting, as a true revolutionary.'

As his struggle had always been in isolation, the occupation had

227

made him realize the impotence of a solitary individual confronted with a hostile world: 'Those terrible years of oppression showed me,' he said, 'that I should struggle not only through my art, but with my whole being.' But his principal motive seems to have been a fear of loneliness which suddenly overcame him and weakened his pride in being alone. Those years of solitary and silent work had chilled his spine and he was now turning to a source of warmth. Just as he had looked for a comradeship he had rarely known by plunging into the controversies of the Spanish Civil War, so now he sought and found it in the Communist Party, 'among all those', as he said, 'whom I most respect, the greatest thinkers, the greatest poets and all those insurgents of Paris with their beautiful faces that I saw during the days of August'. His statement ended with the heart-felt cry: 'I am once more amongst my brothers.' Picasso's profession of faith created an enormous stir. Once again, American journalists smothered him with questions, asking him, for instance, whether, as he was now a Communist, he would change his style.

But Picasso was determined to preserve full freedom of expression and was conscious of being able to do so. He explained patiently to his questioner that he was still the same man he had always been: 'If I was a Royalist or Communist bootmaker I wouldn't make my boots in a special way to show my political convictions.' His previous statements had revived animosity implanted by Nazi propaganda against modern art as an instrument of Bolshevism. 'If I was a chemist,' retorted Picasso, 'and I obtained a red liquid in my experiments that would not mean that I was making Communist propaganda, would it?'

But Picasso supplied the real reason for his joining the Communist Party in a further interview with *New Masses*: 'I was in a great hurry to find a home. I have always been an exile; now I am one no longer.' This helps to explain his continued loyalty to the Communist Party, which has persisted despite some stormy incidents.

The first statements by survivors from concentration camps, the first photographs and eye-witness accounts horrified all those who had not yet realized the depths to which human degradation had sunk. As the news of the attack on Guernica had impelled Picasso to undertake his great canvas, so now he painted the *Charnier* (Walter P. Chrysler Collection, New York), choosing the piled corpses of a man, a woman and a child to personify all those millions who had died under torture or in the gas-chambers. He did not attempt, as in *Guernica*, to symbolize the great tragedy: the mass of tortured limbs, fettered arms, clenched, accusing fists and the eyes of the dead child seemed to him eloquent enough. On the man he implanted the face of one of his familiar monsters. Behind the corpses stands a table still covered with a crumpled cloth on which a saucepan and a pitcher are placed, as though to express the eruption of terror into a peaceful domestic scene. As in *Guernica*, colour is avoided; the picture is bathed in a cold steel-grey, blacks and whites, Picasso worked at this picture intermittently for years and finally left it unfinished.

In the *Charnier* and certain still-lifes painted in early 1945, Picasso seemed to be struggling with a nightmare. At the same time a new female figure entered his art, having already appeared in a composition of 1944 which he had called *Intérieur*. One day in 1943 he had noticed a young girl sitting in a restaurant. She had well marked features, wide green eyes, a slim nose and a small expressive mouth. She was very young, barely twenty in fact, and despite a mass of ripe corn-coloured hair, her extremely slim figure made her look more like a boy. She came from a good family, was well educated and cherished a fervent ambition to become a painter. To her, Picasso was a demi-god and she admired him with all the passion of a disciple for his master, while he himself was profoundly touched by this combination of callow youthfulness and reckless adoration.

According to Françoise Gilot herself, Picasso takes up a new interest when he is bored with his existing ones. But chance always plays a part. Those who have known him best never tire of repeating that he does not go out to meet things, he allows them to come to him. It was in this way that, towards the end of 1945, lithography, in which he had already made experiments, suddenly became a passion. This was a providential encounter for him as Picasso's rapidity of execution, based on the clarity of vision which he had possessed even as a young man doing his first diploma drawing, was particularly well suited to the lithographic technique. When needing a change of surroundings he had often gone up to Mourlot and watched him at work. This fired his enthusiasm and his own first lithograph dates from November, 1945. Another, the *Jeune Fille aux grands cheveux*, done in the same month, was a portrait of Françoise Gilot. On yet another lithograph, this too a *Tête de jeune fille*, Picasso worked for a long time, from 7th November, 1945, to 19th February, 1946, producing ten different versions.

This new and passionate interest in lithography took him back to the themes of his youth, to circus and bull-fight scenes. A certain nostalgia for his own country was also revived by Françoise Gilot who, although of purely French extraction, bore a striking resemblance to Spanish gipsies with their green eyes and slim figures. After a rapid sketch of a bull dated 5th December, 1945, he drew a mountainous beast whose massive body lends menace to rare touches of white on black. In another version (of 18th December) the bull is drawn in minute detail down to the folds in its thick skin, the inside of the ear and the tufts of hair on its tail, as though it was to be used as a study-plate in a manual of natural history. By 24th December this realistic bull was divided into segments and triangles by white lines traced over its black surface and behind these its real aspect gradually disappeared until it became an agglomeration of cubist facets or finally, on 17th January, 1946, the mere symbol of a bull drawn in a few lines.

When Picasso began the portrait of Françoise Gilot on 5th May, 1946, he intended to paint her seated in a chair, but in the course of the work he painted over the chair and her legs and bust with a light background-colour, leaving only a slim strip of the body in the form of a stalk bearing pods and round fruit three-quarters of the way up its length. This thin, unsteady stalk is topped by a flattened ball like the heart of a daisy or a sunflower with petals and fine-veined leaves attached to it. Though the features in Françoise Gilot's face are simplified, the curve of the eyebrows, the straight line of the nose, the small childish mouth with a slightly pouting expression and particularly the wide open eyes represent a striking likeness. The picture is painted in soft pastel colours which accentuate a suggestion of preciosity in the texture of the petals and the fruit. Picasso called it *La Femme fleur*.

In February he left Paris for Antibes and Golfe-Juan, Françoise Gilot at once feeling at home in the countryside. On his return to Paris, Picasso resumed work on his lithographs, drawing ten portraits of Françoise in June, 1946, in pencil on lithograph paper.

A sort of healthy pagan joy seems to have taken possession of him at this time. He had always drawn a line between the subjects of his engravings and those of his pictures and he now painted one of his few large mythological works: *L'Enlèvement d'Europe*. In this picture he took his model on a pilgrimage to the past, to ships' figure-heads in detached sections with spherical breasts in turned wood and a fist

23　Picasso at Vallauris

24 Picasso at Vallauris

25 Picasso and Françoise Gilot

like a club which has seized on to the horns of a bull with a pink, bewildered-looking eye.

In July, 1946, Picasso and Françoise Gilot went for the summer to a villa which had been lent to them in Golfe-Juan. On the beach one day a chance encounter took place. He met the curator of the Antibes Museum, Dor de La Souchère. It was again chance which had put this man in charge of a provincial museum as custodian of certain Roman and other remains which had been discovered in the neighbourhood. The collection was housed in a large medieval building that had once been the palace of the Grimaldi family and had been converted into a museum in 1928. La Souchère asked Picasso to do a painting for his museum. The idea of linking an archaeological collection of purely local interest to an art as revolutionary as Picasso's seemed at first sight fantastic. But the curator realized Picasso's attachment to the Mediterranean tradition, and the latter promised more than the gift or the loan of a picture. He accepted the offer which La Souchère then made to use the upper floor of the museum as his studio. As soon as he entered his new domain Picasso realized that he had found an atmosphere particularly propitious for his work.

One has only to follow the ramparts of Antibes to feel that time here has stopped. The walls heated almost to incandescence by the sun overlook a metallic blue sea. The château, which has been much restored since it housed the Picasso Museum, rears as steeply as the rocks in forbidding and mysterious whiteness, like a suit of armour made for giants. A small courtyard below welcomes the visitor with a pool of goldfish and a thick-leaved plant resembling a solidified jet of water. Overhanging the sea is a terrace like the bridge of a ship where a glacial wind blows and the sun is cruel in summer.

The sea and its fauna entered the still-lifes which Picasso now painted. He has always been fond of what he calls 'natural smells' and sea-urchins with their salty odour seemed to appeal to his sensitive nostrils; at any rate, they were soon dominating his pictures with their warm brown colour and their prickly spurs. After someone had given him a baby owl, this also appeared in his still-lifes, its compact silhouette being particularly well suited to the hieratic forms he was in the process of depicting. As canvases were still difficult to obtain, the curator had put some sheets of plywood at his disposal so that he could always have something to work on, and it was on one of these that he painted the *Hibou sur une chaise et oursins*.

Confronted with so much space and so many large surfaces to cover
—the panels of plywood or hardboard supplied were over 7′6″ by
3′7″ in size—Picasso felt his creative forces redoubled, and a kind of
pagan joy and sensual bliss which swept away the last traces of anxiety
in his mind. The picture he now conceived required no preliminary
studies and the successive stages recorded by the photographer,
Michel Sim, show that it was painted at a speed rare even for him. The
central figure is a nude dancing-girl with a tambourine. The stalk of
the 'woman-flower' has breasts like fruit, but the movement of her
legs in a frenzied dance reveals the curve of her back in the same plane.
A heavy-hoofed centaur has borrowed Pan's flute. Two kids are
bucking as though mad with joy. To start with, one of them is a she-
goat, but in the final picture it has been given a disc-like human head
and its companion has a crescent-shaped smile. During the course of
the work the most radical changes took place in the faun on the right
of the picture and these show Picasso's laborious progress even when
he is improvising. The most rigorous economy was also applied to
the picture through judicious suppression of detail, a process which
always costs Picasso an effort. In the result he believed he had told his
fairy-story in a language that would be universally understood. 'This
time at least I knew that I was working for the people,' he said to his
friends. And he knew that if grief is solitary, happiness is communicative even when it is expressed in very personal terms. He called his
picture *La Joie de vivre* (Grimaldi Museum, Antibes) and as a man
who felt his cup overflowing Picasso had indeed tried to communicate
the simple joy of existence.

Picasso was then working as only he can work when the mood is
on him. Large sheets of fibro-cement were to hand, each the same
size as *La Joie de vivre*, and on three of them he painted a triptych of
his personal mythology in vigorous black strokes on a white background. Only the rigours of the season put an end to his frenzied work.
The château had no heating and he had sung his hymn to the sun
during the coldest months in the year in a glacial atmosphere. In the
middle of January he returned to Paris. There he resumed work in
Mourlot's workshop as though he had just come back from an idle
holiday. Though the 'woman-flower' seemed ill-suited for motherhood, Françoise Gilot was now expecting a child.

From the shores of the Mediterranean Picasso brought back a whole
world of apparitions, and these were duly installed in Mourlot's work-

shop: fauns—the most innocent and the most malicious-looking fauns that a pagan *joie de vivre* could ever conceive—confronting a female centaur with huge breasts; a centaur accompanying a Bacchante with long hair and a wasp-waist. His friend the owl which he had brought back with him to Paris also appeared in these new lithographs preceded by numerous studies. And he drew pigeons again, the companions of his childhood, experimenting with a gouache wash on lithograph paper—a process which was to produce extraordinarily fine technical results.

In the midst of these familiar memories a new subject suddenly aroused Picasso's enthusiasm: Cranach's picture, *David and Bathsheba*. With his engraving after Cranach a taste for the archaic was born in Picasso and for a proliferation of detail corresponding to the pleasure he found in getting close to folklore. From this excursion into the Middle Ages knights in armour and women wearing the *hennin* would one day appear in his pictures. And through the Germany of Cranach Picasso was curiously to find a link with the past of his own Spain. A drawing in pen and wash, the *Portrait de Gongora*, dates from March in that same year. With extraordinarily delicate lines alternating with large liquid strokes and an extreme subtlety of contrasts between blacks and whites, Picasso illustrated the sonnets of Gongora which were to be published in the following year. He transcribed the Spanish text in his own hand and accompanied it with marginal illustrations.

On 15th May, 1947, an important event occurred in Picasso's life: his son Claude was born. The child looked extraordinarily like him and the resemblance was to become increasingly marked. At the beginning of June, Picasso stayed for a short while in Avignon before returning to Golfe-Juan. An apparently insignificant event dating from the previous year now became of great importance for him. Quite close to Golfe-Juan is the small village of Vallauris, the 'valley of gold' where the soil has been exploited by potters for centuries. The village, in 1946, was dying. By degrees, production had been reduced to cooking utensils of poor quality which were liable to crack on heating. During the war when there was a shortage of pots and pans there had been a certain revival of activity, but in 1946 when out of pure curiosity Picasso visited the annual exhibition of ceramics sixteen kilns were already out of commission. One factory, the only one to possess an electric kiln, was still struggling to survive and that was run by a woman, Suzanne Ramié, with her husband Georges. Picasso visited this factory and made the acquaintance of the Ramiés. Pottery manufacture had been a closed book to him until then and he found it enormously interesting. The Ramiés suggested he should try his hand at moulding the clay and before leaving he left three small pieces to be fired in the kiln.

This might seem an unimportant interlude, but Picasso remembered it during the course of that winter and jotted down a few sketches for ceramic designs. In the summer of 1947 he went back to Vallauris to see the pieces he had moulded. 'It was then,' says Georges Ramié, 'that he discovered his vocation.' Several factors played a part in this discovery: the pleasure of moulding material which responded to the slightest touch of the fingers, the magic of the fire which transformed the colours and the joy of communal work which contrasted so pleasurably with his solitary tête-à-têtes with a canvas on its easel. In his impatience with intellectual pretension, he also no doubt found relief in contact with the simple potters of the Madoura factory. Later, Georges Ramié wondered whether this primitive industry had not reminded Picasso of Malaga, where the same kind of pottery is made almost in the same way.

To start with he decorated plaques reminiscent of the Italian *tondos* and innumerable oval platters and round plates, large and small, tracing motifs familiar to him in rapid strokes on to the absorbent surface. Here his sureness of touch and speed of execution were perfectly suited to the material. A few masterly strokes would produce a faun, a goat or a pigeon with ruffled feathers. He seemed to be working with a miniaturist's brush when he painted the *Battle of the Centaurs* or the *Horseman* on an oval plate, but at the same time the composition in the restricted space was so skilful and its effects were so well calculated that it could have been transferred on to a large canvas. Beside what he called these 'grecqueries' he painted still-lifes on the plates: sliced fish, eggs, a lemon and a glass of water with its shadow. The objects ran over on to the rim of the pottery standing out from the background in relief or ringed with sunken contours, a technique he often used to obtain an alternation of roughness and smoothness in the surface.

Picasso showed much imagination and light-hearted inventiveness in the way he decorated the material prepared for him. One bulbous vase is adorned with a woman's body with a very slim waist, prominent thighs and arms lazily extended to form the handles. Some of the pieces offered him he transformed with almost magical fingers into a bird with an open beak, a dove, a vulture or an ibex. He also modelled vases into women's bodies, some of them standing with protruding breasts, others crouching, outlined with a light and continuous stroke, the curve of their thighs forming the bottom of the vase. Certain vessels reveal such a strong erotic inspiration that they seem intended for some phallic cult.

Among the exceptional achievements of his ceramic work is an oval dish showing a bull-fight done in 1951 (property of Picasso), with the shadow in the hollow of the dish slanting across the sunlit arena, and tiers of seats thronged with spectators drawn on the rim, partly in sunlight, partly in shadow.

Still living in Golfe-Juan and visiting the Madoura factory only in the afternoons, Picasso made the stupendous achievement of producing over two thousand pieces in the course of a single year, from October, 1947, to October, 1948. When about 150 of them were exhibited in Paris for the first time in November, 1948, the world saw Picasso in a new light, linked to a minor and more readily intelligible art. As far as he was concerned, the staggering performance he had just achieved in no way exhausted his enthusiasm for ceramics, and realizing he had not yet explored all its possibilities, he decided to live in Vallauris itself so as to be nearer his work.

In August, 1948, he went to Poland, a country he had not yet visited, with Éluard and Vercors to attend the Congress of Intellectuals for Peace which was due to be held in Wroclaw. In Warsaw he was obliged to make a speech and elsewhere he played the role of a political star with a good grace, but not without secret amusement. In Cracow, the ancient capital of Poland, the museum which was still closed to the public after the war years was specially opened for the party so that they could see Leonardo's *Lady in Ermine*. At first sight, this precursor of the *Mona Lisa* did not seem to impress Picasso very much. But as always the visual memory was stored up in his mind and a lithograph of December, 1948, showing a series of classical profiles verging on caricature, is reminiscent of Leonardo's drawings. Exploring the museum, Vercors discovered a small landscape by Rembrandt and this immediately made a stronger appeal to Picasso. They enjoyed themselves studying the minute perfection of detail and after a moment's reflection Picasso said: 'It is impossible to compete with sheet talent.'

From Poland Picasso brought back a peasant costume for his son.

He painted him in broad flat surfaces and lively colours dressed in the small embroidered costume with the cap pulled down over the large ball of his head. There is an air of folklore about the whole picture, with the exception of a window-handle which is painted with the usual insistence.

After his return to France at the beginning of winter Picasso settled definitely in Vallauris. The Ramiés found him a vast studio in an empty distillery and a rather nondescript white-painted house on a hill-side. The modest interior contrasted strongly with the fame of its occupant. But Picasso's intimates were fond of quoting his epigram: 'You must be able to afford luxury before you can despise it.'

Even under the blue sky and sun Vallauris is as unpicturesque as any industrial suburb. One day in 1951, Picasso painted *Les Fumées de Vallauris* (property of Picasso), showing serried ranks of bright red buildings with freshly pebble-dashed fronts and new, unweathered slates below a somewhat bare hill spattered with telegraph poles. The thick, spiralling smoke, black or violet in colour, looking more substantial even than the bricks and mortar, was the result of his handiwork. The whole village with its reviving prosperity was due to him. It was Picasso who had put Vallauris on the map and no doubt the intriguing contrast between his fame and the humble craft which he continues to exercise in his studio has helped to keep it there. Thanks to him the village has become endowed not with a past—for its past was never startling—but with an immemorial tradition. It has become linked to the shades of Don Quixote, bulls, fauns, centaurs, Pan with his magic pipes, women-vases with provocative hips, objects of phallic worship, bird-deities, even prehistoric buffaloes. All this very personal and, in the last resort, very artificial achievement—for the soil of Vallauris yields only a small part of the material required—seems nevertheless authentic and rooted in the place itself. The approach to Vallauris today, with its advertisements and stalls of pottery on sale to the public, seems like any other tourist centre—Toledo or the Ponte Vecchio. A large restaurant serves as a façade to this new-found prosperity. Behind it the village slumbers with suburban shops in the square by the church—nothing exceptional, you would think, except that the lady at the haberdashers does a brisk trade selling picture-postcards of Picasso's works.

In 1950, Picasso was made an 'honorary citizen' of Vallauris. In return he gave the municipality a bronze replica of his *Homme au mouton.* Today it stands inconspicuously in a corner of the church square, close to a war memorial of enormous size and in execrable taste. *L'Homme au mouton* looks a bit skimpy in comparison and rather incongruous in this commonplace setting. Nevertheless, it might have been standing there centuries before Vallauris was ever heard of.

CHAPTER XVI 1949–1954

War and Peace

IN APRIL, 1949, the World Peace Congress met in Paris in the enormous Salle Pleyel. Aragon asked Picasso for a poster. The latter rummaged in his files and found a lithograph which Kahnweiler had already published in 1949. Picasso's friends called it 'The Pigeon'. Picasso had drawn it in wash on a zinc plate in January of that year. The quality of the engraving was exceptional, according to Mourlot it was one of the finest which had ever been made. But the white dove on a black background had nothing revolutionary about it; it was presented sitting, not in full flight with spread wings and it did not even bear the traditional olive-branch.

But Aragon sensed at once that this was the symbol he was looking for and he took it away with him. It was then about midday, he remembers. Thousands of copies were made, and by 5 p.m. posters showing the white dove were covering the walls of Paris. Though the Peace Congress had been organized by the Communist Party for its propaganda effect and was highly suspect to many people, Picasso's dove was strikingly successful as a symbol of peace—the peace for which all men yearned. It was also a work of art of rare perfection. In the autumn of that year, despite its association with the Peace Congress, *The Dove*, which was then being exhibited in New York, was awarded the Pennel Memorial Medal by the Philadephia Academy of Fine Arts. This prize had been founded in 1928 by members of the Club of Artists in Watercolour.

Picasso himself had probably not foreseen the suggestive power of his dove before seeing it in the Salle Pleyel, enormously enlarged and impressive under the glare of spotlights above a dark mass of wildly enthusiastic people who from now on associated it with their own fervour. But the day was exciting for him in another sense. Françoise

Gilot was expecting another child and had been taken to the clinic where her son had been born. Picasso telephoned for news from the Salle Pleyel and was delighted when he was told that he now had a daughter. When asked what name she should be given he had no hesitation in saying 'Paloma', the Spanish for 'dove'. For him the birth of a daughter presented the peak of personal happiness. It was as though he had been given a second youth and fresh reasons for loving life at an age when men begin to detach themselves from it, or rather when the joys of life abandon them.

As soon as the child opened its eyes and began to smile Picasso was overwhelmed with feelings of tenderness. All that he had ever loved in another human being he seemed to find again in this little girl. At the same time, the stresses and strains in his nature became focused in his anxious parental love. With anyone but Picasso the combination of personal happiness and fame such as he could never have foreseen would have had a marked influence on his artistic expression. But in his case no break occurred with the past and his view of the world became no calmer.

Curious evidence of his personal feelings and of the persistence of his artistic vision is supplied by two lithographs. Though Picasso joked to his friends: 'To produce babies at my age is really ridiculous,' his emotions and his gratitude to the young mother sought an outlet. He seemed to recognize her androgynous body, which maternity had not deformed, in the *Venus* of Cranach, a picture which he had often seen at the home of the Vicomtesse de Noailles. Of this picture Picasso made a copy more faithful than any he had done before from a large reproduction lent to him by Marie-Laure. Five days later, he elaborated the drawing in his own style, presenting the body of Venus in a simultaneous view with the back attached to the profile, enormous feet and the face streaked with arabesques. The two plates have a certain autobiographical significance, but they also represent Picasso's reluctance to surrender to the softer emotions. A striking instance of his equal interest in the beautiful and the ugly is supplied by the fact that the celebrated *Dove* and the *Toad* both date from the same month of January, 1949. With its almost human expresssion, the loathsome cavern of its mouth and feet like some dripping, viscous liquid, the *Toad* is in a direct line from the monsters of Bosch.

In 1948, Picasso had embarked on an experiment connected with the plates for Balzac's *Chef-d'oeuvre inconnu*. He now repeated it in

239

two large pictures bordering closely on abstract art and bearing the vague title of *Cuisine*. He covered the surface of the canvas with a network of lines ending with dots or dashes with the object, according to Raynal, of achieving 'flat depth' and avoiding the intersection of straight lines deriving from classical perspective. This treatment of the surface recurs in a portrait of his son, dated 1948. He painted him in his small nondescript bed with the curves of the ironwork ending in balls similar to the dots of the abstract lines. The small body squeezed into schematized clothing is treated in curves which repeat the contours of a child's rattle and the slightly compressed sphere of the face in which roughly indicated features are dominated by large eyes.

Meanwhile, in this seemingly contented period in his life, portraits of Françoise Gilot continued to serve as experimental canvases incorporating all the nightmare visions of his past. The pointed muzzle reappeared with the juxtaposition of a vertical and a horizontal eye. He even returned to the Dinard manner with a nude made of articulated pieces of wood. A new experiment—which was repeated, but was not a complete success—consisted of a lithograph in which the features of Françoise were cut up into separate pieces and assembled like a jigsaw-puzzle. Picasso called this experiment *Figure composée*.

Picasso now sought to combine 'flat depth' and the jigsaw-puzzle effect in the treatment of subjects already familiar to him. The most striking example of this experiment is the *Demoiselles du bord de la Seine* (Kunstmuseum, Basle). 'What is important,' writes John Lucas, 'is the changes which were more radical than any Picasso had ever made when he painted directly from nature. He had never taken more justified liberties in a portrait, a landscape or a still-life than in this transformation which was all three together.'

At first sight nothing seems further removed from Picasso than the saturated and even sedate sensuality which characterizes Courbet's picture; nothing seems harder to reconcile with his prevailing tendencies than the realistic perspective of the landscape. But it is this very difficulty which seems to have tempted him. To achieve a total reorganization he began by reducing the height of the picture to a long narrow strip; he cut off the tops of the trees and reduced them to a rhythmic pattern of leaves. Depth was abolished and all reduced to a single plane. All the elements of Courbet's picture were retained, down to the attitudes of the women represented by their leaf-like hands, a hat with scalloped brim, a stylized bouquet and even a boat on the water; but the picture itself had gone.

The *Demoiselles du bord de la Seine* was painted in February, 1950. Barely a fortnight later Picasso copied El Greco's *Portrait of a Painter* which is said to be that of his son, Jorge Manuel. Here everything is brought to the surface after the coherence of the features has been totally destroyed. But what had attracted Picasso in El Greco's picture was the 'lunar light' of Toledo, and this is faithfully conveyed. Spain, at this time, was once more coming into his work: the horsemen and centaurs, for instance, which he used in his ceramic decorations were nearer to Don Quixote than to Antiquity, and his nostalgia for Spain was revealed one day when he came across a car-load of bull-fighters who had broken down on the road. Picasso hastened to help them and after thanking him the torero handed him a visiting card which bore the words: 'matador de los toros'. Picasso returned the courtesy, writing on his own card: 'matador de los toros de la pintura. . . .'

When Picasso painted his two youngest children at the beginning of 1950, he showed them in contrasting light and shadow, their faces cut up into segments and arabesques, their gaily-coloured clothing conspicuous in the foreground and their fingers spread out like acanthus leaves with an ornamental effect. At this time the very spirit of the sombre Spanish baroque was appearing in his pictures. He spent the winter in the South of France and painted Vallauris with the trees raising their bare and twisted branches to the sky like souls in torment and their knotted trunks writhing like dragons in combat. From covering the surface with a static network, the arabesques in his pictures now began to move, turning round on themselves and playing with shapes as though they were tossing a ball.

The double portrait of Claude and Paloma with their Christmas toys is very characteristic of this increased dynamism. Nothing could be more peaceful than children playing if one imagines the subject treated sentimentally, but Picasso painted the agitation of these young creatures and the turbulence of their games. In keeping with the baroque spirit which possessed him at the moment, the surface of the picture is treated in double arabesques.

Returning to his earlier cycle of Maternities, Picasso now often painted his children with their mother. Despite the disturbing presence of her two offspring, Françoise Gilot had resumed her own artistic

241

work as though anxious to preserve her creative independence in the face of Picasso's crushing superiority. He depicted her leaning over her drawing-board while the heads of the two children beside her seem to float in space like bubbles of soap.

As often when he had achieved a certain degree of plasticity in his painting, Picasso passed to sculpture. The transition was the easier in that he was already in process of modelling such extraordinarily successful ceramic figures as his *Screech Owl* of the same year. For his sculpture he retained the already familiar subject of the she-goat, modelling it directly in plaster. This is a material difficult to handle because it dries too quickly and tends to crumble, but the speed of execution it demands corresponded to Picasso's normal rhythm of work. As armature for this sculpture, which was larger than nature, Picasso used the most varied materials, as photographic records show: wickerwork, palm branches, a tin can and two small earthenware jars. He planted his goat, with a neck too thin for its large head and the pregnant body weighed down with a full udder, leaning heavily on its hind legs. The skin is stretched tightly over its flanks and the bronze conveys the desired effect: the contrast between rough and smooth.

At a time when Picasso was painting his children in their rowdy games, the world was once more on the brink of disaster. During the summer of 1950—another summer of clear skies and peaceful occupations—the Korean War broke out. Though he was living apart from events in a somnolent village Picasso was alert to the distant menace. Soon he became obsessed by the danger; in his own words: 'The anxiety and the hatred came to live in me and, at the same time, the desire to fight them both.'

Picasso is considered to have seen the war in Korea through Communist spectacles, accusing the 'war-mongers', but with an optimistic faith in final 'victory'. But he was moved, in fact, by indignation and compassion for the poor inhabitants of a backward country exposed to modern methods of mass extermination. The vision which rose before his eyes was inspired by his horror of war in itself and by his passionate belief in the sanctity of life. His *Massacre in Korea* (property of Picasso) revealed pity for the weak and a profound dislike of brute force. He did not depict events in Korea or the eternal battle between the forces of light and darkness. He avoided the symbolic and expressed himself in a language as readily understandable as those of a popular orator addressing the masses. Basing his picture on Goya's *Fusillade of 3rd May*, which depicted soldiers of Napoleon massacring Spanish victims, he painted a compact group of armed men, underlining their character as an anonymous death-machine by giving them close-fitting armour and medieval visors and suggesting a link between the Frankensteins of modern war and the barbarity of the Middle Ages by making the commander of the execution squad brandish a naked sword over his victims. These are represented by a line of naked women facing the robots, among them a young 'woman-flower', with a head too large for her thin neck, and two pregnant women, one of them with dangling arms and palms open in a gesture conveying fatalism and incomprehension. Like *Guernica* the *Massacre in Korea* is painted in monochrome, but this time in a clear steel-grey with a touch of yellow in the middle and a suggestion of green.

Today there are about fifteen films on Picasso, but one of the first to make a documentary on the artist was Paul Haesarts. Conscious of his outstanding manual and visual powers, Picasso was quite ready to demonstrate them in the cinema and willingly accepted an invitation to co-operate. Certain parts of the film, called *Visit to Picasso*, which show him 'at work' are as close as possible to a performance of conjuring tricks. He is asked to paint on a pane of glass and the audience watch his brush dipped in white oil-paint run over the transparent surface with breath-taking speed and assurance. He draws a huge dove and one sees the bird come to life with an admiration mixed almost with terror.

In Vallauris there was a deconsecrated chapel which had once belonged to the monks of Lérins. For a long time it had been used as a mill for extracting olive-oil. The municipality now offered the building to Picasso to decorate in any way he chose. The idea attracted him and not only because it offered a field for new experiments. Matisse had just finished decorating the chapel of the Dominican convent at Vence. The emulation that had for so long existed between the two artists now played a certain part in Picasso's anxiety to start work at once. He conceived the idea of painting a sequel to the *Massacre in Korea* depicting the horror of war and the paradise of peace. He was also beginning to fear old age, imitating, according to Kahnweiler, an old man getting with difficulty out of a chair and saying: 'It is that which is so terrible. At the moment I am still capable of doing all I want. But to want and not to be able—that's terrible. I must do

243

the Temple of Peace now, while I am still capable of climbing a
ladder.'

The threat of a world conflict died away and, with the collective
suicide of humanity averted, reasons for living seemed for the moment
even more persuasive. Picasso painted the exuberance of Mediterranean
summers: the sun on white walls, the brilliance of orange trees and
palm-leaves rearing in tall arabesques to the sky. The holiday flourish
which Picasso introduced into his Mediterranean landscapes achieved
its greatest intensity in a picture which he painted in 1952 (private
collection, Paris): white walls, a small red villa with green shutters, a
blue pergola bathed in bright golden sunlight and, against the background of an almost violet-blue sea, a boat raising a silvery sail while
gleams of white streak the azure sky like streamers.

Amidst these activities the great work was slowly incubating.
Picasso seemed to have taken root in Vallauris and to be adopting
immutable habits which might one day become tyrannical. But he
now disturbed his routine by offering the use of his second studio in
the disused distillery to the young painter Édouard Pignon.

Pignon had first met Picasso about fifteen years before in circumstances which he had never forgotten. Prior to a big exhibition in
Paris a violent argument had broken out between Pignon, who
wanted a good position for the works of his young colleagues, and
Fernand Léger, whose main object was to show off the important
canvases to best advantage, those of Matisse or Picasso, for instance.
In the middle of the discussion Picasso arrived and instinctively backed
up the young men who were being cold-shouldered. 'I like a good
argument,' he said. 'I like it a lot. But I won't allow young people to
be treated today as we were treated when we were their age.'

Now, at a time when he was beginning to feel lonely and rarely
visited Paris, he invited Édouard Pignon and his wife to share what he
called 'a painter's life' with him. But once the offer was made and
accepted he regretted it at once and awaited the arrival of his guests
with apprehension.

Picasso had plenty of poet and writer friends, but had never had any
close connection with another painter. In view of the difference in
their ages it seemed possible that a relationship of master and pupil
might establish itself between him and Pignon, but Picasso had never
had any disciples and was never to have one. The women who had
been close to him and were painters themselves had inevitably suc-

cumbed to the tyranny of his vision, but Dora Maar had recovered quickly and developed her own creative style in striking portraits and landscapes. Françoise Gilot was at this time seeking her artistic independence with a stubbornness redoubled by the feeling that Picasso's influence held her prisoner like a vice.

Vlaminck grumbled one day: 'Picasso has stifled the spirit of creativity for several generations of artists.' But Pignon, who came from a mining family in the North, was of a tenacious and solid disposition. Throughout a squalid childhood and embittered family quarrels over his choice of career he had preserved a luminous faith in his vocation and in the value of art. With this young, red-headed giant Picasso at once established frank, man-to-man relations, while Pignon, for his part, felt no fears that his famous host would suffocate him. 'Édouard is a tank,' said his wife laughingly.

A house-warming was held in Picasso's studio at Vallauris with an immense placard hung up in the adjoining kitchen: 'Picasso dîne chez Picasso'. A Spanish artist friend, Manolo Ortiz, sang Flamenco airs. Early each afternoon Picasso went into the garden, set up the canvases on which he had worked the previous day and discussed them with his young friends. Pignon always remembered these discussions. 'Every summer,' he has said, 'Vallauris went to our heads like a good liqueur, providing us with work and reflection for the whole year.'

Among the canvases which Picasso painted in that summer of 1952 were two portraits of Hélène Pignon who, under the name of Hélène Parmelin, is a writer of authentic talent with a great mastery of her craft, freshness of vision and an acute sense of humour. Thus the two young people fitted smoothly into Picasso's daily life and soon Pignon was painting as though on a desert island.

From the end of April to mid-September, 1952, Picasso was preoccupied with his great work, confronting the double theme of war and peace. He knew how he was going to treat it and instead of making elaborate studies like those which had preceded *Guernica* he filled notebooks with rapid sketches and outlines of ideas. Goya was always present in him, like the scenes of childhood live in the hearts of exiles, and the first symbol of war which rose before his eyes was a screech owl sitting on the body of a man. From a Pandora's box, which the man incarnating war holds in his hands, horrible visions escape above a pile of human skulls. A man with a naked sword steps forward to slaughter the monster, while, as a kind of counterpart to

horror, a group of girls dance round a tree. The man-owl becomes a
satyr with short curving horns and a wrinkled belly. Then, at a later
stage, he turns into a robot. Near some horses which have been enlisted
in the service of war, a winged horse riding in a boat with an owl and
a pigeon huddled close together on its head symbolizes the finer
aspirations of humanity.

During this preliminary work the chapel was being cleared. The
oil-cake was removed, but the millstone, being too heavy, was left at
the entrance. A ramp was constructed to enable Picasso to paint over
the joins in the wooden panels of the pictures once they had been set
in place in close contact with the curve of the barrel-vaulting.

When he began to transpose his vision of *War and Peace* on to the
panels, the result seemed, and in part was in fact due to improvisation.
Picasso explained to Claude Roy why this was necessary. 'In modern
painting every touch has become a precise operation like a piece of
clockwork. Suppose you paint the beard of a character. It is red and
this redness makes you rearrange the whole picture, repaint everything
around it, like a chain-reaction. I wanted to avoid that and paint as
quick as thought, as in writing, keeping time with the rhythm of my
imagination.' And he added, as though to underline the urgency of
this new style: 'If I had been born a Chinaman I would not be a painter,
but a writer. I would write my pictures.'

The most impressive part of the picture of War was entirely
improvised and 'written in' at the last moment. These are the silhouettes of demons brandishing axes, pikes and knives which Picasso
supplied as escort to the funeral chariot. This army of shadows accom-
panies the chariot in its assault on a mountainous figure of a man who
is holding up a shield on which a dove appears in place of a Medusa's
head. The man-monument symbolizes armed peace; corn is growing
close to his feet. But it is a peace in justice and equity, as the scales
show which he holds in his hand.

The Hymn to Peace corresponding to the sinister procession of
War is in the form of a ballet, like *La Joie de vivre*. A faun sitting on a
snail on the extreme left of the picture supplies music on his short
pipes. In the centre of the composition a large winged horse driven
by a child through a blue haze seems to be trotting to the frenzied
rhythm of two dancing women with contorted bodies presented in a
simultaneous view from all sides at once. Amid these winged, cavorting
genii there is also a child with an owl on its head, an hour-glass float-

ing in the air, a bird-cage full of fish and an enormous bowl of water with birds fluttering in it. Above the dancing figures a sun with prismatic colours glares from a rose-pink sky with rays escaping from it in the form of branches.

The two huge panels, each measuring 15′5″ by 33′6″, were shown to the public for the first time towards the end of 1953 in Picasso's great retrospective exhibition—and, expecting a repetition of *Guernica*, the public was again disappointed, as it had been by *Massacre in Korea*. In all three pictures, but particularly in *War and Peace*, the complaint seemed to be that Picasso had been *too* intelligible and had employed familiar symbols: Picasso, in short, had not been sufficiently Picasso. But he seems to have expected this attitude. While he was working on the huge panels he had shut himself up in his studio and let no one, not even Françoise Gilot, see them. While he spent whole nights painting, his friends had glimpsed only the great yellow sun of peace gleaming through the windows. In fact, both in form and colouring, *War and Peace* was well suited to the walls and vaulting of the small dark chapel for which it was intended.

The Temple of Peace of which Picasso dreamed remained unfinished. He had intended to complete it and, as it were, conclude his story with a vast panel on the back wall. But the public reaction discouraged him and it was this which probably deterred him. In a bout of bad temper he closed the chapel, but then, after a black cloth had been hung over the empty space, opened it again so that the public could see the already complete story of man's ancestral fears and hopes.

In the same year as *War and Peace* Picasso painted several portraits of his children. Paloma, in particular, was taken on the same pilgrimage through the different periods of his art as he imposed on the women he loved. In one portrait the little girl is seen sleeping naked in her wooden bed in that abandoned attitude common to animals and small children, her body treated in Picasso's familiar ship's-figure-head manner. Paloma in blue, with a composite nose constructed of two profile views in the middle of a chubby face where all the other features have remained in their normal position, is strangely reminiscent of *L'Enfant aux pigeons* of 1943. Paloma in a tartan bonnet is brought up to date, as it were, in Picasso's new manner with the contours traced in double arabesques or single arabesques in relief.

The same treatment in grey-blue or in white on a grey background is used to depict women's faces which look as though they were made of rubber tubes (Galerie Leiris, Paris). Arabesques also serve as a framework for still-lifes featuring the skull of a goat, a bottle or a candle, though the double arabesques are sometimes submerged beneath violent colouring and sharply delineated right-angled planes.

In February, 1953, Picasso painted the *Femme et chien sur fond bleu* in which a woman with massive hands has seized the legs of a bulldog which she holds pinned on its back. In its suggestions of animal violence this picture is far removed from the pale and contemplative 'woman-flower'. During the last ten years Françoise Gilot had greatly changed, though Picasso, absorbed in his creative problems, had hardly realized it. 'The passage of time,' she said later, 'had a different effect on each of us.' For a woman, particularly if she is in love, a whole lifetime can be passed between the ages of twenty and thirty, and in the friction of daily life Françoise Gilot's feelings had necessarily undergone a change. They had been pitched too high at the start to be able to subside into domestic contentment. One day, she left Vallauris, taking her two children with her.

Once again, solitude suddenly descended on the man who had never been able to live alone and who now missed his family terribly. For him, as for all famous people, isolation was harder to bear, for it had to be defended—paradoxically—against intruders and scandal-mongers. Winter had laid its blight on the surrounding countryside. Picasso continued to work, at first in ceramics, as though afraid that if he stopped he might stop for ever. Then, towards the end of November, he let his imagination wander and started to draw with anything that came to hand: charcoal, crayon or indian ink. Barricading himself in his studio he produced a series of images based on personal, artistic or literary memories. He worked in a state of auto-intoxication, at a rapidly increasing speed: eight crayon drawings a day in December, up to eighteen a day in the first week of January, reducing to a dozen or so at the end of the month. In 1954, *Verve* published 180 of his drawings dated 28th November, 1953, to 3rd February, 1954. But this was only a small part of his output for, as Aragon said: 'If, as has been suggested, Picasso followed a single line of thought for more than two months the result would not have been 180 drawings, but, as we know, between a thousand and two thousand.'

This series of drawings has been seen as a sort of journal, pages of autobiography like Baudelaire's 'Mon coeur mis à nu'. But the state of mind in which Picasso worked is more reminiscent of Goya producing his *Caprices* and mingling his own passion with social satire and the *roman picaresque*. This parallel occurred to Picasso himself and in his drawings he deliberately introduced elements borrowed from the *Caprices*.

The series was grouped round a central theme: the relationship of a creative artist, whether painter or sculptor, with his model. In the *Suite Vollard* of 1933–4 he had succeeded in conveying the harmonious curves of the female body with almost unequalled perfection. In the new series of 1953–4 the women's bodies are scarcely less beautiful, but their delineation is quite different. This difference is not only due to the employment of a fluid ink, a change of technique which seems to have been chosen to give the best possible expression to a livelier sensibility. Picasso's nervous stroke, whether light or heavy, changes like handwriting under the pressure of emotion and gives his female bodies a sense of vitality which none of his previous drawings had achieved.

The relationship between the painter and his model provides the thread of the story, but the real theme linking the separate drawings is that of creative impotence. This is symbolized by an aged, distinguished-looking painter smoking a long pipe for whom a provocative girl after the 1900 style is posing, wearing only stockings and hat and sitting in such a way as only partially to conceal the dark triangle of her sex.

Other drawings are invaded by frenzied Bacchantes with small erect breasts who are wriggling their buttocks to the sound of pipes played by a fat, bearded faun. But the old painter pays no attention to what is going on around him. Sometimes he is replaced by a mannish old woman with sagging breasts and a fat belly, who confronts a recumbent model with a lascivious and at the same time disgusted expression. Sometimes a small and ancient monkey appears holding a palette and painting a very young nude wearing only a hat and necklace with a supremely contemptuous expression on her face. All these drawings suggest exasperated eroticism. They also contain Picasso's full cast of characters: buffoons, fauns and pages. But even in this familiar company the tragi-comedy of sexual indifference continues.

When Picasso began to use coloured crayon towards the end of the series, the note of gaiety barely weakened the note of tragic disharmony. In the last of the series Picasso portrayed the theme of creative impotence still more clearly with an underlying suggestion of tragedy in the disparity of age between the painter and his model. In *Vieillard et Fille*, drawn in crayon in two different greens, browns and reds, a bald old man appears with a flabby, naked body, wrinkled stomach, circular beard and eyes concealed behind bushy eyebrows. Facing him a very young girl is crouching with an impassive expression, her nude body traced in extremely pure contours.

But when he depicted the central theme of his *Series* with such virtuosity, Picasso's mood of exasperation had already passed, and his drawings in crayon were as close to Ingres as the drawings and engravings of his Classical period. Resuming his work in lithography, he returned to familiar themes, to the dance in *Répétition* and to pierrots, acrobats and variations on the bull-fight. An old woman, a sumptuously clad torero, a small girl (symbolizing confidence) watch the dance of a beautiful nude who is taunting a bull with banderillas. But the bull is only a mask held by a vigorous man who is kneeling before the young dancer. The Minotaur has reappeared, mask in hand, with all his strength recovered.

For once, Picasso followed the advice he was fond of giving his friends: he went off to amuse himself at bull-fights at Collioure and Perpignan amongst a noisy crowd of male and female admirers. Returning refreshed to Vallauris, he set furiously to work again as though anxious to convince himself that his creative powers had remained intact. His interest had been aroused in a slender, fair-skinned girl of such markedly insular charms that she was known in Vallauris as 'L'Anglaise'. Sylvette David was now taken on the obligatory pilgrimage which he imposed on all his female models. The starting point was an almost realistic painting in which a nude torso with tightly waved hair, transparent eyes and a small, innocent mouth recalls the women of Domenico Veneziano. The delicacy of the forms is matched by the delicacy of the colouring which is in grey monochrome of a hard enamel quality.

But the fair Sylvette was only a passing phenomenon. In June, 1954, Picasso painted the portrait of a young woman wearing a yellow-striped dress sitting on the ground with her arms clasping her knees. The square-shaped neck of excessive length carries a head with a straight nose, a small compressed mouth and a soft chin painted in black strokes. The face, which is presented almost in profile, is dominated by enormous eyes beneath low circumflex eyebrows. This picture was a recognizable portrait of Jacqueline Roque, a young, dark-haired woman with a milky skin. Thus, without knowing she was loved, she made her entrance into Picasso's life and work. Her attitude was still calm, but the expectant look in her eyes suggested that she had a premonition of the exciting days to come.

CHAPTER XVII 1954–1956

Picasso the Magician

IN OCTOBER, 1954, Picasso returned to Paris—no one knew whether for a week, three months or for ever. His first public appearance was at a sale of books organized by the National Committee of Authors. A patient and enthusiastic crowd surged towards his stall. 'It's impossible to get near you,' cried a wild-eyed, ecstatic lady, thrusting her way to the front; 'it's like a rush of believers to a miracle.' Picasso quickly restored her to earth. 'I've got a blister on my finger,' he said tonelessly, 'from signing so many books. . . .'

A visit to Picasso in the Rue des Grands-Augustins is quite an adventure. A steep, winding staircase with worn treads leads to a dark landing at the top of the house. Half way up, a hand-written notice used at one time to encourage the visitor: 'M. Picasso habite au-dessus'. But now callers are so numerous they no longer need this guide. When you ring the bell there is silence for a while until you begin to think no one is at home. Then the tall figure of Paulo is standing in the doorway or Sabartés is scrutinizing you with a disenchanted look that at once makes you feel an intruder.

Once you are inside everything is arranged to encourage this feeling. Midday is the time for visits. In the afternoon Picasso is at home to no one, even if he has no work in hand. So you must make the best of your time. The large room with perpetually closed windows in which you find yourself is about as homely as a railway station. Regular visitors and passers-by eye one another with the hostility of travellers competing for seats in the same train. Kahnweiler surveys them all with the sad and patient smile of a courteous gentleman trying to make some strangers understand that they have come to the wrong address. But if they must stay—let their stay be brief. The room is furnished to encourage this. Apart from kitchen chairs, the only other seat is a solitary armchair in faded velvet with a cigar burn. Piles of pictures—the paternal pigeon well in evidence—are leant against the walls or behind a large brazier. The walls themselves are covered with picture-postcards and photographs, including a framed one of Olga Picasso, while yellowing newspaper cuttings are pinned between them. Besides radiators, the large black stove which reminded Picasso of a negro sculpture supplies the heating. A paraffin lamp without a shade recalls the still-lifes of the old penniless days. A long table is piled with books and parcels which will remain unopened until the routine of Picasso's work allows him time to look at them.

This routine is more important to Picasso than visitors or changes of scene. In his case the need for change felt by every human being seems only to apply to his love life. He does not get bored by familiar sights and never seems to feel the urge to do something different, no matter what so long as it is a change from the day before. Nor does he seem to suffer those bouts of claustrophobia which suddenly descend on those who have lived too long in familiar surroundings. The huge variety of his creative resources no doubt satisfies this need for change; new ideas assuage his thirst for the unknown and act as substitute for the long journeys he has never undertaken.

Now, in October, 1954, Picasso in depressed and dispirited mood was awaiting the release of the creative trigger. Shutting himself up in the Rue des Grands-Augustins, he was reluctant to go out even to have his hair cut. One day, he came down to his visitors with the thick hair on the back of his head cut by himself in irregular slices. 'I have not been out for months,' he said in an accusing tone, as though holding the grey skies of Paris and his friends responsible for his misery.

But one day the news went round among his friends that Picasso was working again. On 13th December, 1954, he painted the two first versions of the *Femmes d'Alger* (property of Picasso). The calm sensuality of Delacroix's picture seems to have attracted him, the placidity of the plump bodies and full throats and the satiated expression beneath low heavy eyebrows. Into his own versions of this picture he injected much of his own private torments, giving them a unity of expression which was no doubt more obvious to himself than to the spectator. Nevertheless, the *Femmes d'Alger* represents a much more striking confession than the series of drawings which he had recently completed.

He seems to have had the two versions of Delacroix's work before his eyes, the large canvas in the Louvre and the smaller one in the Fabre Museum at Montpellier. The main accent is supplied immediately by two of the four women he has borrowed from Delacroix's large painting: the woman sitting cross-legged and the other seen in profile in an indolent pose with bowed head. The first woman, who is clothed and rather sleepy in Delacroix's picture, is transformed by Picasso into a nude hunched in a sleep of exhaustion. The main note is struck by large round breasts placed high with strongly marked nipples and also by a rounded abdomen with a conspicuous navel. In one of the variants of February, 1955, which includes only the cross-legged woman, the tips of the breasts become two small open eyes, while in the last version the navel is hollowed like a small hungry mouth.

In several variations a negress appears, seen from the back in Delacroix, but stretched out naked in Picasso's paintings in a voluptuous attitude. One large study in *grisaille* shows a woman who seems to be falling out of bed. 'She, too, is for the *Femmes d'Alger*,' said Picasso. Her huge face bisected by shadow bears the features of Jacqueline Roque. Picasso studied one of his latest versions: 'No, that's not what I want. But instead of working on the same canvas, I shall start again and do another one in a different way.' Thus these different versions are not successive stages in the same picture, but echoes of former manners mingled with new elements, a pilgrimage, as it were, through the past. The mass of triangles and rectangles returns insistently and above this jumble of geometry hovers a coffee-pot, painted with incongruous realism, held aloft by a servant woman who is represented only by signs. The faceless monsters also reappear and the ones with pin-heads, the figure-head Sphinxes and the tangle of curves representing a simultaneous view of bodies.

Begun on 13th December, 1954, the series on the *Femmes d'Alger* reached its fourteenth canvas on 14th February, 1955. From a striped background painted in bright, contrasting colours emerges a sleeping woman depicted in triangles and rectilinear strips with a blue body and salient breasts, the servant woman with a fat short rump and, further back against an oriental window, two enormous breasts which seem to be attached to a totem-pole. The foreground is dominated by the cross-legged woman dressed like an idol and depicted in a perfectly intelligible manner with a round white face, small chin, soft mouth and, under the almost circumflex accent of the eyebrows, the great calm gaze of Jacqueline.

At the beginning of 1955, Picasso's wife, Olga, had died in Cannes. In the spring, leaving one of his apartments in the Rue Gay-Lussac to Inès and the other to Françoise Gilot and the children, he set off for the South of France intending to find somewhere to live there. He meant to be away for only a few days, but he never returned to Paris, not even for the great exhibition held there in the autumn of 1955, although he regretted not seeing the works from the Moscow and Leningrad museums which it included.

Picasso bought a large villa called 'La Californie' on the hills behind Cannes and immediately started to settle in. Strict necessities like beds, chairs and tables were soon inundated and almost crowded out by a mass of assorted objects arriving from his flat in the Rue des Grands-Augustins, until the new house began to look like some wind-swept beach littered with the jetsam from a shipwreck.

Picasso now found a new interest. He has always been very conscious of his exceptional gifts and he realizes that, other factors apart, the speed with which he transposes reality, shaped according to his own particular vision, on to the canvas is in itself a unique phenomenon. This phenomenon arouses his curiosity, he enjoys surprising himself and this helps to explain why he has always been ready to take part in cinematic or photographic experiments. One of these experiments was based on a new type of coloured ink which made the paper transparent on which it was painted and enabled the different stages of a picture to be followed from the back without the artist himself being visible. The film in which this technique was used to illustrate Picasso's sleight of hand was directed by Clouzot. The first shock which Picasso received when he turned up at the studios in Nice was the heat. It was a particularly torrid summer and this was aggravated by the floodlights centred on the canvas and the artist. The second shock was the name of Clouzot's assistant: Claude Renoir, the grandson of the painter. Whenever the name 'Renoir' was called between shots Picasso started at mention of the great man's name. 'I can't get used to it,' he told Hélène Parmelin. 'Every time someone calls "Renoir", you can't imagine the effect that has on me.' But despite all this and the presence of technicians amidst a jungle of cameras and cables, Picasso did not lose his sureness of touch. The charcoal scratched over the white surface, impelled by the frenzy that has always been in him. He began drawing anywhere on the canvas, at the top, the bottom or the middle, tracing the visions which rose complete before his eyes, and the specta-

tors were dazzled by the *tour de force*, not knowing that even as a child
he had been drawing like this and that the facility he revealed was
deceptive in that it conjured a world already familiar to him: the nude
bodies of young girls, the old men and bearded dwarfs that had featured
in the series of drawings done in 1952.

Clouzot had at first thought of a short documentary, but he was so
impressed by Picasso's magic that he decided to make a longer film,
taking direct views of the canvas in course of execution as well as
shots from the back through the transparent paper. Picasso would sit
between the camera and the painting, work on it for a few minutes,
then step aside for progress to be recorded. 'You have finished with
the red?' Clouzot would ask him. 'Yes.' 'All right, get up.' The camera
would turn, then: 'You can go back now.' To finish the head of a bull
he was seen to stand up and sit down again seventy-eight times in two
hours.

The sweat beaded Picasso's bald head and ran down his back, but
he was enjoying himself immensely. There was a sparkle in his eyes
in spite of the fatigue, and his slightly raucous voice still revealed a
repressed sense of humour. He began by painting flowers. Then he
turned them into a fish, then he gave the fish a turkey's beak and
ended by painting the head of a satyr.

One day during the filming Picasso told Clouzot that he wanted to
paint a beach near Antibes that was familiar to him. To record the
picture, which was going to be on a large scale, Clouzot decided to use
cinemascope. Picasso painted a blue sky, gaily striped tents in yellow
and red, women sunbathing on the ochre sand, multicoloured parasols,
an almost violet sea, water-skiers and swimmers. He also introduced
the nude woman with voluptuous breasts from the *Femmes d'Alger*.
Seen on the cinema screen the details of this picture appear with un-
canny speed like a series of magic-lantern slides. Again Picasso was
required to sit down, stand up and sit down again, more than a hundred
times an hour, so that the progress of the work could be filmed. He
finished at two o'clock one morning after fourteen consecutive hours
in the studio. His friends saw him light a cigarette, then his face relaxed
in a smile of triumph. The heat was intense. Suddenly he felt dizzy and
called out: 'Hold me up, I am going to fall.' The result of his superhuman effort was an alarming rise in blood-pressure which necessitated
a long rest. But he returned once more to the film studio and in two
hours repainted the beach scene on a fresh canvas in lively geometrical

patches of colour from which the contours of a seated woman emerge.

Clouzot wanted to end the film with a last appearance of Picasso on the screen. The artist signed his spectacular signature on a vast white canvas. A fleeting conspiratorial smile appeared on his lips. Then he turned and walked slowly away and the audience saw his back recede through the jumble of lights, cameras and cables till it vanished in the distance.

With his fear of illness and a consequent reduction of vitality Picasso now dutifully submitted to medical examinations, prescriptions and diets. The tests he had to undergo interested him, particularly the little zig-zag traced by the encephalogram, and when he had recovered—very quickly thanks to the persistence with which he followed the treatment—he did some drawings for his doctor with contours repeating the zig-zag pattern.

Picasso was now at work again in his villa, though nothing seemed less suited to steady labour than the atmosphere of idle luxury prevailing in Cannes. With their squat, tasteless houses the hills behind the town symbolized days of unlimited leisure. In a sky fingered by tall palm trees, the bulb of the Russian church—Picasso called it the inkpot—recalled Cannes's most glamorous period, when Grand Dukes used it as their favourite playground. The villa which Picasso had chosen also seemed a curious setting for an artist. Apparently some millionaire had built it as a monument to his financial and social success. It had a pretentious façade with wrought-iron balconies, a vast entrance-hall and a whole suite of reception rooms. Wrought-iron was also prominent in the interior in the banisters to a white marble staircase. But Picasso had already placed his stamp on the place. The hall looked like a railway depot: unopened cases sent from Paris, half-opened cases from Vallauris containing pottery that he was intending to decorate, sacks of cement for work which would probably never be put in hand, and an assortment of packages that had burst open and were losing their contents.

A large bay-window in the main reception room led to some steps looking out over a garden of tall palm trees and mimosa. On this terrace Picasso had collected some of his favourite sculptures. The immense bust in gilded bronze of the woman with the big nose faced the pregnant goat. It was raining. 'Oh, look at her!' exclaimed Jacqueline with childlike enthusiasm. 'Look at the drop of water on her nose!' Picasso laughed. The gilded lady assumed an indignant air. . . .

Picasso looked younger than in the days when he had gazed at the low sky of Paris. He was bronzed, his features were relaxed and his eyes sparkled more brightly than ever. He seemed perfectly at ease in the chaos still reigning in his new house. On the marble mantelpiece there was a collection of hats, among them a Tyrolean felt hat in violent green. Picasso put it on at a slant and looked at himself in the mirror. 'Don't you think I could wear this?' he said, then decided he couldn't and regretfully put it back in its place.

Some of the furniture seemed to have come from the previous owner; other pieces were clearly marked 'Picasso'—an aged chair in a corner of the dining-room, for instance, that had once been covered with red damask, and the brazier from the Rue des Grands-Augustins that had found its way into a corner of the drawing-room already cluttered with papers, books and photographs. The luxurious interior of the house was already looking like a nomad tent set up in the desert for a brief spell before moving on. But it was clear that everything had to take second place before something that was much greater, the only thing of importance in his life.

Picasso had started work again, painting with the same frenzy as in the happiest moments of his incredible youth when Gertrude Stein was amazed that he could paint so many pictures in the course of a single year.

For a while I was alone confronting the pile of canvases he had painted in the last two months. Then Picasso came in with his silent tread. 'You see,' he said, spreading his arms and smiling his peculiar, half ironic, half affectionate smile, 'I am only just beginning.' He had painted Jacqueline in an almost realistic manner, sitting with her knees tucked up in a rocking-chair, the eyelashes shadowing her cheeks and a soft, pink mouth. He had painted her nude with her hands behind her head in an almost monochrome composition of whites and greys, or else in a violent clash of colour wearing a dress of green and violet lozenges. He also painted a number of portraits—which seem like an almost realistic succession to the *Femmes d'Alger*—of Jacqueline in Turkish costume. These portraits introduce a new note into Picasso's art, a thrill of sensuality expressed in a special subtlety of colouring. In a portrait of 20th November, 1955, painted on a dull red background, the whiteness of the slightly inclined face is rendered by mauve and greenish tones in the flesh and a transparent material barely conceals the satin texture of the breasts. In another portrait of Jacqueline in

Turkish costume, where the green-shadowed face is depicted between long flowing hair, the huge eyes drawn in green and black have an extraordinary luminosity conveying the clear candid gaze of the model.

As a studio Picasso was now using what must once have been a card-room or smoking-room. It was lit by three windows through which the trunks and branches of palm trees could be seen. But three enormous floodlamps set up on the easels showed that he was also working at night. A large mirror above the fireplace reflected an odd assortment of objects: a crystal vase, a marble bowl, a candlestick in opaque glass—all seemingly inherited from the previous owner—with below them a mortar, some bottles, a coal-scuttle and a chair littered with paint-brushes. The figured parquet floor was spattered with paint as though Picasso had been using it as a palette. At sunset a rosy light tinted the white walls and sharpened the metallic green of the palm trees. Picasso painted this studio scene giving the walls the colour of Arab buildings in Spanish towns and the windows the appearance of mullions. He painted a whole series of *Interiors* in rose and white with patches of luminous green, the first version being dated 23rd October, 1955. But this transposition into large rose-coloured planes did not satisfy him, and soon he began another and more elaborately drawn series in which he reproduced almost everything in front of his eyes in miniaturist style.

Nothing provides greater insight into Picasso's method of breaking down and reconstructing reality than these studio scenes. If it were possible to isolate each object and see how it is transformed under his brush one would have penetrated the laws of his plastic vision. Everything in his studio is included in these pictures: a ceramic head, a table with three red trays, the chair with its paint-brushes, the bottles, the coal-scuttle and even the design on the parquet floor. But they are portrayed in arabesques which give the canvas a particular rhythm and make them part of an ornamental whole until the position of each object seems governed by some law of necessity.

Another of Picasso's characteristics is revealed in these studio scenes: his indifference to the place he lives in, to the order or disorder which surrounds him. For him, objects only begin to exist at the moment when he transposes them, takes them out of their normal setting and gives them a new aspect: the drinking glass when it becomes cubist, the packet of cigarettes when it is included in a prismatic world. In Picasso's conception of the world things in themselves have never had any reality. To us, the stucco ornamentations on his studio mantel-piece are an eyesore, but to him they are merely the starting-point for transformations which make them into something totally different from what they seem. In the pictures of his studio they become motifs which have been familiar to him since his childhood.

The series of studio scenes, like the portraits of Jacqueline in Turkish costume, introduce a new element into Picasso's art and seem to denote a new feeling for the texture of things. To me it seems that he is about to surprise the world and himself by embarking on new paths. Standing at his door on that day in January, 1956, when rain had blotted all light from the sky, he seemed full of vigour and infectious good humour. Laughing, he waved good-bye. He knew he was on the threshold of fresh creative adventures. His strong voice echoed in my ears: 'You see, I am only just beginning.'

Index

Index